Gender, Welfare State and the Market

This book explores the highly topical issue of the gender divide of welfare. A common characteristic of welfare states of the OECD countries is a profound gender division of paid and unpaid work and care. This affects women's position in the family, the labour market and their access to social citizenship. *Gender, Welfare State and the Market* extends the discussion about the relationship between the welfare state, market and family and its impact on women's economic, social and political (in)dependence in the modern western welfare societies.

The book goes beyond the narrow focus on the labour market/welfare state arrangement to explore the relationship between production and social reproduction, paid and unpaid work and care within the framework of different welfare states. The volume specifically focuses on the shifting gender balance of employment and the restructuring of social care provision. Moreover, using feminist critiques of welfare state research, the book brings gender-specific as well as gender-relational approaches to the analysis of social citizenship, and the importance of the family and other non-public agencies for the provision of social care.

Gender, Welfare State and the Market reveals that any analysis must take into account the care work provided informally or unpaid, in order to understand how welfare policies contribute to gender inequality in the family, labour market and with respect to social citizenship. This volume represents the present state of the art in theoretical debate in welfare state scholarship, drawing on research from western Europe, North America and Japan. It therefore provides a valuable balance of breadth and detail, from the broad international overview to comparisons between specific welfare states and national case studies. It will be a necessary resource for anyone involved in policy making, or research in economics, politics, sociology or gender studies.

Thomas P. Boje is Professor of Sociology in the Department of Sociology at the University of Umeå, Sweden. He is currently editor-in-chief for the ESA journal *European Societies*. **Arnlaug Leira** is a Professor of Sociology in the Department of Sociology and Human Geography at the University of Oslo, Norway.

Routledge Research in Gender and Society

Gender, Welfare State and the Market

Towards a new division of labour

Edited by Thomas P. Boje and Arnlaug Leira

London and New York

First published 2000 by Routledge
11 New Fetter Lane, London EC4P 4EE

Simultaneously published in the USA and Canada
by Routledge
29 West 35th Street, New York, NY 10001

Routledge is an imprint of the Taylor & Francis Group

© 2000 Thomas P. Boje and Arnlaug Leira for selection and
editorial material; individual chapters, the contributors

Typeset in Baskerville by
Rosemount Typing Services, Thornhill, Dumfriesshire
Printed and bound in Great Britain by
TJ International Ltd, Padstow, Cornwall

British Library Cataloguing in Publication Data
A catalogue record for this book is available from the British Library

Library of Congress Cataloging in Publication Data
Gender, welfare state and the market : towards a new division of labour / edited Thomas
P. Boje and Arnlaug Leira.
    p. cm.– (Routledge research in gender and society ; 4)
  Includes bibliographical references and index.
    1. Sexual division of labor–OECD countries. 2. Labor policy–OECD countries. 3.
Welfare state. 4. OECD countries–Economic policy. 5. OECD countries–Social policy.
I Boje, Thomas P., 1944– II. Leira, Arnlaug. III. Series.
HD6060.6 .G468 2000
306.3'615–dc21   00–030428

ISBN 0–415–23531–6

Contents

Figures

Tables

Notes on Editors

Thomas P. Boje is Professor of Sociology at the University of Umeå, Sweden. He was previously Associate Professor and for a period Head of the Department of Social Sciences at the University of Roskilde, Denmark. He has been American Studies Fellow at the Department of Sociology, Harvard University, Cambridge, US and Jean Monnet Fellow at the Department of Political Science and Sociology at the European University Institute, Florence, Italy. He is currently co-editor of the journal *Dansk Sociologi* and editor-in-chief of the ESA journal *European Societies*. He is the Swedish partner in the EU/TSER Research networks: *BETWIXT: Between Integration and Exclusion* and *HWF: Household Work and Flexibility*. Thomas P. Boje has published extensively in Scandinavian languages and English on employment, industrial restructuring, and flexibility and the relationship between women's labour market involvement and family policies. He is the author of *Mobilitets - og beskæftigelsesemønstre på det danske arbejdsmarked 1980–81* (Mobility and employment patterns in the Danish labour market 1980–81) (The Copenhagen Business School 1987); editor of *Work and Welfare in a Changing Europe*, also published as special issues of *International Journal of Sociology*, 1994–5 and joint editor of *Scandinavia in a New Europe* (Scandinavian University Press 1993) and *European Societies: Fusion or Fission?* (Routledge 1999).

Arnlaug Leira is Professor of Sociology at the University of Oslo, Norway. From 1990 to 1995 she was Research Director at the Institute for Social Research (ISR) in Oslo, with special responsibilities for research focusing on women, gender equality and the family. She is the Norwegian partner in the EU/TSER-funded Research Networks *Gender and Citizenship: Social Integration and Social Exclusion*, and *Mothers as Workers and Carers: Social Practices and Social Policies*. She is one of the editors of the *Yearbook of Comparative Social Research* (published by JAI Press). Arnlaug Leira has published extensively in Norwegian and English, in books and social science journals, on poverty and social policy, women and gender issues, family policy, trends in welfare state development, citizenship and social rights. Her list of publications includes *Welfare States and Working Mothers. The Scandinavian Experience.* (Cambridge University Press, 1992), 'The Woman-Friendly Welfare State? The case of Norway and Sweden' in J. Lewis (ed.), *Women and Social Policy in Europe* (Edward Elgar 1993), 'Gender, Caring and Social Rights' in P. Koslowski and A. Follesdal (eds) *Restructuring the Welfare State* (Springer Verlag 1996), 'The Modernisation of Motherhood' in E. Drew, R. Emerek and E. Mahon (eds), *Women, Work and the Family in Europe* (Routledge 1998), and 'Caring as Social Right: Cash for Child Care and Daddy Leave' (*Social Politics*, vol. 5, 1998).

Notes on Contributors

Anna-Lena Almqvist is Researcher at the Department of Sociology, Umeå University. She is currently working on her dissertation analysing the relationship between family policy and women's labour market participation in France and Sweden. Anna-Lena Almqvist has been visiting scholar at MSH Ange-Guepin, Nantes, France. She has published with Thomas P. Boje 'Who Cares, Who Pays and How is Care for Children Provided? Comparing Family Life and Work in Different European Welfare Systems (DK, D, F, S, and UK)' (in Denis Bouget and Bruno Palier (eds) *Comparing Social Welfare Systems in Nordic Countries and France* MIRE/MSH, Nantes 1999).

Cecilia Benoit is Full Professor at the University of Victoria, Canada. In autumn 1999 she was Visiting Research Professor at Åbo Academy University. Cecilia Benoit has done research in several areas – e.g. gender, work, social rights, occupations and professions and comparative health and welfare systems. Her major publications are 'Mothering in a Newfoundland Community: 1900-1940' (in *Delivering Motherhood*, Eds K. Arnup, A. Levesque, R. Roach Person, Routledge 1990), 'Paradigm Conflict in the Sociology of the Professions' (*Canadian Journal of Sociology* 1994), 'Midwifery in Canada and Sweden: A Cross-National Comparison' (*Health and Canadian Society.* 1998), and *Women, Work & Social Rights: Historical and Cross-National Perspectives* (Prentice Hall, Canada, 2000).

Mary Daly is Professor of Sociology at the Department of Sociology and Social Policy, Queen's University, Belfast, Northern Ireland. She was formerly an Assistant Professor at the Institute of Social Policy at the University of Göttingen, Germany. Her current research interests include the stratification effects of welfare states and transformation and change in social policy. Her recent publications include *Social Security, Gender and Equality in the European Union* (Brussels EC 1996), 'Welfare states under pressure: cash benefits in European welfare states over the last ten years' (*Journal of European Social Policy* 1997), and 'A More Caring State? The implications of welfare state restructuring for social care in the Republic of Ireland' (in *Gender, Social Care and Welfare State – Restructuring in Europe*, Jane Lewis (ed.) Ashgate 1998).

Anne Lise Ellingsæter is Research Director at the Institute for Social Research, Oslo, Norway. She is the Norwegian member of the EU/EEA expert network on gender and employment. Her major publications in English include 'Gender Relations and the Norwegian Labour Market Model' with J. Rubery (in J. E. Dølvik and A. Steen (eds) *Making Solidarity Work? The Norwegian Labour Market in Transition*, Scandinavian University Press 1997), 'Dual Breadwinners Between State and Market' (in R. Crompton (ed.) *The Decline of the 'Male Breadwinner'*? Oxford University Press 1999), and 'Dual Breadwinner Society. Provider Models in the Scandinavian Welfare States' (*Acta Sociologica* 1998).

Janet C. Gornick is Associate Professor of Political Science at Baruch College, and at the Graduate Center, City University of New York. She is currently working on several reseach projects: the interplay between unemployment insurance and public assistance in the OECD countries, supporting the employment of mothers, and anti-poverty policy analyses. Her most recent publications include, together with Jerry A. Jacobs, 'A Cross-National Analysis of the Wages of Part-Time Workers: Evidence from the United States, the United Kingdom, Canada, and Australia' (*Work, Employment and Society* 1996) and 'Gender, the Welfare State, and Public Employment: A Comparative Study of Seven Industrialized Countries' (*American Sociological Review* 1998), with Marcia K. Meyers and Katherin E. Ross, 'Supporting the Employment of Mothers: Policy Variation Across Fourteen Welfare States' (*Journal of European Social Policy* 1997), and 'Gender Equality in the Labor Market: Women's Employment and Earnings: Women's Employment and Earnings' (in Diane Sainsbury (ed.) *Gender Policy Regimes and Welfare States*, Oxford University Press 1999).

Jørgen Elm Larsen is Associate Professor at the Department of Sociology, University of Copenhagen. He is a member of the Board (deputy member) of the Nordic Institute for Women's Studies and Gender. Elm Larsen was Visiting Research Scholar at the Social Policy Research Centre in Sydney 1990-1 and 1997. His list of publications in English includes, together with John Andersen, 'Gender, Poverty and Empowerment' (in *Critical Social Policy* 1998), 'The Underclass Debate – a Spreading Disease?' (in Nils Mortensen (ed.) *Social Integration and Marginalisation*, Copenhagen 1996) and, with Søren Carlsen (eds), (1993) *The Equality Dilemma: Reconciling working life and family life, viewed in an equality perspective. The Danish example* (Munksgaard, Copenhagen).

Jane Millar is Professor of Social Policy and Director of the Centre for the Analysis of Social Policy at the University of Bath. She was the UK representative on the EU Observatory on National Family Policies between 1994 and 1996. She has carried out extensive research on lone-parent families and social policy in the UK, comparative EU research on the socioeconomic circumstances of solo women, family obligations in law and policy and studies of employment and social exclusion, both at national level and in comparisons of EU countries. Her list of publications includes, with J. Bradshaw, *Lone-parent families in the UK* (HMSO 1991), with C. Glendinning, *Women and Poverty in Britain: the 1990s* (Wheatsheaf/Harvester 1992), 'Family obligations and social policy: the case of child support' (*Policy Studies*, 1996), with H. Jones, *The politics of the family* (Avebury 1997), and, with S. Webb and M. Kemp, *Combining work and welfare* (Joseph Rowntree Foundation 1997).

Ito Peng is Associate Professor at the School of Policy Studies, Kwansei Gakuin University, Sanda, Japan. She has worked at policy level with the Ministry of Health and Welfare in Japan and with the Ontario provincial government in Canada. Her most recent publications in English include *Boshi katei: a theoretical and case analysis of Japanese lone mothers and their relationships to the state, the labour market and the family, with reference to Britain and Canada* (London School of Economics 1995) and 'The East Asian Welfare States: Peripatetic Learning, Adaptive Change, and Nation-Building' with Roger Goodmann (in Gösta Esping-Andersen (ed.), *Welfare States in Transition*, Sage Publication 1996), and 'A Fresh Look at the Japanese Welfare State', *Social Policy and Administration* 34(1): 87–114.

Chiara Saraceno is Professor of Family Sociology at the University of Turin, Italy. She was the Italian expert in the EC Observatory on Policies for Combating Social Exclusion from 1990 to 1994. At present she is chair of the Commission on Poverty and Social Exclusion at the Prime Minister's Office in Italy. Her most recent publications include 'The Changing Italian Welfare State' (with N. Negri) (in *Journal of European Social Policy* 1994), 'The Ambivalent Familism of the Italian Welfare State' (in *Social Politics* 1994), *Sociologia della Famiglia* (Sociology of Family) (Il Mulino 1988/1996), *Le Politiche contro la Povertà in Italia* (Il Mulino 1996) (with N. Negri), 'Family change, family policies and the restructuring of welfare' (in *Family, Market and Community*, OECD 1997), 'Growth, Regional Imbalance and Child Well-Being: Italy over the Last Four Decades' (in G.A. Cornia and S. Danzinger (eds), *Child Poverty and Deprivation in the Industrialized Countries, 1945–1995*, Clarendon Press 1997), *Mutamenti familiari e politiche sociali in Italia* (Il Mulino 1998), and *Separarsi in Italia* (Il Mulino 1998) (with M. Barbali).

Introduction

Gender, welfare state and the market – towards a new division of labour

Thomas P. Boje and Arnlaug Leira

For decades the modern welfare states have been under growing constraints, and calls for restructuring, roll-back or overhaul are commonly voiced across the western world. Labour markets, families and welfare states are changing as are the interinstitutional arrangements. The relationship between women and men is taking new forms within the labour market as well as in families, which has crucial consequences in defining social citizenship; thus the dominant 'gender contract' is under pressure.

Whatever the character of the welfare state being discussed, the future of the 'welfare state' is high on the political agenda. This is a major analytic theme whether the welfare systems in question are classified as institutional or residual, in the tradition from Wilensky and Lebeaux (1958), and, following Richard Titmuss (1974), as residual, institutional-redistributive or industrial achievement-performance models, and, in the terminology of Gøsta Esping-Andersen's (1990) elaboration, as social-democratic, corporative-conservative or liberal welfare state regimes, respectively. Generally, the crisis of the welfare state is analysed with reference to the ongoing comprehensive structural and institutional changes: globalization of economies, rapid restructuring of labour markets, deregulation, flexibilization, widespread deskilling and demands for reskilling of the workforce and shifts in the balance between labour and capital as well as in the gender balance of employment.

This book starts from the profound gendered division of paid and unpaid work and care. It examines the gender outcomes of processes of restructuring within the labour market, the welfare state and the family. The contributions also explore, in different ways, the interplay between social change and policy reform in western Europe, North America and Japan. The main field of research is the welfare state approach to the combination of work and family responsibilities, and the gendered outcomes of welfare state intervention. The current economic constraints do form a background for several of the contributions, but not a major theme. From different perspectives, and examining different forms of the welfare state, the book deals with the impact of two processes that in particular have triggered discussions about policy reform: the first is the comprehensive change in the demographic structure and in family relations, the second is represented by the mass mobilization of women for labour market participation. Both processes highlight the importance for social theory of rethinking gender relationships in the labour market, the family and the welfare state, and underline the necessity of gender-sensitivity in the formulation of welfare state policies.

In all the welfare states examined in this book, the family institution is undergoing comprehensive transformation. The European welfare states, in particular, are experiencing the impact of comprehensive demographic change, sometimes referred to as a 'second demographic transition', characterized by falling birth rates and an ageing of the population. Increasing 'flexibilization' of family formation and rising break-up rates among married and cohabiting partners and parents are often interpreted as expressions of a fragmentation of family obligations, a dilution of traditional relations of responsibility between gender and generations (see the contributions of Millar and Saraceno in this volume). The family model of the early postwar welfare state is on the decline; in the OECD countries the gender-differentiated nuclear family is being replaced by the dual-earner family as the dominant family form, even among families with young children (EC Childcare network (1996), Almqvist and Boje (1999); see also the contributions of Benoit, Ellingsæter and Gornick in this volume). Several countries have experienced an increase in the proportion of single person households and of single parent families (Elm Larsen in this volume). The ongoing diversification of family forms, currently more predominant in the northern regions of Europe than in the southern or elsewhere in the OECD area, poses challenges to the welfare states, since the traditional definition of family obligations that includes the unpaid provision of care and welfare cannot be taken for granted.

Economic constraints, demographic change and a high proportion of economically active women have actualized questions concerning the social rights of citizens and the capacity and willingness of welfare states to accommodate the needs and demands of different population groups for benefits and services. The problems go to the core of the modern welfare state project as they challenge the economic promises entailed: to safeguard the population from economic need when income from the market fails. Moreover, the concept of the welfare state as a 'service state' is questioned when the state does not deliver as promised or anticipated, with respect to health, education, welfare provision and social services. In several countries social benefits and services have been reduced and/or changed to encourage private responsibility, and to promote the involvement of a number of non-public agents in the provision of care and welfare. Thus, the concept of the welfare state is questioned and fears are raised about its capacity to provide economic security and social care, health and welfare services. According to the theories of 'reflexive modernity' globalization processes apparently enhance more general processes of individualization (Beck 1992) that challenge the social solidarity so important to the ideological underpinning of the welfare state.

From a different perspective, some of the problems mentioned are also examined in various OECD analyses (1994, 1997), which identify as main problems of the western welfare states their inability to combat unemployment and generate processes of social integration in societies that are economically, socially and culturally diversified. Differences with respect to race and ethnicity, gender and generation have become increasingly visible. The OECD reports do not offer a general blueprint for policy reform. However, labour market marginalization and social exclusion are addressed as challenges for the welfare state; the generational conflicts and upkeep of social solidarity represent a call for welfare state concern and intervention. Thus, one of the more important challenges for the welfare state societies (or welfare societies for short) is how to create an institutional context promoting or facilitating social coherence. No easy task in a situation where the authority and power of the nation states are often regarded as being undermined both by regional cleavages and/or in Europe by the European Union (EU) 'suprastate'.

The call for families to take on greater responsibility, a 'refamilialization' in the sense of returning to the family obligations and patterns of the past, is voiced in the political debate (for an overview, see, e.g. Saraceno 1997). For a number of reasons this approach does not offer a viable solution to the problems raised by the ongoing demographic change. A recent report from the European Union member states points to the formidable problems connected with care provision, focusing especially on the gap between resources demanded and the provisions supplied when it comes to caring for the very young and the very old (Bettio and Prechal 1998). Let us reiterate some of the more obvious: as witnessed in care of the elderly, a considerable proportion of the very old and very frail do not have close relatives or other family members living nearby. The capacity of families to care for frail elderly relatives, and for young children, is also limited by the families' need for two incomes. However, families still do provide care. Data from the mid-1990s show that a large proportion of Europeans do spend a considerable amount of time caring for their elderly relatives, friends and neighbours (EUROSTAT 1997). State-sponsored and other extra-familial childcare supplement parental care, which still represents the larger share of childcare in society (Millar and Warman (eds) 1995; Saraceno in this volume).

The gap between resources and demand, referred to as a 'caring deficit' (Hochschild 1995), generated by the rapid growth in women's employment and the popularity of the dual-earner family, the ageing of the population and the large number of frail elderly single persons, implies that the demand for extra-familial care is increasing and the traditional supply of women's labour less available for providing informal, private, unpaid care for family members.

The need of individuals who are not able to provide and care for themselves, particularly the very young and the very frail elderly, has raised the debate about 'care' as a right of citizens, that is, as a right to receive care when in need, and as a right (or responsibility) to give care (Knijn and Kremer 1997; Boje and Almqvist in this volume). Increasingly, the division of responsibility and costs of caring for children and the frail elderly is questioned: who is to provide the care, and who to bear the cost? (Jenson 1997). This is not only an issue to do with the division of labour, responsibility and costs between the welfare state, market, family and the voluntary organisations, or the third sector, it is also a highly gendered issue, as demonstrated particularly in feminist scholarship from the past decades (e.g. Lewis 1998). Changing family patterns and practices indicate that the gendered division of unpaid family-related care and welfare provision cannot be taken for granted in the future. In all countries women have the principal responsibility of caring for dependent family members. Therefore, it is obvious that the untapped reserves of time and labour available for unpaid family-related work and care largely rest with the men.

As shown in scholarly debate and in political discussions, the restructuring of the provision of care for the very young and the very old is multifaceted and complex. State-sponsoring of care varies in form and content across the OECD area. The Protestant countries of the 'social-democratic' north have apparently accepted state intervention in care provision to a larger extent than is the case in some of the southern European countries, where the subsidiarity principle advocated by the Catholic Church has made a more profound impact on family and care-related policies. In some of the Anglo-American countries the market is the main provider of care services. Thus, as comes out very clearly in Chiara Saraceno's contribution, 'refamilialization' or 'defamilialization' might imply very different policy strategies depending on the political context. Consequently, the implications of care-related policies for the paid employment of women as well as men need to be analysed in more detail and the consequences need to be evaluated.

Across the welfare states discussed in this volume recent policy reforms give evidence of different tendencies at work. In some of the OECD member states new forms of 'refamilialization' are supported by the state, as witnessed for example in the institution of parental leave schemes (OECD 1995), that offer not only employed mothers but also employed fathers a right to care for their children with some form of wage compensation arranged. The cash benefits for childcare established in some countries might also be interpreted as state support for family care, alternatively as state support for the private arrangement of childcare (e.g. Leira in this volume). Different forms of 'defamilialization' are also witnessed, for example in the state-sponsoring of extra-familial services for childcare and elderly care, and in the development of commercial services for the very young and the very old. In the Nordic countries, since the late 1970s, feminist scholars in particular have analysed social reproduction going public. Taking a special interest in the ascription of care responsibilities and caring work to women, they have advocated the necessity of examining all forms of care provision together, whether private or public, formally or informally organized, and to study the gender effects of different forms of care provision. In the 1990s the concern in several countries (e.g. the UK) has had more to do with social reproduction going commercial, as marketization and quasi-marketization of services have been of growing importance to welfare provision (see Lewis (ed.) (1998) and the contributions of Saraceno, Peng, and Boje and Almqvist in this volume). Thus, in several welfare states, the state–family arrangment is being renegotiated and 'family obligations' are redefined. More generally, the public–private mix of service provision is being restructured and the institutional arrangements for care provision are increasingly diversified.

The ongoing redrawing of the division of labour and responsibility between public welfare systems and families influences the often fragile balance between individual needs or demands and the public resources available. To the material problems is added a so-called legitimation crisis, i.e. a widening gap between popular expectations and welfare state promises (nurtured to no small extent by welfare state rhetoric). In all western societies the resources available for social welfare are scarce and this obviously raises major concerns over the welfare state's capacity to deliver as promised (Boje 1998).

Changing the 'gender contract'?

The comprehensive restructuring of labour markets and families, mentioned above, has affected the traditional gender arrangement in the labour market and in the family institution, and the relationship among and between women and men. In all welfare state societies analysed in this volume the gender balance of employment is changing; women have taken on more of the economic provider responsibilities. However, the gendering of unpaid family-related work and care remains remarkably unchanged. Even in those countries where women's employment rates are approaching those of men, women still spend more time than men on unpaid, family-related domestic work and care.

The everyday life of individuals in the family, in the labour market and in society at large is structured by various social contracts among which an employment contract, and more metaphorically speaking, a gender contract, are of particular importance (OECD 1994). The gender contract (Hirdman 1988), or 'sexual contract' (Pateman 1988a), sets the general framework for distributing rights and responsibilities between women and men in society in general and in the family in particular. The employment contract, on the other hand, specifies the regulation of the relationship between capital and labour, the rights and duties of employers and employees. In the industrialized societies of the western world the gender-differentiated nuclear family became predominant, and was integrated as the main family model of the postwar welfare states. This family model takes the father/husband as the economic provider of the family, charged with the responsibility to provide materially for his dependent wife and children. The housewife/mother is the main carer and nurturer for children and often for the frail, elderly relatives. Providing unpaid family-related domestic work, social and care services for the husband, she is in return protected economically and socially by the social status of her mate.

According to the very influential family theory of the 1950s and 1960s, presented in the tradition of Parsonian structural-functionalism, this family arrangement was functional for the family, the labour market, and for the capitalist economic system as such. The 'gender contract' underlying this family type generally prescribed full-time wage-work as the norm for adult able-bodied males, while women's labour market participation – if any – was not to interfere with the primary housewifely and motherly duties in the home.

The employment contract, on the other hand, generally presumes that the labour force is free and mobile, and not charged with caring commitments. Thus, to a very considerable extent, the employment contract has assumed an underlying gender contract as described above. Put differently, the organization of the labour market presumes an organization of social reproduction that does not interfere with the demands of production.

Since the 1950s and 1960s the mass mobilization of women to labour market participation changed the gender balance of employment in the Scandinavian countries, and a similar development took place in central and southern Europe and North America some decades later. The male breadwinner family was replaced by the dual-earner family as the numerically predominant family type. However, these processes have not dramatically challenged the gender segregation in the labour markets (see, for example, the chapters by Benoit, Ellingsæter and Gornick to this volume). In countries where women's participation rates are approaching those of men, women on average put in fewer hours in paid work than men do. Despite equal opportunity legislation in all western countries, women have not, on average, achieved equal pay for equal work or career possibilities comparable with those of men. One explanation of the gender inequalities in working hours, payment and career advancement is the, often tacit, assumptions of the gender contract and its corollary: unequal division of unpaid family-related work and care work which disadvantage women in the labour market. Thus, the influence of traditional gender roles and behavioural patterns does still make a strong impact on the employment contract which takes as a norm the full-time wage-working male.

The dual-earner family (or one and a half-earner family as the Scandinavians rapidly termed it) has become increasingly common; in the mid-1990s it made up more than half of the families with young children in the EU member states (EC Childcare Network 1996). As noted in a considerable literature from recent years, and in several of the articles in this volume as well (see, for example, Boje and Almqvist; Saraceno), changes in women's labour market participation have not to any dramatic extent changed the gendered division of domestic labour; the gender contract is still at work in the household. Most unpaid family-related domestic work and care is 'gender-typed' in the sense that it is considered as women's work; largely, but not exclusively it is done by women. Despite the very comprehensive family changes mentioned above, the lasting practical as well as ideological influence of the gender contract should not be underestimated.

As Peter Taylor-Gooby (1991) observes:

> If state policy fails to ensure that women have a comparable status in waged work to that of men, it becomes an irrational work strategy in many households not to pursue a gender division of unwaged work that mirrors that of waged work.

While Taylor-Gooby obviously makes an important point, empirical observations also point to a different 'logic'. Across the western welfare states a considerable number of women have, from necessity or choice, headed for other options. Without waiting for equal pay or for the state to shoulder the caring commitments or for their partners to share in unpaid care and housework, they have pursued strategies that allow for the combination of work and family responsibilities. As long as motherhood tends to outlast marriage and partnership, heading for the labour market appears as a perfectly rational strategy for many women, even if wage and career discrimination persists.

Only very gradually have welfare state policies and labour market organizations responded to the changing gender balance of employment and the increasing demand for extra-familial care generated by the growth in women's employment rates. For example, the extent to which the labour market participation of both fathers and mothers is facilitated by maternity, paternity and parental leave schemes varies throughout the OECD countries (OECD 1995; Moss and Deven eds, forthcoming), as does the provision of publicly sponsored childcare and elderly care (Anttonen and Sipilä 1996). The implementation of the EU directive on parental leave may signal a new approach, providing as it does an interesting example of both mothers and fathers being considered as both workers and carers. However, gender neutral parental leave schemes do not seem to make any great difference with respect to fathers' take-up of this right (OECD 1995; Bruning and Plantenga 1999; see also Leira in this volume). Even in the dual-earner families where both men and women have a significant labour market involvement, the combination of work and family obligation is largely considered as a 'women's issue'. From the Scandinavian countries there are some indications that this may be changing in the younger generation.

Against this background it is no wonder that the past decades have seen a flourishing debate concerning the future of the western welfare states, the outcome and effect of the ongoing processes of restructuring and the efforts at redefining the rights and responsibilities of the individual and families in relation to the welfare state. The institutional organization of the welfare system, the arrangement between welfare state, market, family and institutions of civil society is in flux; the gender outcomes are questioned, as is the future of welfare provision.

Rethinking social citizenship?

In the tradition from T.H. Marshall, originating in his influential essay on Citizenship and Class (1965), the male wage-worker has served as the prototype of the citizen. In Marshall's analysis, citizenship includes three components that are of equal importance: civil rights, political rights and social rights. We shall not enter here into the comprehensive debate on Marshall's conceptualization, such as the critique of his Anglo-centredness, or the efforts in later critical analyses to address race and ethnicity within the citizenship framework or to rethink citizenship in a human rights framework. For the contributions to this volume one aspect of Marshall's perspective is particularly important, meaning that it has strongly influenced present-day thinking, namely his taking the male as the norm of the citizen.

According to Marshall, 'citizenship is bestowed on all those who are full members of a community. All who possess the status are equal with respect to the rights and duties with which the status is endowed' (1965: 92). However, although citizenship is conceptualized as a system of equality, in everyday practices the system tolerates far-reaching inequalities. As indicated by the essay title, Marshall's main concern is with the impact of citizenship as a system of equality contrary to the impact of social class as a system of inequality.

Throughout Marshall's analysis of the historical development of the rights and duties of citizenship, including the social rights of the twentieth-century welfare state, focus is on the male worker. Thus, the analysis ignores the very different ways in which women and men have been integrated as citizens (Hernes 1987; Pateman 1988b; Leira 1992; Boje 1998). Noting that there were 'some peculiarities' in the position of married women, Marshall did not, however, explore these in any detail.

Marshall's essay has often been regarded as a contribution to the theory of democratization. As pointed out by Carole Pateman (1996) in an interesting assessment of Marshall's work, discussing the rights and duties of citizenship, Marshall's concern is with the male; the democratization processes refer to the male population only. For Pateman, the democratization of citizenship is not only represented by the struggle of the male wage-workers, but also includes the struggle of women for civil, social and political rights. The political history of women's rights is often different from that of men (see also Hernes 1987). Pateman notes in passing that when Marshall first presented his essay in Cambridge in 1949 women had gained admittance as students only the previous year. However, Marshall's essay does not address the obvious differences with respect to rights and duties of women and men. (For a more comprehensive discussion of Marshall's work, see Pateman 1996.)

As is often noted, the mainstream welfare state literature has largely been preoccupied with the relationship between the state and the market. Accordingly, the development of the modern welfare state is often interpreted as a series of compromises between capital and labour and between welfare and control. What has been less often observed is that the welfare state also represents compromises between women and men, mediated via their different relationship to the family and the labour market (Leira 1997). Put differently, until relatively recently, welfare state research has generally been more concerned with the labour–capital compromise and the employment contract than the gender contract. Thus, the social citizenship of the male wage-worker is more thoroughly analysed than is that of his mate (Hernes 1987, 1988; Pateman 1988a, 1988b; Siim 1993). As more is known about the employment-relatedness of welfare states, it has been argued that the 'care-relatedness' of welfare states deserves more attention as do the theoretical challenges represented by the organization of social reproduction, and of social care in particular, for welfare state analysis (Leira 1992).

The dominant welfare state typologies from the 1950s to the 1990s have largely followed the Marshallian way of thinking about citizens as being predominantly male. Indeed, feminist scholars have argued that concepts such as 'worker' and 'citizen' have strong male connotations, and some have questioned whether they travel well when applied to women (for an overview of this debate see Lister 1997). From the 1980s feminist scholarship in particular has challenged the neglect of 'the peculiarities' of women's social citizenship in the mainstream approach, and called attention to its 'gender-blindness', which limits the understanding of welfare state functioning and neglects the different ways in which women and men are integrated in the welfare state. As has been documented from various forms of welfare states, to a very considerable extent the gendering of access to social rights is mediated by the different participation of women and men in the labour market and in family matters (for example Hernes 1987; Pateman 1988b; Lewis (ed.) 1993; for a useful overview of the literature see O'Connor 1996). The lively debate in the 1970s and 1980s concerning the character of the welfare state's relationship with women as 'patriarchy' or 'partnership' also emphasized the necessity of examining the processes that generate a gendering of access to the social rights of citizenship (see, for example, Hernes 1987; Borchorst and Siim 1987; Leira 1992).

In the 1990s the discussions about the gendering of welfare states have been much stimulated by the highly influential work of Gøsta Esping-Andersen (1990), and particularly his typology of welfare state regimes. In his analysis of the three worlds of welfare capitalism, Esping-Andersen takes the arrangement between the welfare state, labour market and the family as the basis for his (above-mentioned) classification of regimes. The regime types are also identified by the extent to which they provide social rights, including 'decommodification', and whether the welfare state upholds or reduces social stratification. 'Decommodification occurs when a service is rendered as a matter of right, and when a person can maintain a livelihood without reliance on the market' (pp. 21–2). According to Esping-Andersen, the welfare state is a system of stratification, and the main question is how social policies affect stratification, or 'what kind of social stratification is promoted by social policy' (p. 23).

As has often been pointed out, Esping-Andersen's main concern is with the labour market–welfare state relationship, while the family does not really play an important part in his analysis. Provision of welfare, however, includes not only state and market, but also the family, social networks, and voluntary organizations, the so-called 'third sector', where the care work of women – and men – plays a crucial role. Esping-Andersen largely overlooks the division of labour by gender in extra-market work, and the importance of the family in welfare provision. The level of decommodification and the type of social stratification generated by social policy are influenced not only by employment status but also by gender. However, the different ways in which women and men are affected by decommodification – or commodification for that matter – are not an issue in his analysis, and he does not look into the gender effects of the social stratification generated by the social policy system. Thus, the analysis misses the gender differentiation of access to social citizenship. In Esping-Andersen's most recent book (1999), in which he rethinks his regime typology and responds to some of his critics, the family is at centre stage, but the gender differentiation with respect to social citizenship is not really explored.

Looking at the welfare state from a different vantage point, and starting with the family models promoted, offers interesting alternatives to the typologies of 'mainstream' research, as argued, for example, by Jane Lewis (1992) who distinguishes between strong, modified and weak male breadwinner states (see also Lewis 1997; Daly in this volume). Starting from the public–private division of responsibility for care provision shows the very different approaches of the welfare state to social reproduction (Anttonen and Sipilä 1996), as does the study of family obligations (Millar and Warman 1996). Bringing the family, gender and responsibility for care provision into the welfare state analysis provides the basis for different classifications (see, for example, Sainsbury 1994; Siaroff 1994).

As mentioned above, the dominant welfare state typology of the 1990s, Gøsta Esping-Andersen's, has also been reworked to include gender. In an influential critique of the 'power resources school' in comparative welfare state research, Ann Orloff (1993) elaborates on Esping-Andersen's discussion of the three welfare regimes, by explicitly gendering the main dimensions of his analysis, and including two additional dimensions, namely access to paid work and the capacity to form and maintain an autonomous household (see also Hobson 1990). Orloff's analysis further illustrates the different approaches of welfare states to different family forms and to social reproduction in a broader sense. Some differences are perhaps most clearly evidenced in the policies concerning single provider households with children, where the policies of the US, for example, contrast strongly with those of the Scandinavian countries (Sørensen 1999; see also the contributions of Larsen and Millar in this volume).

Challenging the narrow focus on the relationship between capital and labour and the state–market interaction, the feminist critique has made two particularly important points: first, focusing on the welfare state–market relationship to the exclusion of the family, the voluntary associations and other institutions of civil society obviously gives a limited perspective on the production of welfare in society. Thus, the many ways in which the welfare state depends upon the family and other institutions and agencies for the provision of social care and welfare are easily neglected. The second aspect of the critique points to the implicit or explicit male-centredness of much of the comparative welfare state literature, in that the focus on the state–market arrangement easily misses the importance of the gendered division of paid and unpaid work and care, and thus its importance to the gendering of access to social rights (Boje and Almqvist, Daly and Saraceno in this volume). Focus on the construction of the social rights of wage-workers (typically men) has often entailed a neglect of the very different basis from which unpaid carers (who are typically women) may make claims for social rights (Leira 1992).

For the analysis of how the restructuring of labour markets, the family institution and welfare state affects the social rights of women and men as workers and carers it is important to consider in more detail the relationship of the welfare state to gender and class. In this volume the added challenges represented by race and ethnicity are not specifically addressed.

Content of the book

This book starts from the gender divide of welfare. A common characteristic of the welfare states of the OECD countries is a profound gender division of paid and unpaid work and care, which affects women's position in the family, the labour market and their access to social citizenship. One of the major purposes of this book is to take further the discussion about the relationship between welfare state, market and family and its impact on women's economic, social, and political (in)dependence in the modern western welfare societies. The book aims to reach beyond the narrow focus on the labour market–welfare state arrangement and to explore the relationship between production and social reproduction, paid and unpaid work and care within the framework of different welfare states. Special attention is paid to the shifting gender balance of employment and the restructuring of social care provision. An analysis of the different ways in which men and women are integrated in the labour market, the family and the welfare state has to make explicit the tacit assumptions concerning the gendered division of paid and unpaid work and care.

The feminist as well as others' critiques of the mainstream literature on welfare state typologies have contributed to a broadening of the scope of welfare state research by emphasizing the need for gender-specific as well as gender-relational approaches to the analysis of social citizenship, and the importance of the family and other non-public agencies for the provision of social care. Throughout the book it is argued that without a better understanding of the relationship between paid and unpaid work and care it is not possible to understand the different ways in which men and women are integrated into the labour force, the gendered division of family obligations or the different conditions for women and men in getting access to social citizenship.

Thus, theorizing the gender arrangements of welfare states, labour markets and families is a central concern of the book, and the combinations of work and family or of paid and unpaid work and care made by women and men are the main frame of reference for the empirical studies. An analytic approach that excludes the care work provided informally or unpaid in the family or household makes it impossible to understand how welfare policies contribute to gender inequality in the family and the labour market and with respect to social citizenship.

From a gender perspective the contributions reflect on the present state of the art in the theoretical debate in welfare state scholarship, and discuss the impact on gender relations of the ongoing restructuring of labour market, family institution and provision of social care. Drawing upon research from western Europe, North America and Japan, the book strikes a balance between broad international overviews, comparisons between specific welfare states and national case studies.

The first part of the book takes the changing gender balance of employment as a starting point for discussing the restructuring of welfare state and family-related policies, while in the second part the contributions largely start from the ongoing restructuring of care provision and examine the interplay of welfare state policies, labour market developments and family changes.

Mary Daly introduces the first part of the book giving a critical overview of the feminist debate concerning gender and welfare state. During the recent decades a substantial literature on the gender dimension of welfare states has appeared but most of this research on gender and the welfare state has struggled to render the mainstream concepts more adequate in understanding the gendered relations and processes of paid and unpaid work and care. According to Daly most of the feminist-oriented literature is centred around three approaches: first, the concept of care in revealing the links between care and the gender dimension of welfare state provision, second, the gendered aspects of the welfare state to be explored by analyses of differences in access to social citizenship for men and women, and, finally, the breadwinner/housewife typology to be used as a way of understanding the organizing principles of welfare states from a gender perspective. Daly gives a critical overview of these three approaches and evaluates their potential for capturing the gender dimension of welfare states and she ends by arguing for a theoretical model combining the three approaches. Rather than forcing the individual approaches to overreach she suggests a framework where they are combined and used in analysing the different dimensions of the welfare state for which they are most suited. Furthermore, she recommends a reorientation of methodology in welfare state analysis. The many countries/few variables comparative analyses have reached their limits, she argues, and have to be replaced by few countries/multi-variables studies combining quantitative overviews with detailed qualitative national case studies. The research strategy she recommends has been applied in several of the studies presented in this book.

Boje and Almqvist take a different starting point, looking at the different approaches of welfare states to women's combination of paid work and unpaid care, and discusss the policies instituted to meet the demands of carers and the persons cared for. They assess the impact of family policy on women's labour market involvement in five different European welfare states – Denmark, France, Germany, Sweden and the UK. In their conceptualization of citizenship they argue for a definition which, on the one hand, includes the rights and the obligations to labour market participation but, on the other hand, also recognizes citizens' rights to receive and to give care. This extension of the concept of social citizenship is in line with the recommendations by Knijn and Kremer (1997) and is discussed in the study of Boje and Almqvist by a distinction between the right to receive care and the right to time for care. The analysis concludes that the divergencies in women's labour market involvement during the different periods of their lives are determined in a complex relationship between national differences in family policy as well as differences in labour market regulation and patterns of family formation. Furthermore, the gendered character of paid work, unpaid work and welfare provision differs between the five countries to such a degree that any use of the conventional welfare regime typologies does not make sense and has to be replaced by national case studies.

In their analyses of labour market changes and policy reforms Cecilia Benoit and Anne Lise Ellingsæter make a critical examination of labour market developments, discussing the use of common terms in welfare analyses such as 'globalization', 'flexibilization', 'deregulation' and what the social processes behind these concepts mean for women's labour market participation and for their social rights in different types of welfare systems. Benoit's analysis and comparison of the liberal welfare states, Canada and the US, offers an interesting elaboration of some of the themes addressed by O'Connor, Orloff and Shaver (1999) in their discussion of the liberal welfare states. In several respects the study by Benoit responds to the various calls from feminist scholars to incorporate gender into the comparative welfare research, to restrict the studies to few countries/multi-variable analysis and to analyse the cross-national differences in a longer time perspective. In her concluding remarks Benoit states that the concept of liberal welfare state regime, which is the usual connotation of the two countries, probably fits the organization of the US welfare policies but has little value for understanding the complex nature of the Canadian welfare system. The two national welfare systems are different in their response to globalization and post-Fordism. In some respects the effects of post-Fordism have been more dramatic in Canada than in the US – growth in part-time employment, level of unemployment, and growth in self-employment – while in others the opposite has been true – size of the public service sector, union strength or deregulation. Therefore, in comparative studies it is important 'to keep our eyes open for continuing differences between the two OECD country cousins' – just as it is important in other studies comparing countries normally considered as similar in welfare systems.

Ellingsæter looks in a similar way at the Scandinavian social-democratic welfare states and analyses what has happened with welfare policies and labour market institutions in a period of increasing external pressure. She examines how policy changes and restructuring of the labour markets in the Scandinavian countries in the 1990s influence gender relations in work and employment and thereby are transforming prevailing gender structures in welfare states normally considered as 'women-friendly' (see Hernes 1987; Siim 1987). Taking this focus she illustrates the role played by the labour market structures in shaping gender equality. Ellingsæter finds no trends in her study towards a dismantling of the Scandinavian welfare model but rather an emphasizing of the differences between the countries included in the Scandinavian welfare model. Her analysis thereby provides another illustration of the limits of the welfare state typologies. From an OECD perspective she concludes that the Scandinavian welfare states are still the countries with the largest share of women in the labour market and the highest level of gender equality in labour market relations. Futhermore, most of the registered changes in labour market structure and policy regulation cannot be related to economic globalization or deregulation but are primarily coloured by the countries' own historical legacies.

The first part of the book concludes with a chapter in which Janet C. Gornick presents a broad overview of trends in women's labour market participation and cross-national variations in public policies supporting mothers' employment. Despite a strong increase in women's labour market participation in nearly all OECD countries, substantial gender differences in levels of employment, division of labour, industrial affiliation and earnings persist in all labour markets; differences which can only partly be explained by the cross-national variations in public policies. The causal links between policy and outcomes have to be clarified, she argues. In her conclusion Gornick raises two important issues concerning the relationship between family policy and women's labour market integration. First, the effects of the ongoing labour market restructuring and welfare state retrenchment for women's future labour market position. Second, the possibilities of reducing the sexual division of labour in unpaid care work through public policy measures. The latter issue is a core question in several of the studies presented in the remaining part of this book.

The second part of the book takes the welfare state's response to changing family forms as the point of departure and discusses the ongoing renegotiations of the state–family relationship in different forms of the welfare state. The contribution of Chiara Saraceno offers a broad overview of the arrangements between families and markets in the welfare states of the West. The differences between welfare states with respect to their family policies have to be historically contextualized, she argues, to acknowledge in current arrangements the influence of how issues of gender relations and family obligations were framed in the early origins of the national welfare states. Saraceno's chapter outlines the multiplicity of meaning and contents in the conceptualization of family obligations, and brings out the variations across western Europe with respect to how family obligations are formally defined. Saraceno further illustrates the different approaches of welfare states to new family forms. While all the welfare states in question experience an increase in the labour market participation of women and mothers, the policy response to working mothers is far from uniform, for example as regards the provision of maternity, paternity and parental leave, or the state-sponsoring of childcare facilities. The chapter also comments upon the call for 'refamilialization' of care and welfare provision, demanding that families take on more responsibility for members and relations. Although the unpaid labour available for family care is diminishing as women are entering the labour force, arguments for the strengthening of family responsibilities and extending obligation in relation to caring for both children and the elderly are often voiced. In several welfare states the division of labour between the public and the private sectors, the state and families is renegotiated, often with the aim of limiting public spending and upholding or extending family or individual obligations.

Saraceno's chapter provides a backdrop for the following chapters. From different perspectives and dealing with developments across different welfare states, they deal with the renegotiation of the state–family relationship, and particularly with the welfare state approach to the combination of work and family.

The chapters by Arnlaug Leira and Ito Peng examine developments in family policies in the welfare states of the Nordic countries and Japan, respectively, and focus on the restructuring of childcare provision necessitated by mothers' employment. The increase in women's labour market participation, and particularly that of mothers of young children, has everywhere raised questions concerning the combination of job and family commitments. The two chapters discuss the different approaches to childcare provision developed within the very different welfare state traditions of Japan and the Nordic area.

Focusing on recent reforms related to the combination of work and family for both fathers and mothers, Arnlaug Leira examines similarities and differences in the approach of the Nordic countries, which are commonly classed together as social-democratic welfare state regimes. The reforms are linked with more or less explicit family models, she argues. For example, the expansion of state support for childcare facilities is regarded as benefiting the dual-earner family; the extension of parental leave to include a special quota for fathers promotes the dual-earner, care-sharing family; and the institution of a cash benefit for childcare, introduced with the aim of increasing 'parental choice' with respect to childcare, as a support of the traditional gender-differentiated family. The chapter pays special attention to the 'daddy quota' and the cash benefit, and their reception in the Nordic countries. The 'daddy quota', potentially a very radical reform, was hardly debated at all, while the proposal for a cash benefit for childcare caused heated political debate.

Ito Peng gives an analysis of important developments in postwar family policy in Japan. Since the early 1990s, actualized by the increase in women's employment, Japan has debated the provision of childcare: who should care for children, where and by whom should care be provided, and who should shoulder the costs? Peng presents an overview of the public support for childcare established to meet the demands of children and parents in need, and discusses the shortcomings of the traditional system in meeting the demands of dual-earner families. Some of the problems to be addressed in Japanese policy reforms, stemming from the change in mothers' economic activity, are rather similar to those reported from across the OECD area. However, policy reforms do not necessarily travel well. Peng's chapter emphasizes the importance of an historically situated analysis that brings out the meaning and content of public and private involvement in childcare provision in the Japanese context. The analysis of recent developments in childcare policies also provides an insight into the character of the Japanese welfare regime.

From different perspectives the last two contributions analyse the gender assumptions underlying the welfare state's response to family change, taking the single provider or lone mother family as the main case. The comprehensive transformation of family formation witnessed in the widespread popularity of cohabitation without marriage and the increase in parental split-up have changed the content and meaning of 'lone parenthood' and actualized the questions concerning the economic and social situation of the single parent family with young children, and particularly the lone mother family.

Jørgen Elm Larsen's chapter starts from a discussion of two main approaches in social research to the study of lone parents. One is primarily concerned with the increase in lone parent families, poverty risks and the difference in policy response of welfare states to this family form. The other approach takes lone parents as a 'litmus test' of how welfare states approach the 'woman question'. From an overview of the change in 'lone parenthood', the rising proportion and the changing recruitment, Elm Larsen goes on to discuss the poverty rates of this family form, poverty rates being regarded as the outcome of labour market participation, social services and benefits, and family support. Drawing upon comprehensive survey data sets, he finds no simple answer to the question concerning which policy regime is most efficient in combating poverty among lone parent families. Apparently, different policy regimes may produce similar effects on poverty regimes, and similar policies apparently produce different poverty rates. However, two policy approaches stand out as opposites when it comes to taking lone mother families into or out of poverty: that of the US, which goes together with high poverty rates, and that of the Scandinavian welfare states, which keeps poverty rates low.

Jane Millar's contribution starts from a broad overview of the reformulation of family obligations in Europe. Based on a sixteen-country study of how family obligations are formally defined in law and politics, the chapter explores the influence of changing perceptions of family obligations on policy, taking the changing obligations surrounding partnering and parenting as the main case. European welfare states have pursued different policies in relation to the lone-mother family, Millar argues. Some are promoting maternal responsibilities for childcare and upbringing, while others aim at strengthening the economic provider aspects of motherhood, e.g. the 'workfare' initiatives. In several countries policies towards lone-mother families are being changed. Taking the British case as a main example, Millar discusses the problems inherent in policies that apparently aim at strengthening the economic provider responsibilities of lone motherhood, without providing generously for high-quality, low-cost childcare. As Millar aptly concludes: 'Who bears the costs of children and who bears the costs of care are likely to be among the most central questions of the next century.'

References

Almqvist, A.L. and T.P. Boje (1999) 'Who cares, who pays and how is care for children provided? Comparing family life and work in different European welfare systems (DK, D, F, S, and UK)', in D. Bouget and B. Palier (eds) *Comparing Social Welfare Systems in Nordic Countries and France*, MIRE/MSH, Nantes 1999.

Anttonen, A. and J. Sipilä (1996) 'European social care services: is it possible to identify models?' *Journal of European Social Policy* 6: 2.

Beck, U. (1992) *Risk Society. Towards a New Modernity*, London: Sage Publications.

Bettio, F. and S. Prechal (1998) *Care in Europe. Medium-term Community Action Programme on Equal Opportunities for Women and Men (1996–2000)*.

Boje, T.P. (1998) 'Welfare, citizenship and social solidarity', in Bent Greve (ed.) *What Constitutes a Good Society?* London: Macmillan.

Borchorst, A. and B. Siim (1987) 'Women and the advanced welfare state. A new kind of patriarchal power', in Sassoon, A. S. (ed.) *Women and the State*, London: Hutchinson.

Bruning, G. and J. Plantenga (1999) 'Parental leave and equal opportunities: experiences in eight European countries', *Journal of European Social Policy*, 9: 3.

Deven, F. and P. Moss (eds) (2000) *Parental Leave: Progress or Pitfall? Research and Policy Issues in Europe*, Brussels: NIDI CBGS Publications 35).

Esping-Andersen, G. (1990) *The Three Worlds of Welfare Capitalism*, Cambridge: Polity Press.

Esping-Andersen, G. (1999) *Social Foundations of Postindustrial Economies*, Oxford: Oxford University Press.

European Commission Childcare Network (1996) *A Review of Services for Young Children*, Brussels.

EUROSTAT (1997) 'Family responsibilities – how are they shared in European households?' *Statistics in Focus* 1997: 5.

Hernes, H.M. (1987) *Welfare States and Women Power*, Oslo: Norwegian University Press.

Hernes, H.M. (1988) ' Scandinavian citizenship', *Acta Sociologica*, 31: 2, 199–215.

Hirdman, Y. (1988) 'Genussystemet – reflexionor kring kvinnors sociala underordning' *Krinnovetenskapligs tidsskrift*, No. 3.

Hobson, B (1990) 'No exit no voice: Women's economic dependency and the welfare state', *Acta Sociologica*, 33: 235–50.

Hochschild, A. (1995) 'The culture of politics: traditional, postmodern, cold-modern, and warm-modern ideals of care', *Social Politics*, Fall: 331–46.

Jenson, J. (1997) 'Who cares? Gender and welfare regimes', *Social Politics*, 4, 2: 182–7.

Knijn, T. and Kremer, M. (1997) 'Gender and the caring dimensions of welfare states: yoward inclusive citizenship', *Social Politics*, 4: 3.

Leira, A. (1992) *Welfare States and Working Mothers*, Cambridge: Cambridge University Press.

Leira, A. (1997) 'Social rights in a gender perspective', in Koslowski, P. and Føllesdal, A. (eds) *Restructuring the Welfare State*, Berlin: Springer.

Lewis, J. (1992) 'Gender and the development of welfare state regimes', *Journal of European Social Policy*, 2, 3: 159–73.

Lewis, J. (ed.) (1993) *Women and Social Policies in Europe. Work, Family and the State*, Aldershot: Edward Elgar.

Lewis, J. (1997) 'Gender and welfare regimes: further thoughts', *Social Politics*, 4, 2: 160–77.

Lewis, J. (ed.) (1998) *Gender, Social Care and Welfare State Restructuring in Europe*, Aldershot: Ashgate.

Lister, R. (1997) *Citizenship. Feminist Perspectives*, New York: New York University Press.

Marshall, T.H. (1965) *Class, Citizenship and Social Development*, New York: Anchor Books.

Millar, J. and Warman, A. (eds) (1995) *Defining Family Obligations in Europe*, Bath: Bath Social Policy Papers.

Millar, J. and Warman, A. (1996) *Family Obligations in Europe*, London: Family Policies Study Centre.

O'Connor, J.S. (1996) 'From women in the welfare state to gendering welfare state regimes', *Current Sociology*, 44: 2.

O'Connor, J.S., Orloff, A.S. and Shaver, S. (1999) *States, Markets, Families. Gender, Liberalism and Social Policy in Australia, Canada and the United States*, Cambridge: Cambridge University Press.

OECD (1994) *OECD Societies in Transition: The Future of Work and Leisure*, Paris: OECD.

OECD (1995) 'Long-term leave for parents in OECD countries', Ch. 5 in *Employment Outlook*, pp. 171–96.

OECD (1997) *Family, Market and Community. Equity and Efficiency in Social Policy*, OECD Social Policy Studies, no. 21, Paris: OECD.

Orloff, A. (1993) 'Gender and the social rights of citizenship', *American Sociological Review* 58: 303–28.

Pateman, C. (1988a) *The Sexual Contract*, Cambridge: Polity Press.

Pateman, C. (1988b) 'The patriarchal welfare state', in Gutman, A. (ed.) *Democracy and the Welfare State*, Princeton: Princeton University Press.

Pateman, C. (1996) *Democratisation and Citizenship in the 1990s. The Legacy of T.H. Marshall*, Oslo: Institute for Social Research.

Sainsbury, D. (1994) 'Women's and men's social rights: Gendering dimensions of the welfare states', in Sainsbury, D. (ed.) *Gendering Welfare States*, London: Sage.

Saraceno, C. (1997) 'Family change, family policies and the restructuring of welfare', in *Family, Market and Community. Equity and Efficiency in Social Policy*, OECD Social Policy Studies, no. 21, Paris: OECD.

Siaroff, A. (1994) 'Work, welfare and gender equality: a new typology', in Sainsbury, D. (ed.) *Gendering Welfare States*, London: Sage.

Siim, B. (1987) 'The Scandinavian welfare states: towards sexual equality or a new kind of male dominance', *Acta Sociologica*, 30, no. 4.

Siim, B. (1993) 'The gendered Scandinavian welfare states: the interplay between women's roles as mothers, workers, citizens in Denmark', in Lewis, J. (ed.) *Women and Social Policies in Europe. Work, Family and the State*, Aldershot: Edward Elgar.

Sørensen, A. (1999) 'Family decline, poverty and social exclusion: the mediating effects of family policy', in Engelstad, F. *et al.* (eds) *Yearbook of Comparative Social Research*, vol. 18: 57–78.

Taylor-Gooby, P. (1991) 'Welfare state regimes and welfare citizenship', *Journal of European Social Policy*, 1, 2: 93–105.

Titmuss, R.M. (1974) *Social Policy*, London: Allen and Unwin.

Wilensky, H.L. and Lebeaux, C.N. (1958) *Industrial Society and Social Welfare*, New York: The Free Press.

Part I

Women's employment and welfare systems

1 Paid work, unpaid work and welfare

Towards a framework for studying welfare state variation

Mary Daly

Introduction

The study of welfare state variation proceeds apace. Much of the recent impetus in scholarship on the welfare state has come from gender-focused work. As a result, one has a choice of approaches to study the gender dimension of welfare states. But there has been little critical comment on the gender-focused work. Even though it has provided a critique of the conventional perspectives on the welfare state, feminist work has itself been subjected to little by way of review and appraisal. This is in some ways surprising for a perspective that is critical in origin. While one may speculate about the reasons for the absence of critique, some appraisal of feminist work on the welfare state is overdue. It is time to take stock. Towards this end, I intend in this chapter to undertake a review of some of the main approaches to understanding and studying variations in how welfare states treat and influence gender relations. This analysis sounds several key notes of a theoretical, conceptual and methodological nature.

One could say that three main approaches to the welfare state prevail in the feminist-oriented literature today. The first centres on the concept of care, employing it to uncover the characteristics of caring as labour and a set of relationships and to reveal the links between care and the gender dimension of welfare state provision. Work that explores the gendered aspects of the welfare state from within the paradigm of citizenship forms a second bulk of feminist scholarship on the welfare state. Third, feminists have proffered the breadwinner/housewife typology as a way of understanding the organizing principles of welfare states from a gender-sensitive perspective. While they have some common links, each approach tends to adopt a different perspective on how to theorize and identify the gender dimension(s) of the welfare state. Each of the three frameworks will be reviewed in this chapter for its capacity to countenance the key elements involved in the relation between gender and the welfare state and associated variations. The thrust of my analysis with regard to these approaches will demonstrate that each has strengths and weaknesses which enhance, but at the same time delimit, analytic capacity. Second, I want to consider the main methodological approaches adopted by feminist work in recent years in order to identify the general methodological principles of this work as well as the direction in which it is heading. In particular, the merits and demerits of typologizing need to be carefully debated. In the third part of the chapter I suggest some ways in which it is possible to move towards a better conceptualization of the relationship between state, market and family in terms of how they embody and shape gender relations. It will be interesting to ascertain if it is possible to do so by undertaking a synthesis of the three approaches of care, citizenship and breadwinner models. The key challenge is to rework these concepts into a comprehensive framework capable of countenancing variation and complexity in how welfare states embody and affect gender relations. This third part of the chapter will also consider how methodological approaches can be rendered more satisfactory.

To the extent that what I undertake here is a review or evaluation of feminist work on the welfare state, the evaluative criteria should be made explicit at the outset. Some such criteria are easily identifiable. It goes without saying that the overriding criterion of the utility of an approach is that it be able to capture the gender dimension of social policies. The meaning of this is not, of course, straightforward, but I am specific in my use of it. What I mean is that an approach should be capable of countenancing the position of both women and men, their relations and the state/family/market relation as they are envisaged in and shaped by social policies. Second, any satisfactory approach should be able to cope with variation. With welfare state research becoming increasingly comparative, an essential evaluative criterion is the capacity of perspectives to accommodate and account for variation. Third, this piece is guided by the conviction that welfare state analyses must become more comprehensive and for this purpose it is necessary, somewhat paradoxically perhaps, that they become more differentiated. More precisely, the difference between the content or design of policies, the processes which policies set in train and the outcomes which they bring about must be registered. These have tended to be elided in the literature. I do not wish to imply that these are in practice separate but a distinction between them for analytic purposes seems to me to be essential, especially for work that searches after the analytic strengths and weaknesses of particular approaches to the welfare state. A key goal of the review of the feminist work that follows, then, is to ascertain the potential of each approach on the basis of these lines of evaluation.

Critical overview of work on gender and the welfare state

Gender as a practice and process of social differentiation and a key constituent of identity has proved to be one of the major growth areas in the social sciences over the last decade and a half. In the welfare state, as in other domains, it has yielded a rich legacy of concepts and approaches. This work is especially good on the nature and content of social policies. We can, for instance, analyse gender in the welfare state in terms of the underlying institutional and normative models underlying policy (conceptualized either as breadwinner models, gender regimes or models of marriage), the quality of social rights (conditions of access and entitlement to benefits, the range of risks covered and the extent to which hierarchies exist between women and men's risks), or the different roles for women and men which are envisaged by welfare state provisions. Alternatively, we may take the outcome side as our starting point and focus upon women and men's lives as they are influenced or affected by welfare state provisions. Here we have the choice of examining how welfare states help to shape gender roles, how they act to distribute paid and unpaid labour and time, and, over the longer run, women and men's life chances and opportunities.

This review engages not with the details of each of these strands of analysis but rather with the general principles that underpin them. It is useful to begin with an attempt to differentiate the conceptual and methodological dimensions of existing work.

Conceptual approaches

Feminist work on the welfare state is impossible to understand apart from its historical context. This is a body of work that is, and should be seen as, a critical response to either the downgrading of women and gender in mainstream work or their outright exclusion from it. The originating critique by feminism of the conventional work on the welfare state focused upon the failure to consider gender as a constituent element of political identity, the role that female political agency played in shaping welfare states, the contribution of female labour, both paid and unpaid, to welfare in societies and the fact that welfare states may have both shaped these and led to gendered outcomes. Concepts, if not theories, have been at the forefront of the feminist critique. Looking at the body of feminist work on the welfare state as a whole, it could be said to have proceeded along two lines, the tracks of which were laid out by the critique of existing perspectives.[1] Either scholars felt that they had to develop new concepts and approaches or they, implicitly or explicitly, reworked existing frameworks so as to render them more 'gender-friendly'. The latter comprises the greater bulk of the work, although the former would probably have been the more sought-after goal.

Three core approaches have guided the most recent wave of feminist work on the welfare state. They are the care-centred work, that focused on citizenship and the scholarship around the breadwinner model. There is surprisingly little conversation between the different approaches – while their relationship is not competitive or adversarial, it is not complementary either. Work on the different strands proceeds more or less independently of each other. This is a pity for, as the analysis to follow will demonstrate, the three conceptual approaches have something to say to each other and complement one another at important junctures.

The concept of care[2]

Care, one of the truly original concepts to emerge from feminist scholarship and arguably one of the most widely used in feminist analyses of welfare states today, has its origins in an attempt to define the work that makes up caring for others and to analyse how that work reinforced the disadvantaged position of women. The nature of the labour involved in caring was a key consideration from the outset, the goal being to define in its own right the set of activities that make up caring for others, to identify its specific if not unique features and to analyse how both the activity and responsibility for caring reinforced the disadvantaged position of women. Caring was, initially at any rate, conceived of in relation to the unpaid domestic and personal services provided through the social relations of marriage and kinship. So defined, the concept turned attention on the material and emotional processes that made up care and at the same time confirmed women as (for the most part unpaid) carers. The pioneering work on care (Finch and Groves 1983; Waerness 1984) focused mainly on unpaid, informal care in the family. The approach could be said to have served the feminist analytic purpose well, having led to a body of scholarship which demonstrated the ubiquity and specificity of the activity of caring. In this regard, it drew attention to the fact that care was more than just unpaid personal services. Not only was it inherently defined by the relations within which it was embedded and carried out but care, conceived as responsibility and/or need, played a powerful role in defining the life situation of women and men and the nature of family life. The specificity of the relations of care was elaborated and they were shown to be characterized by personal ties of obligation, commitment, trust and loyalty (Leira 1992).

Over time, the concept of care was broadened, reflecting both the changing nature of arrangements for caring in practice and the complexity introduced by the increasingly comparative nature of scholarship. Across nations and over time within them, care-giving has shifted between the realms of paid and unpaid work, a movement that has never been solidly in one direction. Moreover, the interpretation of the meaning and significance of care-related policies for women is not straightforward. Early Scandinavian feminist analysis of social policy argued that the entry of women into jobs in day-care centres, schools, hospitals and old people's homes – in the service of the welfare state – represented a form of 'public patriarchy' (e.g. Siim 1987). Women were now doing in the public sphere the work which they had traditionally carried out in the home. Others have been more eager to claim this shift as an unequivocal gain (e.g. Kolberg 1991). As these and other debates were unfolding, care was maturing as an academic concept. Graham (1991), for example, sought to include non-kin forms of home-based care so as to enable the concept to embrace relations of class and race alongside those of gender. Leira (1992) drew attention to how care involves the interface of public authorities, especially the welfare state, and private agents. Tronto (1993) elaborated a view of care as both practice and disposition. Thomas (1993) further developed the concept, identifying seven dimensions to it.

These pertain to the identity of the providers and recipients of care, the relationship between them, the social content of the care, the economic character of the relationship and of the labour involved, and the social domain and institutional setting within which care is provided.

Care has, therefore, matured into both a complex concept – it does not dovetail, for example, in any simplistic way with the paid/unpaid work differentiation – and one with considerable analytic potential in relation to the welfare state. Part of its beauty is that it is enlightening about the content and context of a defining element of women's life situation and how welfare states relate to and reinforce that. This is a strength, indeed a not inconsiderable one, and it has led to a number of insightful analyses of welfare state provision from the perspective of care (Knijn and Kremer 1997; Boje and Almqvist in this volume). This and other strengths notwithstanding, the concept of care is both ambiguous and contested. Part of the problem may lie in its very popularity – it has been used in such diverse ways that it is in danger of losing its core meaning. If one is to employ the concept of care as a category of analysis in relation to the welfare state, one must find a way of retaining its capacity to reveal important dimensions of women's lives (indeed, the human condition) as well as developing further its capacity to uncover more general properties of public arrangements for the fulfilment of personal needs and welfare. Some pressing questions remain in regard to the latter. The extent to which one can make general statements about welfare states by virtue of the nature of their care-related policies alone remains to be established. While I am not disputing that all welfare state policies have consequences for caring, I am claiming that not all welfare state policies were designed and instituted with care in mind. This, while it may seem like a minor point, has important analytic implications. Its main significance is two-fold. First, the nature and distribution of care in society is influenced not just by explicit care-related policies but by the entire range of welfare state provisions. Having said this, I would argue, secondly, that care is a concept that speaks more readily to the processes and outcomes of welfare states than to the content or architecture of their policies. That is, while one will find some traces of care in all welfare state policies, the essence of the relation between welfare states and care is larger than any single policy and is to be found especially in the processes generated by welfare states and the outcomes which these processes bring about. In other words the real strength of the care concept lies not in what it has to say about welfare state policies *per se* but in what it can reveal about the processes set in train by such welfare state provision. This set of points will be further developed in the third part of the chapter.

Citizenship

Citizenship has led one of the main flanks of the feminist advance on conventional welfare state scholarship. The two different historical traditions of citizenship – the liberal rights approach which conceptualizes citizenship as

status and right and the civic republican approach which emphasizes practice
and participation – have each received critical attention and some scholars have
seen a better future to lie in a synthesis of the two (Lister 1997). One of the most
long-standing concerns in relation to citizenship or citizenship theory on the
part of feminists has been the concept's exclusionary tendencies. Questions of
inequality have been given a central place. Feminists trained the spotlight on the
assumption that citizenship was undifferentiated, in essence asking whether
social rights are of equal value for women and men (Pateman 1996: 7). The
answer is a resounding 'no' and the path leading to this conclusion has
furnished a critique of the false universalisms of the mainstream discussions of
citizenship (in relation to women especially but also on the basis of race and
ethnic identity) (Lister 1996: 6). Issues of dependence and independence as they
are embedded in the conditions of citizenship have been raised in this context.
This debate has increasingly embraced the issue of care, of late wandering into
the terrain of how carers can be given adequate rights. Some have even gone so
far as to claim that welfare states' treatment of care defines women and men's
citizenship status (Knijn and Kremer 1997). Different routes and past and
current political approaches to women's social citizenship have been considered.

One of the most sought-after goals in the feminist critique of citizenship has
been to elaborate it as a soci(ologic)al and contingent concept. According to
Lister (1996: 1): 'what is involved is not simply a set of legal rules governing the
relationship between individuals and the state in which they live but also a set of
sociological relationships between individuals and the state and between
individual citizens'. This focuses attention on the interplay between the social
and political aspects of citizenship. Siim (1997: 5) makes the argument that a
gender-sensitive framework of citizenship must conceptualize two relatively
independent dimensions: women's social welfare rights and women's political
presence, identity and power. She makes a first attempt to insert gender into a
comparative approach to citizenship by developing Turner's (1992) model with
its two dimensions: active/passive and public/private citizenship. But, since she
does not go any distance in actually applying this model across a range of
welfare states, it is not yet clear whether this development of the citizenship
concept would contribute significantly to making this whole field of study more
dynamic and more comparative.

One of the main strengths of the citizenship approach is its capacity to bring
politics and provision together. In relation to the welfare state for example, the
use of this concept can help to reveal the relationship between political
engagement around welfare and the nature of welfare policy and provision
within and across national settings. To the extent that it has this potential, one of
its strengths is a sensitivity to how welfare states and social politics develop over
time. A second strength is that it speaks in very large terms. For citizenship is a
'big' concept, one with the potential to address not just individuals' relationship
with the state but, indeed, state/society relations themselves. So the citizenship
perspective lends itself to quite a macro-level analysis; being oriented to the

societal level it is a concept that is larger than the welfare state or indeed any particular domain of social policy. As things stand at present though, it is my opinion that the potential of the concept remains to be realized in that citizenship is one of the least comparative areas of feminist scholarship on the welfare state.[3] While it has, among other things, offered a critique of the periodization implied by T.H. Marshall's depiction of the development of civil, political and social citizenship, this scholarship has engaged in little comparative analysis of citizenship from place to place. As a result, this body of work has contributed but little to the analysis of variation in welfare state provisions and has had little to say about trajectories of change around citizenship. More than that though, it is not immediately clear what kind of analysis it invokes of the welfare state, other than a general analysis of social rights (which in my view is not hugely revealing when used comparatively). As it stands now, then, the citizenship domain offers little substance from the point of view of the analysis of the gender dimension of welfare states in a comparative perspective.

Breadwinner models

From around the mid-1980s on welfare state research became consciously comparative. As a result, the most interesting aspects of welfare states were seen to reside in how they compare with each other (most often as regards either policy content or outcomes). Feminists soon followed suit with their own brand of comparison. The latest round of feminist work, therefore, took its cue or initial impetus from mainstream work. This has tended to have the effect of redirecting the focus of feminist work on the welfare state from a concern with the complexity of particular welfare states to an approach that is preoccupied by variation across a (large) number of states.

The male breadwinner concept, the main axis of recent comparative feminist scholarship on the welfare state, speaks directly to the content of welfare state provision and how this varies from place to place. The wish to develop a gender-specific typology led Lewis (1992) and Lewis and Ostner (1991) to examine the organizing logics of welfare states from a gender perspective. Focusing primarily on the content and design of social policies, these authors highlighted the assumptions regarding the role of women that lie embedded in welfare policies. More precisely, a number of European welfare states are compared on the basis of whether they recognize and cater for women solely as wives and mothers and/or also as workers. In large part, Lewis represents this as a dichotomous choice and the general tendency, she says, has been to treat women as mothers. Put simply, this means that women's ties to welfare states are conceived in terms of their family role rather than on the basis of their status as individuals. From this framework, Lewis derives a three-fold categorization of several European welfare states: those with strong, moderate and weak breadwinner models. Britain and Ireland are categorized as strong male breadwinner countries. They are marked by their tendency to draw a firm dividing line between public and private responsibility and to treat married women as dependent wives for the purposes of social entitlements. France is categorized as a moderate male breadwinner state because women there have gained entitlements as both citizen mothers and citizen workers. Female labour market participation is encouraged but, at the same time, the policy framework is strongly supportive of families. Motherhood is treated as a social function rather than a private matter by family-centred, pronatalist-inspired social policies. Post-1970 Sweden and Denmark constitute the third variant in the typology, being weak male breadwinner states. Swedish social-democratic governments took conscious steps to bring all women into the labour force and to make the 'two breadwinner family' the norm. The basis of women's social entitlement was transformed: they have been treated as workers and have been compensated for their unpaid work as mothers at rates which they could command as members of the labour force (Lewis and Ostrer 1991: 169). Lewis's work remains the most influential typology in the gender-focused welfare state literature.[4]

In seeking to make the concept travel, Lewis has transcended a simplistic application and demonstrated that, while common, the family wage is by no means uniform. Another strength of the male breadwinner model is its inherent dynamic and implicit trajectory of change. Although Lewis does not develop a change-related analysis – indeed her characterization seems to be set some time around the 1970s/early 1980s – the male breadwinner typology has the potential to generate hypotheses about welfare state change and transformation. It has another merit as well in that it focuses centrally on how welfare state provision, as it is structured and organized, differentiates between women and men. Lewis's formulation of the model requires further development, however. While it may be occasioned by the degree of generality required by a typologizing methodology, too little attention has been devoted to specifying the attributes of the male breadwinner model. In particular, a specification of the terms of the model as it pertains to all women and to men is missing. This raises a number of problems. For one, the dichotomous treatment of women as mothers or workers is an (unacceptable) over-simplification of welfare states' gender dimension. While the need for a shorthand indicator is appreciated, the treatment of mothers is unlikely to serve as the template for the experience of all women at the hands of welfare states. Other work suggests that one should differentiate between the subsidization of marriage as against parenthood (Scheiwe 1994), that different models of motherhood are envisaged in and sustained by public policies (Leira 1992) and that states may and do support a wifely as well as a motherly role for women (Shaver and Bradshaw 1993). A second problem with the mother/worker dichotomy is that the treatment of mothers has no one-dimensional interpretation – it could be revelatory of a societal or state position on mothering, marriage, the family or a combination of all three. Third, it is undoubtedly important to note that high male wages, especially for men with families, are a condition of the male breadwinner model. In other words, to differentiate among women welfare states must also differentiate among men. This is perhaps one of the biggest failings of work on the breadwinner model to date – that it treats a gendered concept as a woman-specific one.

The framework has potential, though, not least because the breadwinner model offers a powerful way of conceptualizing welfare state variation. The integration of men and of a more differentiated set of female roles could, I suggest, render the model more discriminating and lend it an empirical applicability beyond a few states. The work of Diane Sainsbury (1996) is helpful for further elaborating the model. Through a consideration of the bases of entitlement to welfare benefits and services in the Netherlands, Sweden, the UK and the US, she demonstrates that the principle of supporting motherhood is only one of a number of principles contributing to the gender dimension of welfare state provision. Sainsbury's work leaves no doubt that a simplistic version of the breadwinner approach fails to do justice to the complexity of how welfare states govern access to their resources and have developed social programmes over time. Revealing the universe of variation represented by just the four welfare states which she studies, Sainsbury proves the need to differentiate between the support of women as wives (which, translated into social policy terms, means a principle of maintenance) and as providers of care (whereby mothers and other carers get benefits in their own right independent of their marital status). In the four welfare states which she studies, Sainsbury finds evidence of the following five principles in social provision as it relates to women and men:

- the principle of maintenance (the classic breadwinner ideology which celebrates and privileges marriage and reinforces a traditional sexual division of labour);
- the principle of care (whereby mothers and other carers get benefits in their own right independent of their marital status);
- the principle of citizenship or residence;
- the principle of need or want;
- the principle of labour market status and performance.

Searching for the broad distributive principles that underpin welfare state provision is therefore an important route to uncovering how welfare state benefits are organized and how this organization is gendered. The underlying point speaks to the complexity of welfare states: they can, and most do, operate to a number of principles simultaneously.

Overall, the main point to be emphasized at this stage is that each of the concepts or approaches has particular strengths and weaknesses. This has tended to go unrecognized – a fact which itself has had two consequences. First, the individual approaches have tended to be utilized in isolation, in essence being viewed as capable of taking a comprehensive perspective on the welfare state when, I would argue, each is (in different ways) partial. Second, the approaches have been used in an all-inclusive fashion when in fact a more differentiated application may well have yielded greater fruit. While the distinction is often a fine one, the conceptual referent of each is different. The 'natural' constituency of the concept of care is in my view the processes set in train by welfare state programmes. That is, this is a concept which is at its best in capturing the activity, conditions and relations of care and hence of women's (and men's) work as paid or unpaid. While the extent to which care can tap the constituent elements of social policy or the welfare state is questionable, the breadwinner model is strong on this very dimension. That is, the breadwinner model speaks especially to the structure and content of welfare state provision and to the institutions and ideologies embodied in policy; in essence what we might call the input side – the ideological, material and organizational dimensions of social programmes. The citizenship concept I view as being the 'largest' concept of the three considered here but also the one that has been least applied. While it may also address the constituents and content of policies, its primary referent in relation to the welfare state is to outcomes, in terms of whether women are enabled to be independent or autonomous individuals or not, gender-related and other forms of inequalities, and the relationship between the form of the (social) state and the nature of the society. In summary then, while each of the approaches has the capacity to be deployed for general analyses of the welfare state, their strengths lie in what they have to contribute to particular dimensions of the relationship between gender and the welfare state. In the last section I will attempt to utilize the strengths of each to develop a comprehensive framework for studying the gender dimension of welfare states.

Methodological issues also represent an important contribution of feminist work on the welfare state.

Methodological approaches in feminist work on the welfare state

There are at least two methodological traditions in feminist work on the welfare state. The first, and the original, is of a detailed focus upon the institutions of policy and their impact upon (women's) power relations. This approach lays emphasis upon processes and is concerned especially to identify the types of relations and activities which receipt (and sometimes non-receipt) of public benefits precipitate for women. It focuses more often than not upon micro-processes, piecing together the story of how welfare state provisions lead to particular experiences of people at the receiving end. Much of this work, reflecting a general tendency in feminist scholarship, has concentrated on the details of social programmes, how they have conditioned women's experience of (in)dependence and wellbeing and how they have led women to engage in relations and processes that are empowering or disempowering. It is a scholarship that has tended to relish the complexity of the everyday, emphasizing relations especially.

This type of approach has tended to be eclipsed in recent years as comparative work has assumed precedence. This is now the dominant idiom in welfare state research, for both the feminist and conventional scholarship. In taking this direction, feminists were following developments in conventional work which for the last two decades anyway has been consciously comparative. Furthermore, a particular orientation to comparison has prevailed. The many countries/few variables approach has dominated with ideal types as the favoured comparative device. It is a scholarship which is for the most part preoccupied with typologies and the act of typologizing. Esping-Andersen's (1990) book is perhaps the most famous approach to typology-building in the conventional welfare state literature. While they have been critical of his particular indicators and also of his resulting clusters, feminists have tended to replicate his approach by undertaking their own clustering, in practice thereby accepting the validity of the method and the approach. As outlined earlier, the most influential gender-inspired clustering is that of 'strong', 'moderate' and 'weak' male breadwinner models (Lewis and Ostner 1991; Lewis 1992).

This type of approach has many advantages. For one, forcing concepts and explanations to travel across a number of national borders introduces a degree of rigour and a breadth of explanation that can be missing in one- or two-nation studies. For another, this kind of comparative work demands a high degree of clarity about factors and variables and the nature of the causal processes that are involved in particular outcomes in a large number of countries. The few variables/many countries approach is not uncontroversial, though. The nature of the typologizing methodology, the coherence of the regime clusters identified and the appropriate characterization of particular countries are each problematic. There are, in my view, two points in the entire debate about welfare state regimes worth retaining. First, some country cases are definitely problematic for the purposes of regime clustering. Failing to emerge clearly from his empirical work, they had to be dragged by Esping-Andersen into particular clusters. Australia, France, Germany, Ireland, Italy, the Netherlands and the UK are the most obvious outsiders. Of course, with so many problem cases the legitimacy of clustering itself comes into question not least because the regimes, with fewer and fewer exemplar countries, serve an ever more compromised heuristic function. Second, there is a valid critique to be made about the completeness of both Esping-Andersen's and Lewis's clusters. Focusing upon the latter for a moment, to all intents and purposes, the breadwinner model awaits a proper empirical application for it appears that the country cases described are those that best fit the model. In any case, only a handful of countries are covered in Lewis's work and real doubts linger about the wider application of the breadwinner model, in particular its ability to differentiate further among countries. Where, one might ask, do the southern European welfare states fit in – are they not also strong male breadwinner countries? And what about the welfare models of New Zealand and Australia as well as those of Canada and the US? Cursory consideration of these countries and others suggests that they are all versions of the strong male breadwinner model. This leaves the Lewis framework overweighted at one end and hence unable to satisfy a basic criterion regarding the discriminatory properties of typologies.

Apart from matters of empirical application, some more general doubts persist about typologizing as method. Legitimate questions can be raised about an approach that assumes that the complexity of individual welfare states can be meaningfully categorized on the basis of a small number of general criteria. In relation to the, admittedly more primitive, dualistic institutional/residual framework, for example, Sainsbury found that just four countries – the Netherlands, Sweden, the UK and the US – represent hybrids uniquely combining various attributes of each dimension (Sainsbury 1991: 17). But, more tellingly in terms of the models' analytic utility, she found no coherent pattern in the relationships between dimensions conforming to the logic of the ideal types. Second, the dualistic nature of the schema led to difficulties in forcing characteristics to be reduced to two discrete categories (concerning programmes into selective versus universal; concerning funding into contributions versus taxation). Sainsbury also found the dualistic logic incapable of differentiating the ideologies underlying welfare states and the role of private organizations in welfare provision. The underlying point here speaks not only to the act of selecting a small number of criteria to represent national policy configurations but, also, to the degree of constraint and generality that is acceptable. There is a salutary lesson here: typologizing has high costs, forcing one to forfeit especially the richness and complexity of welfare state provision within and across national contexts.

By way of overview, one can say that enabling concepts and explanations to travel can yield and has yielded substantial fruit. It enriches scholarship by compelling us to think in larger categories and in the welfare state domain it has brought together types of welfare state models which were formerly treated in isolation. However, the scale of its contribution to the methodological development of welfare state scholarship and the extent to which many-country comparisons should detain us further can be questioned. In regard to feminist work it is important to appreciate that the many countries/few variables approach has been imported and has to some extent supplanted an older tradition of feminist work which was to identify and piece together, mainly through more qualitative methodology, the different ways in which welfare state and other public provisions contributed to the identity and position of women and the inequalities between them and men. If earlier feminist work was comparative, it tended towards the few countries/many variables approach. One could say, then, that this is the original 'comparative tradition' in feminist work.

Towards a comprehensive framework

The ultimate goal is the conceptualization of the welfare state in a manner that is both sensitive to gender and comprehensive. I suggest that two exercises are involved in this endeavour. The first is to find ways of theorizing gender as internal to the welfare state and the second is to theorize the relationship between the welfare state and gender in terms of surrounding institutions. Obviously these are related and are considered separately here only for analytic purposes.

With regard to a satisfactory theorization of the welfare state itself, the essential exercise is to link together the content or design of policies, the processes set in train by welfare state provisions and the outcomes which they bring about. One could summarize these in terms of structure, relations and outcomes. The first refers to the architecture and institutional design of policy, the second connotes the processes and sets of relations which social policies and the welfare state in general influence and/or set in train, and the third invokes the social effects or consequences which they bring about. In the last case one can take a narrow or broad view of outcomes, seeing them in terms of the financial resources made available by the welfare state or more generally in terms of levels and conditions of living.

As demonstrated throughout this chapter, the different feminist concepts and perspectives tend to be stronger on one aspect than another. For example, Lewis's framing of the male breadwinner model, together with the work of Diane Sainsbury (1996) and my own work to a lesser extent (Daly 2000), analyse welfare states in terms of how the architecture, principles and design of policies grant women and men access to public benefits and services. Similarly, the concept of care, although it also has something to say about the content of welfare state policies, speaks most readily to the processes and relations set in train by the welfare state in telling us how welfare state (and other) provisions construct particular types of labour and relations as paid or unpaid and formal or informal. And then there is the work on citizenship which is somewhat problematic in the present context in that not only has it not so far yielded much by way of welfare state variation, but it also lends itself to a level of analysis that is larger than the welfare state itself. If anything though, citizenship connotes outcomes in society, illuminating the meaning and conditions of membership of the polity. Rather than forcing the individual approaches to overreach, I suggest that we capitalize on the strengths of each and use them to analyse individually the dimensions or elements for which they are most suited. The comprehensiveness of the framework will come from putting them together. Figure 1.1, overleaf, then, is in diagrammatic form my suggested framework for a comprehensive approach to the welfare state.[5]

If one wants to identify how welfare states may be gendered in content or structure, the breadwinner model, with its notion of the possibly gendered nature of the distributive principles and role conceptualizations that are embedded in welfare, is helpful. Programmatic structure and the conditions underpinning receipt of cash benefits, relevant social services and tax allowances are at the empirical coal face as are the conditions and unit of entitlement and the treatment of 'dependants'. This model recognizes that welfare state provisions embody both institutional elements and normative prescriptions in regard to male and female claims on public resources. As I have indicated above, Sainsbury's (1996) work has expanded the principles which comprise the male breadwinner model.

Structures and content – male breadwinner

```
IDEOLOGICAL MATERIAL AND
ORGANIZATIONAL PRINCIPLES OF CASH BENEFITS,
TAXATION AND SOCIAL SERVICES
```

Processes – care

```
FAMILIALIZATION/DEFAMILIALIZATION OF CARE WORK AND
FINANCIAL MAINTENANCE RESPONSIBILITIES
```

Outcomes – citizenship

```
RESOURCE-BASED RELATIONS BETWEEN WOMEN AND MEN
```

Figure 1.1 The different dimensions of the welfare state as gendered

These components lead in turn to a set of processes which span the gulf between provision and outcomes. Such processes are connoted by the concept of care and may be generally described as 'familialization/defamilialization' (Lister 1994; McLaughlin and Glendinning 1994). Two aspects of this are crucial for gender-sensitive analyses: the construction of caring labour as paid or unpaid and as located inside or outside family relations and the construction of maintenance of family members as a private or a public responsibility. Such processes allow us to explore how welfare states serve to set up roles and circuits of redistribution for women and men individually and as members of families.

Finally, there is the matter of outcomes. At their core welfare systems are designed as redistributive processes. While the association of welfare states with equality is problematic, it can be reasonably assumed that:

• resources (re)distributed through the state will be less unequal than those distributed by market forces;
• through its redistribution functions the state effects some reduction in inequality overall;
• through these activities the state has a strong shaping hand on resource-relations (broadly conceived) between women and men.

The second conceptual task in developing a comprehensive conceptualization of the welfare state and gender is to theorize the welfare state in relation to other domains in society, in the present case those that are crucial for gender relations – the family and the (labour) market. Much work exists already on this set of relations – they have tended to be conceived, for example, in terms of a triangle. The problem with the triangular formulation is that it can only conceive of each set of relations independently of the others. To overcome this, rather serious, limitation I have proposed elsewhere (Daly 2000) that the three institutions should be seen as interacting spheres. Such a formulation, presented in Figure 1.2, views the welfare state, family and market as domains that interact in key ways, both as sets of two and as all three together. Life courses and the wellbeing of both women and men are constituted at the intersection of welfare state, family and market.

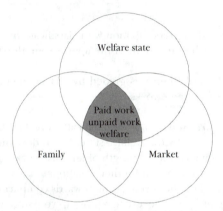

Figure 1.2 The gender dimensions of and the welfare state itself in a societal context

The essence of the interaction between the welfare state, family and market from a gender perspective is how they constitute and affect paid work, unpaid work and welfare. This has both micro and macro dimensions. At the former level, the focus of analysis would be how people's lives are organized in terms of the interaction between paid work, unpaid work and welfare. Expressed in more prosaic terms: who does what? under what conditions? and with what consequences for welfare? What one is essentially doing here is problematizing the relationship between gender and the welfare state in terms of how individual lives are organized around paid work and unpaid work and the consequences of existing arrangements for individual and family welfare. The set of interacting relations also has purchase at the macro level. Here the key analytic dimension is the actions of and interaction between the state, family and market in affecting the distribution and form of paid work, unpaid work and welfare themselves. What kinds of arrangements exist within spheres and how are these related across spheres? The three institutions together play the pivotal role in shaping welfare (and its gender dimension) by virtue of how they serve to construct paid and unpaid work and indeed work as paid or unpaid. Paid work is carried out in the market but it is shaped by both market and state. Unpaid work, in contrast, is primarily carried out in the family and is shaped mainly by the interaction of state and family. Welfare is in turn constituted by these definitions and practices.

These conceptual/theoretical concerns also speak to issues of methodology. In fact, suggesting that the welfare state has to be studied in terms of its structure, process and outcome is effectively to state the need for a more plural approach to methodology. I share Adams's (1998: 10) view of the need to avoid polarized methodological choices and indeed the opinion that methodological openness is best, for now. In a nutshell then, it is my view that feminist work on the welfare state has to become more diversified methodologically. The recent preference for the many-country type of comparison is part, but only part, of the problem. The focus on comparison is not in itself problematic but it needs to be recognized that:

- typologizing tends towards a preoccupation with classification;
- there are other approaches to comparison apart from the typologizing methodology;
- comparison only works well when it is guided by a clear intent and strong conceptual and theoretical frameworks.

It is also the case that comparison does not automatically foreclose the option of studying the relations set in train by the welfare state. My underlying point here refers to the manner in which a classical strength of feminist work on the welfare state – the focus upon the power and other relational aspects of welfare recipiency – has been eclipsed by the recent swing towards comparison. The loss of the study of the complexity of the everyday or, if you prefer, the micro aspects of welfare states, would be a huge cost to feminist scholarship. Similarly, the absence of agency and actors from the more recent feminist work represents a turning away from another of its classical strengths.

With regard to comparison, I am of the view that typologizing should be set aside in favour of few countries/many factors type of work. In other words, the many countries/few variables approach has reached its limits in the welfare state field. A different approach to comparison is needed. Comparative energies, especially in periods of transformation, are best concentrated upon developing concepts and modes of analysis which do justice to the rich detail of welfare state provisions considered in their context. Hence, country case studies would appear to offer a better way forward. Furthermore, given the general methodological underdevelopment of much of the new feminist scholarship on the welfare state, work that advances a bold line of interpretation and causality is especially beneficial. There is also a need not to forget our roots for the conditions that gave birth to feminist work on the welfare state and other domains still prevail. Within the welfare state scholarship one need only look at the burgeoning literature on globalization and new forms of governance, among others, to see how blind this scholarship is to the 'possibility of gender'. Ultimately this chapter rests on the belief that all perspectives, including feminist ones, need constant reworking, critique and development.

Notes

1 Orloff (1996) identifies four different feminist perspectives on the welfare state. A first, and relatively early, perspective saw the welfare state as reproducing gender hierarchies. Over time this approach was complemented by a second which viewed the welfare state in terms of its ameliorative impact on social inequalities, including those based on gender. As it matured further, feminist work became more comparative and more complex (in the sense of perceiving the welfare state as either/both independent and dependent variable). This work can be divided into a third and fourth set of approaches. The third was historical in focus, seeking to identify the development process which shaped and the agency which underlay different types of policies within and across states. The fourth has been explicitly comparative, looking to develop axes of variation in the nature and effect of social policies as they relate to gender.
2 Parts of this section are drawn from Daly and Lewis (1998).
3 With the exception of the work of Lister (1997).
4 For other gender-focused typologies see Siaroff (1994), Mósesdóttir (1995) and Daly (1996).
5 This is outlined in greater detail in Daly (2000).

References

Adams, J. (1998) 'Feminist Theory as Fifth Columnist or Discursive Vanguard? Some Contested Uses of Gender Analysis in Historical Sociology', *Social Politics* 5, 1: 1–16.
Daly, M. (1996) *Social Security, Gender and Equality in the European Union*, Brussels: Commission of the European Communities.
Daly, M. (2000) *The Gender Division of Welfare*, Cambridge: Cambridge University Press.
Daly, M. and Lewis, J. (1998) 'Introduction: Conceptualising Social Care in the Context of Welfare State Restructuring', in J. Lewis (ed.) *Gender, Social Care and Welfare State Restructuring in Europe*, Avebury: Ashgate.
Esping-Andersen, G. (1990) *The Three Worlds of Welfare Capitalism*, Cambridge: Polity Press.
Finch, J. and Groves, D. (1983) *Labour and Love: Women, Work and Caring*, London: Routledge and Kegan Paul.
Graham, H. (1991) 'The Concept of Caring in Feminist Research: The Case of Domestic Service', *Sociology* 25, 1: 61–78.
Knijn, T. and Kremer, M. (1997) 'Gender and the Caring Dimension of Welfare States: Toward Inclusive Citizenship', *Social Politics* 4, 3: 328–61.
Kolberg, J.E. (1991) 'The Gender Dimension of the Welfare State', *International Journal of Sociology* 21, 2: 119–48.
Lewis, J. (1992) 'Gender and the Development of Welfare Regimes', *Journal of European Social Policy* 2, 3: 159–73.
Lewis, J. and Ostner, I. (1991) 'Gender and the Evolution of European Social Policies'. Paper presented at workshop on 'Emergent Supranational Social Policy: The EC's Social Dimension in Comparative Perspective', Center for European Studies, Harvard University, 15–17 November .

Leira, A. (1992) *Welfare States and Working Mothers*, Cambridge: Cambridge University Press.

Leira, A. (1993) 'Concepts of Care: Loving, Thinking and Doing', in J. Twigg (ed.) *Informal Care in Europe*, York: University of York, SPRU.

Lister, R. (1994) 'She Has Other Duties – Women, Citizenship and Social Security', in S. Baldwin and J. Falkingham (eds) *Social Security and Social Change: New Challenges to the Beveridge Model*, Hemel Hempstead: Harvester Wheatsheaf.

Lister, R. (1996) 'Citizenship: Towards a Feminist Synthesis'. Paper presented to conference 'Women and Citizenship', University of Greenwich, 16–18 July.

Lister, R. (1997) *Citizenship Feminist Perspectives*, Basingstoke, Hampshire: Macmillan.

McLaughlin, E. and Glendinning, C. (1994) 'Paying for Care in Europe: Is There a Feminist Approach?', in L. Hantrais, and S. Mangan (eds) *Family Policy and the Welfare of Women*, Loughborough: Cross-National Research Group, European Research Centre, Cross-National Research Papers, Third Series.

Mósesdóttir, L. (1995) 'The State and the Egalitarian, Ecclesiastical and Liberal Regimes of Gender Relations', *British Journal of Sociology*, 46, 4: 623–42.

O'Connor, J.S. (1996) 'From Women in the Welfare State to Gendering Welfare Regimes', *Current Sociology*, 44, 2: 1–127.

Orloff, A. (1993) 'Gender and the Social Rights of Citizenship: State Policies and Gender Relations in Comparative Research', *American Sociological Review*, 58, 3: 303–28.

Orloff, A. (1996) 'Gender in the Welfare State', *Annual Review of Sociology*, 22: 51–78.

Pateman, C. (1996) *Democratisation and Citizenship in the 1990s: The Legacy of T.H. Marshall*, Oslo: Institute for Social Research, Report 96: 17.

Sainsbury, D. (1991) 'Analysing Welfare State Variations: The Merits and Limitations of Models Based on the Residual-Institutional Distinction', *Scandinavian Political Studies*, 14, 1: 1–30.

Sainsbury, D. (1996) *Gender, Equality and Welfare States*, Cambridge: Cambridge University Press.

Scheiwe, K. (1994) 'Labour Market Welfare State and Family Institutions: The Links to Mothers' Poverty Risks', *Journal of European Social Policy*, 4, 3: 201–24.

Shaver, S. and Bradshaw, J. (1993) *The Recognition of Wifely Labour by Welfare States*, Australia: Social Policy Research Centre, The University of New South Wales, Discussion Paper no. 44.

Siaroff, A. (1994) 'Work, Welfare and Gender Equality: A New Typology', in D. Sainsbury (ed.) *Gendering Welfare States*, London: Sage.

Siim, B. (1987) 'The Scandinavian Welfare States – Towards Sexual Equality or a New Kind of Male Domination?', *Acta Sociologica*, 30, 3/4: 255–70.

Siim, B. (1997) 'Towards a Gender Sensitive Framework for Citizenship – Implications for Comparative Studies of Welfare States in Transition', paper presented to conference 'Gender and Citizenship: Social Integration and Social Exclusion', University of Turin, 4–5 April.

Thomas, C. (1993) 'Deconstructing Concepts of Care', *Sociology*, 27, 4: 649–69.

Tronto, J.C. (1993) *Moral Boundaries. A Political Argument for an Ethic of Care*. London: Routledge.

Waerness, K. (1984) 'Caring as Women's Work in the Welfare State', in H. Holter (ed.) *Patriarchy in a Welfare Society*, Oslo: Universitetsforlaget.

2 Citizenship, family policy and women's patterns of employment[1]

Thomas P. Boje and Anna-Lena Almqvist

Introduction

In order to understand gender differences in citizenship rights and employment patterns in modern welfare state systems the complex relationship between work, care and welfare provision has to be taken into consideration. The risk of mothers in losing their labour market position and consequently their independent income when caring for a child is closely connected to the relationship between labour market organization, family structures and welfare state institutions. And this risk takes different forms depending on the family policy pursued in the individual welfare states.

In all European countries we have seen a progressive increase in women's labour market involvement. This trend is a result of several inter-related dimensions in women's social behaviour. First, in a still more comprehensive way, women are shaping their own future by active participation in economic and social processes. They have in large number acquired higher education, have chosen paid work instead of unpaid care work and full-time instead of part-time jobs where available. Increases in women's labour-force participation have obviously taken place despite economic recession, falling general levels of employment, high rates of unemployment and lack of childcare facilities (Rubery and Smith 1996: 1).

Second, integration of women in the labour market has been facilitated by restructuring of the labour markets and changes in patterns of employment. Growth in the service sector and in part-time jobs and different types of temporary employment has on the one hand increased the demand for women's labour in most labour markets but on the other hand has also led to a segregation of the labour markets and restricted women's access to well-paid and senior occupational jobs.

Third, and probably most influential for the integration of women into continuous employment, is the development of the welfare state system. The impact of the welfare state includes two different dimensions. On the one hand, a growth of job openings in the public sector services has been essential for the demand for female labour. In several labour markets the overwhelming proportion of growth in employment has taken place in the public sector and for women. On the other hand, this growth in public sector employment has been accompanied by an expansion in public family services and an extension of social transfers. This expansion of public responsibilities in relation to the family has been a precondition for women's capacity to take up paid work in the labour market.

Family policy of the welfare states influences women's position in the labour market in many different ways. Provision of public social services relieves women of their burdens of care. Furthermore, access to paid leave and public transfers enables women to combine family responsibilities and continuous labour market involvement. In this chapter we want to analyse the relationship between social citizenship rights and women's labour market participation in different European welfare systems. What impact do various institutional arrangements concerning parental leave and child-rearing have on women's labour market involvement? How do variations in caring arrangements in the welfare system influence women's capacity to reconcile labour-force participation and family responsibilities?

In this book we argue for a conceptualization of citizenship which, on the one hand, includes the rights and the obligations to labour-force participation but, on the other hand, also recognizes citizens' rights to receive as well as to give care. In this perspective the social rights of citizens – men as well as women – include the right to paid work, unpaid work and care (see Lister 1997; Knijn and Kremer 1997). Care can take many different forms. It can be paid work outside the family provided by family day carers or in public or private institutions and it can take place inside the family with or without income replacement. Caring work in the family is paid when one of the parents – usually the mother – takes paid maternity or parental leave.

The five countries chosen for comparison in this chapter are Denmark, Sweden, France, Germany and the UK. These nations have many things in common. They are all highly developed industrial countries and they are members of the European Union. But under the surface significant differences are obvious. The Scandinavian countries, Denmark and Sweden, are known to have a comprehensive and generous family policy that encourages female labour market participation and which emphasizes equality in the family as well as in society generally. Germany is considered as having a more conservative family policy, favouring a division between wage work and domestic work and with a strong emphasis on the protection of the integrity of the family. France, although regarded as having a traditional welfare regime, has a quite generous family policy and is supportive of women's efforts to combine family responsibilities and labour market involvement. Finally, the liberal free market regime of the UK is usually considered as an individualistic society not encouraging reliance on the welfare state and considering childcare responsibilities as a concern for the individual family to solve through the market.

Citizenship, work and gender

Most comparative studies of welfare systems focus on the differences in the criteria for social citizenship and how different welfare state systems, by the provision of social protection, enable the citizen to maintain a livelihood without reliance on the market. It is the concept of social citizenship as it has been developed by T.H. Marshall which is normally used in welfare state analyses. In his lecture 'Citizenship and Social Class' from 1949 citizenship is defined as 'a status bestowed on those who are full members of a community. All who possess the status are equal with respect to the right and duties with which the status is endowed' (Marshall and Bottomore 1996:18).

Marshall gives us an overview of the emerging modern citizenship and its content in the beginning of today's welfare societies. He emphasizes that the right of individuals to be citizens involves two general elements. First, citizenship includes a right to be accepted in all economic, legal, political, and social relations as full members of the society and, second, it includes the idea that all individuals on equal conditions share the social heritage of the society (ibid: 6). With the social rights of citizenship it follows that the citizen has the personal autonomy to participate in the social community and the capacity to make informed choices about what is to be done in society and how it is done (Lister 1997: 7).

In the Marshallian conceptualization of citizenship, wage labour is fundamental in determining the rights and obligations of social citizenship. Participation or not in paid work defines the rights of social citizenship for the individual. It is through participation in paid work that individuals become eligible for social benefits but these benefits are further conditioned on the individual's prepareness to take up wage labour when it is available and offered. The close connection between paid work and social citizenship rights means that individuals are differentiated in relation to social benefits and that the already existing inequality based on access to labour and income is reinforced through the criteria determining access to welfare transfers and services. This close connection between social citizenship rights and paid work has been questioned by many researchers. Here we shall discuss two different types of critique coming to the same conclusion; namely the need for a broadening of the concept of citizenship to include both paid and unpaid work.

Work and citizenship

A strong relationship exists between citizenship rights, economic prosperity and the political involvement of citizens in society. How citizenship is defined is thus crucial for the social inclusion of citizens in the social life of the community and for their capability in organizing the economic, political and social institutions of the society (van der Veen 1993). As mentioned above, in most research on welfare states the social citizenship rights are defined as being closely related to the individual's position in the labour market. Both the extent of social rights attributed to citizens and the quality of the social rights are dependent on their labour market involvement. The ability to maintain a livelihood without reliance on the labour market – the level of decommodification – depends thus on the generosity and universality of the social rights. If the citizens can freely leave work when they consider it necessary for themselves then the social citizenship is comprehensive and the level of decommodification high (Esping-Andersen 1990: 22). According to this argument social citizenship rights promote a decommodification of labour by separating the living conditions of citizens from their dependency on being able to sell their labour power in the labour market.

Following the conventional definition of social citizenship, the relationship between social rights and paid work must be considered as an asymmetric relation. According to Leisink and Coenen (1993), employers are not forced to employ unemployed individuals, but these are forced to look for waged labour – and to accept the work offered them – if they want to remain eligible for welfare benefits. The limits of the definition of social citizenship mentioned above are, thus, that it does not give individual citizens as much influence in the economic system as, for instance, a vote according to their political citizenship would enhance the impact on political life. The question of whether work should be regarded as a basic citizenship right, an obligation or both is of great importance for the social rights of individuals and includes an exclusionary tendency in its distinction between different kinds of rights and possibilities according to the individual citizen's involvement in the labour market.

With the present lack of work and consequently a high level of unemployment the close connection between social rights and paid work differentiates rather than equalizes the distinction between citizens and, as a consequence, an increasing number of citizens are excluded from social rights and hence from being active in the social community. The political claim is often raised that work is essential for eligibility to welfare benefits. In this respect there has been a policy shift in many nation states towards more obligations on the claimants and more severe sanctions against those not accepting work being offered (Leisink and Coenen 1993: 14). To get rid of the asymmetric relationship between social citizenship rights and work in regulating the social rights of the individuals it is necessary to extend the social citizenship rights to include the right to welfare benefits in case of both paid work and other types of work.

In this context other types of work mean unpaid work which has value for the society and makes it possible for citizens to contribute to the general welfare of the community and this may include community work and care work in and outside the family. In this respect Leisink and Coenen (1993: 19) talk about a 'citizenship right as well as a citizenship obligation' and they mention three aspects crucial for the argument of seeing work in a broader sense as a citizenship obligation. First, having paid and unpaid work is an important form of social participation. Second, all kinds of work involve people in social networks and contribute to social integration. Third, for a welfare state to be sustainable it is necessary to have a high working participation among its citizens. Notably, these arguments contain not only obligations for the citizen, but also for the welfare state.

The feminist critique of the concept of citizenship takes another stance. It is argued that the strong connection between paid work and citizenship rights ignores the importance of unpaid work in the family. This is despite strong evidence that the family is still the major provider of welfare and, within the family, women are mainly responsible for unpaid care and welfare. By neglecting the unpaid work and by focusing on the connection between social rights and the individual's position in the labour market, the consequence has been that social citizenship rights are primarily defined as rights of a 'typical' male full-time worker (see Orloff 1993). While men were expected to be breadwinners, women were expected to support the society in their role of unpaid caretakers and educators of new generations (Pateman 1992). This has as a consequence that women have been incorporated into the emerging welfare societies differently from men.

The relationship between paid work, unpaid work and welfare provision is gendered (Taylor-Gooby 1991). The gender division in paid work has declined because a substantial number of women have entered the labour market in all European countries during recent decades. This development has, on the other hand, not led to decisive changes in the gender division of unpaid work. Women are still doing the major part of the unpaid caring work in the family and in society as a whole. When women have still not – despite equal opportunity legislation in all the western economies – achieved the same career possibilities as men it can mainly be explained by the unequal divison of labour in unpaid work.

The feminist critique argues that an analytic approach in defining social citizenship rights which excludes the unpaid work provided within the private sphere makes it impossible to understand how welfare policies are contributing to gender inequality in the informal sector (care and reproduction) and are maintaining the inequality between men and women in the formal sector (paid work) (Sainsbury 1996). Most welfare policies aiming at promoting decommodification of labour are thus also gendered. Typically decommodification of women's work results in their doing more unpaid caring – parental leave, leave to care for sick children, etc. are primarily taken by the mothers. Recognizing these gender differences in social citizenship has led to a reformulation of welfare state theories emphasizing the position of women in relation to citizenship and the importance of the family for providing social services (see, e.g. Langan and Ostner 1991; Lewis 1992; Orloff 1993; O'Connor 1996; and Lewis 1997). Orloff argues strongly for questioning the dominant relationship between employment and welfare in defining social rights and instead she wants the criteria for social rights to focus on the right to personal autonomy and self-determination in both the public and personal relations of the citizens. Orloff therefore proposes that the consequences of welfare provision on gender relations should also be evaluated on their capacity to give women access to paid work and to form and maintain an autonomous household (Orloff 1993: 318–19).

Work and care

Most welfare states are characterized by a 'dual' system for welfare provision which is gendered. On the one hand, the individualized insurance programmes related to labour market involvement are focusing on the citizens as wage earners and, on the other hand, the family-related programmes which are directed towards citizens as care-givers. Typically the labour market-related programmes are more universal and have higher rates of replacement than benefits according to family-related programmes. This duality of the welfare systems can only be eliminated if paid and unpaid work are equalized and it is recognized that care has always had an important position in public welfare programmes. It would thus lead to a fundamental change in the analyses of welfare states if welfare programmes including both paid and unpaid work were considered, then unemployment and other labour market-related programmes would no longer be the flagship programmes of the modern welfare state (Jenson 1997: 184).

Provision of care is recognized by the welfare states but it has seldom been considered as part of the basic needs of citizens. Care-giving and care-receiving were supposed to be provided by the family and the social network rather than by the welfare state and consequently were excluded from the citizenship rights defined according to Marshall's conceptualization (see Knijn and Kremer 1997: 331). Without an understanding of the relationship between work and care – it may be paid or unpaid – it will, however, not be possible to understand the different conditions by which men and women are integrated into the labour force.

In focusing on care Jenson argues that it is important not to treat unpaid work as the equivalent of caring work. New types of caring have emerged during recent decades and have blurred the previous distinctions between work and care. The male breadwinner model may be weak – as in the Scandinavian countries – but women are still the major care-givers in the family and in society as a whole. Today care-giving within the family in several welfare systems is paid through parental leave and other types of care allowances and care-giving outside the family is provided in many different contexts, but in both cases it is mainly women who are responsible for the care-giving. Consequently 'we need to distinguish between employment and payment for caring as much as between paid and unpaid care' (Jenson 1997: 184).

All welfare states are characterized by a certain caring regime and the differences between various welfare states in caring regimes have become more and more evident during recent decades. The study of gender relations in caring and unpaid work cannot be separated from the gendered character of paid work.

However, combining these two approaches implies a shift of focus in the understanding of the welfare regimes from decommodification of labour to the relationship between welfare state, family and individual in provision of work and care. By such a change in the analytical perspective the concept of citizenship has to include the right and obligation to paid work as well as the right to receive care and the right to time for care (see Knijn and Kremer 1997). Lewis thus argues that all welfare regimes have a caring regime and that caring work has to be included in studying the relationship between paid work, unpaid work and welfare. She continues that in recognizing the social rights of citizenship based on both work and care-giving women's complicated relationship to paid work, unpaid work and welfare may be solved. In defining social citizenship broadly, she argues, we have to consider women's rights not to engage in paid work (decommodification) and thereby their rights to do unpaid work, but at the same time also their right to do paid work (commodification) and thereby their right not to engage in unpaid work (Lewis 1997: 173–4).

The growing female labour market participation, however, depends on others doing the unpaid care work women have done traditionally in relation to children, sick relatives and the elderly (Langan and Ostner 1991). Here the organization and level of family-related measures such as childcare and leave programmes play a significant role for women. In the more developed and highly regulated welfare states, such as in the Scandinavian countries, this care work has been taken over by the welfare state or women have been paid for doing the care work within the family. Here the care work has been defamilialized, but has to a large extent remained women's work – now carried out as commodified paid work in the public service sector. In the more restricted and market-oriented welfare states, like the UK, some parts of the care work have been commodified, but most responsibility for care work still rests with women and is unpaid – in spite of their growing involvement in paid work.

In contemporary welfare states work and care have normally been construed as mutually exclusive. For men this means that the concept of work is completely internalized in the male concept of citizenship, but for women it leads to a complicated dilemma between their caring work in the family and their search for independence through wage labour (Knijn and Kremer 1997: 350). In solving this dilemma feminist researchers have proposed that to the concept of decommodification should be added the concept of defamilialization. Lister defines defamilialization as a criterion for social rights by 'the degree to which individual adults can uphold a socially acceptable standard of living, independently of family relationships, either through paid work or through social security provisions' (Lister 1997: 173). This concept comes close to Orloff's suggestion that decommodification has to be complemented by two additional criteria for social rights: access to paid work and the capacity to maintain an autonomous household (Orloff 1993). The consequence is that welfare regimes might then be characterized according to the degree to which individuals – both men and women – are able to provide a socially acceptable livelihood

independent of both the family and the market. By focusing on both
decommodification and defamilialization in defining social citizenship rights it is
implied that paid work no longer has a privileged status compared with unpaid
work and care (Sainsbury 1996).

Women's labour market involvement in different European welfare systems

The lives of individuals within the family as well as in the labour market are
organized around various social contracts which include at least two major
elements: a gender contract and an employment contract (see OECD 1994). The
gender contract describes the responsibilities in the family and here we normally
distinguish between the male breadwinner model and the dual-earner model. In
the male breadwinner model the economic wellbeing of the family is the man's
responsibility while family care is undertaken by the woman. In the dual-earner
model the economic wellbeing of the family is individualized and both men and
women are increasingly involved in paid work while the unpaid work has mainly
remained feminized. Despite trends in all European welfare systems towards
defamilialization, women still have the main responsibility for family care.

The social roles and behavioural patterns defined through the gender
contract have a strong impact on the organization of the employment contract.
In welfare states dominated by the male breadwinner model men clearly follow
a pattern of continuous full-time and whole-year employment while women's
labour market involvement is expected to be combined with extensive family
responsibilities. This pattern is modified in countries where the welfare regime
has considered a dual-breadwinner family as the norm and women have been
encouraged to take up paid employment by individual taxation, comprehensive
leave and childcare programmes. A crucial question in this chapter will be to
what extent welfare policies can change the gender and employment contracts
in the division of work and care?

Women – and men – are making a lot of decisions in relation to their labour
market involvement and the outcome of these decisions will be analysed in this
section. Women's decisions are conditioned by different factors – e.g. their
individual economic and social resources, their acccess to private and public
child-rearing services and work arrangements which make it possible to combine
family obligations and work commitments. Based on variations in these factors
women come out with markedly different patterns of labour-force participation
in the individual welfare states. In Table 2.1 we give an overview of some of the
main differences in women's labour market involvement in our five countries.

Compared with the other EU countries the five countries included in this
study have high rates of female labour-force participation (OECD 1998: 202).

Table 2.1 Women's labour market involvement in selected European countries for the age group 25–54, 1998

	Labour market participation	Employment/ population ratio	Part-time employment proportions < 30 hours	Unemployment rate
			%	
Denmark	82.8	77.7	25.4	6.1
France	77.9	68.0	25.0	12.7
Germany	73.5	67.6	32.4	8.0
Sweden	85.4	79.1	22.0	7.3
UK	75.1	71.7	41.2	4.5

Source: OECD 1999: Appendix, Tables C and E.

Women's overall labour market involvement is highest in the two social-democratic welfare regimes – Denmark and Sweden – where about 85 per cent of women in the age groups 25–54 are active in the labour market. Next to the Scandinavian countries we find French women, while Germany and the UK are placed in the bottom with about three-quarters of the female population aged 25–54 active in the labour market.[2] The rates of employment are also highest in the Scandinavian countries. Next comes British women while French and German women have the lowest rates of employment. This ranking has to be qualified and modified in several respects. Most important, the proportion of part-time working women is clearly higher in the UK than in any of the other countries and next comes Germany while the other three countries have significantly fewer women in part-time employment.[3]

Women's as well as men's labour market involvement throughout their lives forms different patterns in the five welfare systems. Among the European labour markets it is possible to distinguish between three different patterns of female labour market behaviour (Rubery *et al.* 1998). One type of female labour market behaviour can be characterized as the continuous pattern where individuals are active in the labour market throughout their working lives. This pattern is dominant in welfare systems characterized by a weak breadwinner regime.[4] A second type of female labour-force participation is the returner pattern characterized by a decline in participation in the age group of 25–45 in connection with childcare for a significant group of women. This pattern of labour-force participation we find in countries with both modified and strong breadwinner regimes. Finally a third type of labour market behaviour for women is the so-called curtailed or 'left-peaked' pattern of labour market involvement. This pattern is typically dominant in countries characterized by a strong breadwinner regime.[5] In Figure 2.1 we have illustrated the age-specific employment pattern for men and women working full-time and part-time in our five countries.

Denmark

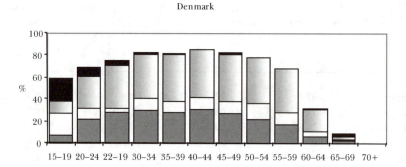

Former West Germany

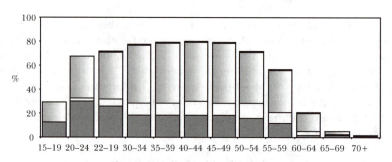

Former East Germany

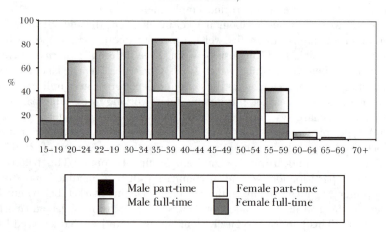

Figure 2.1 Employment rates by age and work time for men and women in Denmark, Germany (West and East), France, Sweden and the UK (continues)

Sweden

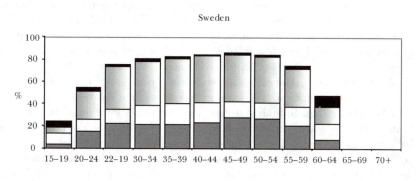

UK

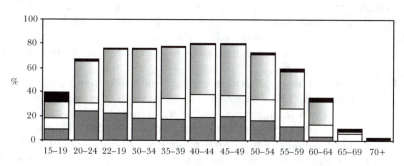

France

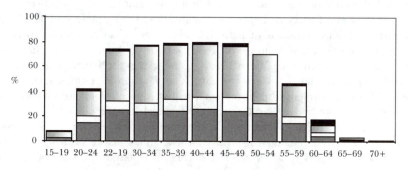

| Male part-time | Female part-time |
| Male full-time | Female full-time |

Figure 2.1 (continued)

Source: Jill Rubery *et al.*1996.

We start with an overall description of the age-related employment pattern and in the next section we analyse the proportion of full-time and part-time working women in the different age groups in more detail. A continuous pattern of employment has characterized labour market involvement of men in all European labour markets including our five countries. This employment pattern we also find for women in Denmark, Sweden and to some extent in France. Especially in the two Scandinavian countries the overall female rate of employment is close to the male rate while the gender gap is more pronounced in France. In Denmark and Sweden women's rates of employment increase until their late thirties and in both countries the rate peaks for women in the early forties.[6] Then it starts declining until the age of pension – more rapidly for Danish women.[7] For women in their twenties the rate of employment has declined in both countries because more women attend higher education and the years in education are extended. The French pattern for women's labour market participation becomes still more similar to the Scandinavian. During the last decade the rates of employment for French women aged 25–50 have increased significantly but a group of women still leave the labour market in their early thirties and slightly reduce the participation rate for these age groups. However, this fall in employment has diminished over the years (see Eydoux *et al.* 1996).

The m-shaped returner pattern[*] in employment can be found for women in Germany (W) and the UK. For both countries, however, the employment rates of women in the child-rearing years have been growing and the m-shaped curve has shifted upwards meaning that the overall rate of female employment has increased and the gender gap is being reduced (see Rubery *et al.* 1995b: 7). In the UK the increase in women's employment in the 25–45 age group seems to have stopped about 1990 and consequently the m-shaped pattern of labour market participation has remained. We find significant differences between the former West and East Germany in the female pattern of employment. The West German women's employment pattern is characterized by a returner pattern while the employment pattern of East German women is more like the Scandinavian continuous pattern.[8] During the 1990s the female employment patterns in the two parts of Germany have, however, become more similar. High levels of unemployment and heavy cuts in provision of childcare in the New Länder have forced many East German women back into the family.

Looking at the overall pattern of labour market involvement for women shows that this pattern has changed in nearly all five labour markets during the past two decades (Rubery *et al.* 1998). The decline in labour market activity in the child-rearing age groups has been reduced and the general female pattern of participation becomes still more similar to the male pattern (see Rubery *et al.* 1996). This development has been most pronounced in the Scandinavian

---

[*] An m-shaped returner pattern is characterized by a decline in labour-force participation in the age group 25–45 and then a return to the labour force after this age.

countries but is in process in all five countries. On the other hand, this overall pattern of growing female rates of employment in the five countries conceals different patterns of female labour market behaviour.

Women's part-time employment

Women's labour market involvement in the five countries is divided into full-time or part-time employment as shown in Figure 2.1. Looking at the employment patterns for these two groups separately changes the previously described pattern and the ranking between the countries. Sweden has the highest overall rate of employment for women but a significant proportion of employed women have part-time jobs. Comparing the five countries based on the proportion of women in full-time employment brings Sweden – where about 40 per cent of employed women are working in part-time jobs – below Denmark, France and Germany (E) (see Rubery and Smith 1996).[9] In Denmark, France and especially Germany (E) the large majority of employed women have full-time employment while this is the case for about 60 per cent of the Swedish women.

Comparing the three labour markets with the continuous pattern of labour market activity for women – Denmark, Sweden and France – we find that Swedish women aged 30–44 are employed on a part-time basis more frequently than Danish women in the same age group. The labour market behaviour for Swedish women in full-time work looks more like a returner pattern with a decline in full-time employment during the childcaring period while most Danish women remain in full-time employment even during periods with extensive childcare obligations. The labour market pattern for French women working full-time is almost the same as the pattern for Danish women. Most French women also remain in full-time employment during the period of childcare and they typically return to full-time employment after they have ended their parental leave.

For Germany (W) and the UK the difference among employed women in overall rates of employment and the full-time rate is pronounced. For both countries fewer than half of the employed women aged 30–49 have full-time jobs (see also Rubery and Smith 1996). The pattern of labour market involvement among German and British women in full-time employment can thus be characterized by an employment pattern with high rates in the twenties and declining employment rates in the years thereafter. This pattern is more like the southern European curtailed pattern than the returner pattern found for the total group of German and British women in employment. The West German and British women who return to the labour market at a later stage do so on a part-time basis although both countries have a slight increase in the proportion of women in full-time employment in their forties when their children have reached school age.

Working hours and part-time work among women

The number of working hours women have in periods of part-time employment is crucial in evaluating women's level of labour market involvement during the period of child-rearing and, thus, their ability to return to full-time employment later in their labour market career if wanted. Those women who work part-time on few hours are more marginalized in the work organization than women who work part-time on more hours or have full-time jobs, and they have markedly greater difficulties in being integrated fully in the labour market at a later stage (see, e.g. Fagan and O'Reilly 1998: 8; and Rubery 1998). Concerning the hours women in part-time employment actually work we find significant differences between the five countries (see Table 2.2).

Table 2.2 Women's part-time employment pattern in selected European countries in the mid-1990s

	Proportion in part-time employment (1995)		Usual hours worked in part-time employment	Unemployed seeking part-time employment	Absent from work because of children
	< 30 hours	*< 35 hours*	*Average hours*	*Per cent of unemployed*	*Per cent of employment*
Denmark	22.6	36.1	21.3	16.5	18.4
France	23.7	32.4	22.6	22.1	9.4
Germany	27.7	34.1	18.9	23.5	19.9
Sweden	26.6	43.4	24.9	19.3	21.7
UK	36.7	43.7	18.3	41.9	13.7

Sources: OECD 1997; Statistics Sweden 1995 and EUROSTAT 1998

It is possible to distinguish between three different patterns of part-time working. One pattern is the Scandinavian where women in part-time jobs work long hours. In Denmark and Sweden a large proportion of women are employed in part-time work for at least twenty-five hours a week. In Sweden about one-third of women in part-time employment work more than thirty hours a week, close to the official standard for full-time employment (forty hours) and Swedish women have the longest usual hours in part-time among the five countries (Rubery *et al.* 1995a). On the other hand, a significant number of Swedish women are absent from work because of caring for a child. Most Scandinavian women in part-time jobs have a working time pattern similar to the full-time working employees and many of these women change from part-time to full-time jobs when their children have grown up (for Denmark see, e.g. Leth-Sørensen and Rohwer 1993).

A radically different pattern of work time exists in Germany and the UK. In these two labour markets more than three-quarters of women employed in part-time jobs work short hours – fewer than twenty hours a week – and only a minority works more than thirty hours a week. Women working part-time in these two labour markets also have the shortest usual working hours in their part-time jobs among the five countries. It is particularly in the UK that the work time pattern for women is diversified. One-quarter of the part-time employed mothers work less than ten hours a week while more than 30 per cent of mothers in full-time employment work more than forty-one hours a week (see Rubery *et al.* 1995a: 93). The labour market integration of the first group of women is precarious. This precarious labour market connection for large groups of part-time working British and German women becomes even more problematic from an equal opportunities perspective considering that they represent the majority of all working women in these two countries.

Finally, French women represent a work-time pattern in between the two extremes. The part-time working group of women is nearly equally divided into two groups with one group working fewer than twenty hours and the other working more than that. The usual working hours for women in part-time jobs are relatively long in France and few women are absent from work because of childcare obligations. Two different strategies for labour market involvement of French women can be registered. Those women working part-time on short hours are primarily care-givers and have childcare as their main responsibility while those working part-time on long hours are more focused on continuous labour market involvement and rely on public institutions for childcare. Many women included in the group working long hours part-time shift to full-time employment when their children have reached school age (see Eydoux *et al.* 1996).

Women's employment and family status[10]

The importance of motherhood and family status in determining women's labour market involvement in Europe has been summarized in Rubery *et al.* (1995a) based on national surveys from the individual EU countries. Not surprisingly they find that changes in family status of women from single to married and from non-mother to mother are strongly influencing women's labour market involvement. On the other hand, the effect of marriage and motherhood on continuity of women's employment differs in the individual European labour market depending on several factors such as the individual attitudes of working women, the organization of the family system, the demand-side organization of the labour market and the national system of family policy.

In their statistical analysis of the effect of marriage and motherhood Rubery *et al.* (1995a) find that the national differences correspond neatly with the classification of the welfare regimes based on the typology of breadwinner regimes mentioned earlier. In the two Scandinavian countries – Denmark and Sweden – characterized as dual-earner breadwinner systems, the impact of marriage on women's labour market involvement was weak. Single and married women have similar activity rates in their twenties while married women in the 30–49 age group have higher rates of activity than single women. Motherhood among Scandinavian women even has a positive impact on women's labour market involvement in sharp contrast with all other European countries. In Sweden, however, mothers' strong labour market involvement is to some extent overestimated considering the high proportion of mothers on parental leave or in part-time jobs.[11]

In France – characterized as a modified breadwinner system – marriage has no effect on young women's labour market involvement as is also the case in the Scandinavian countries. For older French women marriage reduces the level of labour market activity: this might be explained by the generational effect. Motherhood, on the other hand, has a weak negative impact on women's labour market involvement but the effect depends strongly on the number of children a woman has. Motherhood has little effect on women's labour market involvement for the first child but significant negative impact with two or more children. According to the French pronatalist family policy, parental leave is first paid from the second child.

In Germany (W) and the UK – both welfare regimes described by Lewis as strong male breadwinner systems – the impact of motherhood is strong and reduces mothers' level of labour market participation by more than 30 percentage points compared with non-mothers (Rubery *et al.* 1995a: 30). The number of children has an additional impact on mothers' labour market involvement and reduces it still more. The impact of marriage, on the other hand, differs in Germany (W) and the UK. Among British women the effect of marriage on labour market involvement is low but a large proportion of married British women in employment are working short hours part-time. For women in West Germany marriage has a strong impact on their labour market involvement. West German women in all age groups leave the labour market in large numbers when they marry and this pattern is even stronger when they have children. Only a minority of German mothers seem to return to the labour market on a part-time basis later in their life.

Citizenship, family policy and care of children

In all European countries the majority of women combine work and childcare. More than two-thirds of the female population aged 25–54 were in employment in the five countries included in this study. These figures are markedly higher for women in Denmark and Sweden while women obviously have great difficulties in reconciling work and childcare in Germany and the UK. These constraints take many forms and vary across countries depending on both the national labour market conditions and the type of family policies implemented in the different welfare states.

In a previous section of this chapter we discussed the relationship between social citizenship rights, work and care. Here we shall continue this discussion by looking at two aspects of this relationship in connection with care for dependent

Table 2.3   Criteria for the right to receive care and for the right to time to care for children in selected European countries, 1996–8[(a)]

The right to receive care	The right to time for care
DENMARK	**Leave: medium**
	Maternity:
State/municipal responsibility for childcare. No market role/non-profit private institutions play a significant role	Length: 18 weeks (14 weeks)
	Compensation: 55.2 per cent. According to the collective agreements all employed in the public sector and many employees in the private sector have their regular salary paid by the employer who then is compensated with the amount of benefits.
Coverage (percentage of age group)	
Age 0–2: high[(b)]	*Paternity:*
Vuggestue[(c)] 17.5 per cent,	Length: 28 days
Family day-care: 27 per cent	Compensation: 55.8 per cent. See maternity leave
	Parental:
Age 3–school age: high	I. Length: 10 weeks per family
Børnehave: 64.5 per cent	II: Length: 13 weeks per child aged 0–9
Family day-care: 4 per cent	(for child aged 0–1 the leave can be
Børnehaveklasse: 9 per cent	extended up to 26 weeks and prolonged up to 52 weeks with acceptance by the employer)
	Compensation: I: 55.7 per cent and
Fee:	II: 26.85 per cent
Vuggestue/Børnehave:	
Related to income and number of children. Average monthly fee for 0–2 years old DKr2,075 and for 3–6 years old DKr1,159 (1998)	**Possibilities for part-time work: low**
	Part-time work gives restricted social security rights.
Family day-care:	It is not possible to be on part-time
Dependent on income and hours a day. Average DKr1,580 a month for full-time	employment when receiving leave benefits, social assistance or unemployment benefit.
Børnehaveklasse: Free	All types of leave must be taken full-time.
	Sickness leave: low
	No statutory rights, but paid leave first day of child's sickness according to the major collective agreements.

For explanation of (a), (b) and (c) please see notes at the end of table.

Table 2.3 continues

children; namely the right to receive care and the right to time for care.[12] Time for giving care is a citizenship issue usually negotiated between the care-giver, the state and/or the employer. Receiving care has not been considered as a citizenship right to the same extent and the receiver of care does not often have the possibility of claiming her/his rights. In regard to caring for children this is obvious since small children do not have the ability to negotiate or purchase the right to receive care. In Table 2.3 we have listed the conditions for receiving care

Table 2.3 *(continued)*

The right to receive care	The right to time for care
FRANCE	
State/local authorities and non-government organizations responsible for care.	**Leave: medium**
Tax relief supporting payment of childcare.	*Maternity:*
	Length: 16 weeks (10 weeks). 10 weeks extra with birth of the third child.
Age 0–2: medium	Compensation: 100 per cent (up to FFr358 per day, 1998)
Crèches: 12 per cent	*Paternity:*
Family day-care: 11 per cent	Length: 3 days
	Compensation: 100 per cent
Age 3–school age: high	*Parental:*
École maternelle: 98.1 per cent	Length: 146 weeks (shared or alternated)
	Compensation: first child unpaid, second and subsequent child: 59 per cent (up to FFr2,964 per week for full-time leave)
Fee:	
Crèche: 28 per cent of costs	
Family day-care: Income related	**Possibilities for part-time work: medium**
École maternelle: free	Government policy encourages transition to part-time work. Parental leave can be taken part-time.
	Policies are implemented creating part-time jobs in connection to redundancy schemes.
	Sickness leave: medium
	Each parent has 3 days a year paid care for a sick child under the age of 16. In the public sector all women have 12 days a year.

Table 2.3 continues

and for giving care to dependent children in the five countries covered by this analysis.

The right to receive childcare

It might be possible to rank the five countries into three categories with respect to the right to receive publicly supported childcare as follows: it is low in Germany and the UK, medium in France and high in Denmark and Sweden.

In Denmark the coverage of childcare institutions is high in a European context but definitely insufficient in relation to the demand. There is a comprehensive coverage of childcare for all children aged 3–6 years but shortage of childcare places for the youngest children when considering the total length of

Table 2.3 *(continued)*

The right to receive care	The right to time for care

GERMANY

The principle of subsidiarity makes the family responsible for childcare
Tax relief combined with relatively high transfer for payments of families with three or more children.
Substantial provision by non-governmental organizations.

Leave: low
Maternity:
Length: 14 weeks (8 weeks).
Compensation: 100 per cent
Paternity:
No statutory scheme
Parental:
Length: 3 years – can be shared
Compensation: 24 months: 16.9 per cent

Age 0–2: low
Krippe: 4.5 per cent (West);
33 per cent (East) and 7.5 per cent (total)
Family day-care: 4.0 per cent

Possibilities for part-time work: medium
Government policies encourage transition to part-time work.
Parental leave can be combined with up to 19 hours of paid work without reduction in benefits.
Guarantee of full-time unemployment benefits if losing job when moving from full-time to part-time.

Age 3–scool age: medium
Kindergarten: 59 per cent (West); 89 per cent (East) and 65 per cent (Total)
Most institutions are only open few hours a day.

Fee:
16–20 per cent of the total costs (1998)
0–2 years: DM0–300 per month
3–6 years: DM0–240 per month
Family day-care:
Minimum and maximum payment: DM250–959 per month depending on municipality.

Sickness leave: medium
10 days of paid leave per year for each child under the age of 12 for each parent. For single parents it is 20 days per year.

Table 2.3 continues

maternity and parental leave. Childcare is publicly supported and considered as a social right. In 1993 it was declared by government that all children aged 1–6 years were guaranteed a publicly funded childcare arrangement but in reality only a few municipalities have followed this declaration. For children up to 12 months old it is taken for granted that they are cared for at home by their parents during the first half-year through maternity and parental leave, followed by a new scheme introduced in 1994. According to this scheme the leave period can be prolonged for up to one year after maternity/parental leave for children aged 0–1. The new scheme for parental leave is, however, so badly paid that only parents living in couples where one of the parents – usually the father – has a high income can use it.

Table 2.3 *(continued)*

The right to receive care	The right to time for care
SWEDEN	
State and municipal responsibility for right to childcare. Little market role.	**Leave: high** *Maternity/parental:* Length: 64 weeks – can be shared but 30 days are reserved for the other parent. Compensation: Full leave period (450 days): 71.9 per cent Restricted leave period (360 days): 80 per cent
Age 0–2: medium Daghem: 31 per cent Family day-care: 9 per cent	
Age 3–school-age: high Daghem: 54 per cent. Family day-care: 13 per cent Förskola (5–6 years): 29 per cent	*Paternity:* Length: 10 days Compensation: 80 per cent
	Possibility for part-time work: high There is a statutory right to work 75 per cent of full-time, until the child is 8 years. Leave can be taken as 25 per cent, 50 per cent, 75 per cent or full-time.
Fee: Depending on income, number of children and hours of day-care.	
	Sickness leave: high Each parent has right to 30 days a year paid leave for a child's illness until the child's 2nd year. Parents of children aged under 12 are entitled to 60 days extra leave in case of a child being ill long-term.

In France parental employment is the primary criterion for being admitted to services for children under 3 years. A programme, *contrat enfance,* introduced in 1988 has increased the amount of public childcare for children under 6 years of age and the number of places in childcare centres has grown. In 1994 a new law was implemented to make it easier for women to reconcile employment and family life. The conditions were improved for parental leave and different forms of support and allowances were improved for families who employed a carer in their home or used a family day-carer. Finally, tax relief is also available for children under 6 years of age to subsidize parents' payments for publicly funded services or for private non-subsidized services (ECNC 1996).

In both Sweden and France – and also in the UK – the right to attend publicly funded childcare institutions is restricted to parents in employment or education. Parents who are unemployed or on parental leave normally have to

Table 2.3 *(continued)*

The right to receive care	The right to time for care
THE UK	**Leave: low**
	Maternity:
The state intervenes only for children 'in need'.	Length: 40 weeks (29 weeks).
The market is of vital importance for childcare.	Compensation: 18 weeks: 53.7 per cent.
	Rest: unpaid
	Paternity:
	No statutory scheme
Age 0–4: low	*Parental:*
Day nursery: 6 per cent	Three months leave, unpaid, introduced
Family day-care: 12 per cent	in 1999.
Nursery schools: 6 per cent	
	Possibilities for part-time work: low
Age 4–school age: medium	Few social security rights for part-time
38 per cent of children provided with	workers. Unemployed on benefit have to
publicly funded nursery schools (1996).	be available for full-time employment.
Fee:	**Sickness leave: low**
Local authority nurseries: means-tested	No statutory arrangements.
Independent nurseries: £55–160 per week (1998)	
Average hourly cost is £1.30	
Family day-care: Private arrangements.	
Average payment of £1.30 per hour	
Nursery schools:	
Schools run by municipalitiy: Only payment for meals.	
Independent schools: £400–800 per term.	

(a) It is important here to note that the right to receive care and to give care is considered from the positions of the parents and not the children. What favours the parents is not always best for the children. It could often be argued that the children would be better off if the parents stayed at home for a longer period but this would definitely hurt the parents' (mothers') labour market careers.
(b) The ranking of the countries in high/medium/low does not say anything about the relationship between supply of and demand for childcare but places the countries in a European context concerning the coverage of childcare for the relevant age groups and the generosity of leave.
(c) In the table we have used the national names for the childcare centres for clarity, i.e.

Denmark	(0–2 years) Vuggestue	(3–6 years) Børnehave
France	(0–2 years) Crèche	(3–6 years) École maternelle
Germany	(0–2 years) Krippen	(3–6 years) Kindergarten
Sweden	(0–2 years) Daghem	(3–6 years) Daghem
UK	(0–2 years) Playcentre	(3–6 years) Playcentre

Sources: Almqvist and Boje (1998); ECNC (1996); Gornick *et al.* (1996); Halskov (1994); Knijn and Kremer (1997); Löfström (1995); Maier *et al.* (1996); OECD (1995); Rostgaard and Friberg (1998); Rubery, Fagan and Smith (1995a)
Notes: **Grading** – the countries are graded as *high, medium* and *low* according to an EU average taking into consideration both the coverage and length of childcare/leave programmes and the level of payment/compensation. **Length for maternity leave** is divided into total period and the maximum time (in brackets) after giving birth. **Compensation** is calculated based on earnings for an *average production worker* (APW). For maternity and parental leave: APW for a woman working part-time and for paternity leave: APW for a full-time working man (see Hansen 1998). Compensation rates do not take into account the taxes paid on the benefits.

take their children out of the daycare institutions. This clearly creates a barrier for many unemployed women looking for employment. Before they can take an offered job they have to organize regular childcare for their children.

Since the reunification of Germany in 1990 harmonization has taken place in family policy. In practice this has meant that the system of childcare in Germany (E) has been changed and adapted to the system in Germany (W). In Germany (W) the provision of childcare has traditionally been extremely low and, according to the principle of subsidiarity, the family has the primary responsibility for care of children (see Langan and Ostner 1991). Consequently, only about 5 per cent of children aged 0–2 years are cared for in public childcare centres and a further 4 per cent are reared by family day-carers. In addition to the public institutions, the church and charity organizations have established childcare facilities but most of these institutions are only operated part-time and have long lunch-breaks, not matching women's usual working hours. The predominance of private institutions in German (W) childcare is reflected in the composition of the staff. In 1990, about 61 per cent of all pre-primary teachers and nurses worked in the Catholic and Protestant churches and charity organizations. Only 35 per cent worked in the public institutions and the remaining 4 per cent were privately employed (Maier *et al.* 1996).

In Sweden the right to receive childcare is comprehensive, as in Denmark, although the composition of parental and public childcare differs. Most Swedish children are not in institutional childcare during their first year but are reared by their parents (mothers) who are on leave which is highly paid for quite an extensive period. The Swedish public system of childcare for children above one year old is comprehensive and, since 1995, all parents with children aged 1–12, who are employed or studying are eligible to a place in a publicly funded childcare institution. A substantial number of private but publicly funded institutions have been established during the 1990s. They are typically managed by parent co-operatives but non-profit organizations and companies are also engaged (ECNC 1996).

For the UK the right to receive care is restricted. However, the reason for this is different than for Germany. A liberal-oriented ideology has emphasized the role of the market and the publicly funded childcare services are primarily restricted to children 'in need'. Therefore, only about 6 per cent of children aged 0–4 are cared for in public institutions and additionally 12 per cent are in family day-care of which most are private and costly. Legislation emphasizes that the local authorities have a duty to provide services appropriate for children 'in need'. Since the local authorities do not have an obligation to provide childcare for children with employed parents, nearly all services for this group are handled by private, non-subsidized institutions. During recent years there has been a significant increase in the number of places provided by the private, non-subsidized sector, e.g. private day nurseries and child-minders (ECNC 1996).

The right to time for care

We shall now look at how the right to time for care is defined in the five countries and here focus on two aspects, namely: the right to maternity/parental leave and possibilities for combining caring of children and part-time work.

The right to parental leave

Parental leave schemes exist in all of the countries studied, but they differ in length and level of economic replacement. If we compare the parental leave schemes in the different countries – both paid and unpaid – we find that the criteria for being eligible for parental leave vary from no restriction at all in Germany and Sweden to requirements of employment experiences in Denmark and the UK (OECD 1995).

Being eligible for paid parental leave is more restricted than for leave generally. In all countries except Germany paid parental leave is related to some kind of labour market involvement. France has the strongest eligibility criteria followed by Sweden and Denmark. In France the right to paid parental leave is restricted to parents with two or more children, emphasizing its pronatalist policy (see Lewis 1992; and Pitrou and Gaillard 1989). Finally, in the UK a low flat rate benefit is available for all women for fourteen weeks of maternity leave, but a minimum period of twenty-six weeks of continuous employment with the same employer is a condition for the higher level of benefit.

When analysing the leave arrangements in the different care regimes we have to take into consideration both maternity and parental leave. The duration of maternity leave is longer in Denmark than in the other countries, while the period of statutory parental leave in Denmark is shorter than in the other countries except for the UK.[13] Denmark has the lowest replacement rate for maternity leave among the five countries except for the UK.[14] For extended parental leave in Denmark the replacement rate is only a quarter of the income of an average paid worker. This is markedly lower than in Sweden and France but more than in Germany. In France the length of maternity leave is similar to the other countries while the duration of paid parental leave is the most comprehensive. Paid parental leave in France is, however, restricted to families with two or more children which makes the system less generous than the Danish and Swedish systems despite its longer duration (OECD 1995: 139).

Germany has full replacement for maternity benefit, although with a ceiling. The duration for parental leave in Germany is second in length to France but the level of benefit is extremely low. In Sweden maternity and parental leave are combined. Sweden has the highest level of replacement. The duration of leave with a high replacement rate is long but the total length of the Swedish leave period ranks fourth – only the UK has a shorter period of total leave. The British system for maternity leave is a combination of flat-rate benefit and earnings-related benefits for the first six weeks followed by a flat-rate benefit system with a low replacement rate for the next twelve weeks.[15] Before 1999 the UK had no parental leave scheme and it still has the shortest period of statutory parental leave and is the only one of the five countries where parental leave is unpaid.

In this comparison of length and replacement level of maternity/parental leave in the five countries we find that France and Germany have the longest periods of leave but in the German case with low levels of benefits. The duration of leave in Sweden is shorter than in Denmark, France and Germany but the level of benefit higher than in the other three countries. In Denmark the extended period of parental leave introduced in 1994 is used by still fewer parents because of falling rates of replacement. The right to benefits during leave in Denmark and, most of all, in the UK is strongly related to labour market performance. In France, on the other hand, this right is linked with the number of children in the family in addition to previous labour market experiences while parental leave is a citizenship right in Germany and Sweden.

Possibilities for part-time work

Part-time work is normally considered as a typical female pattern of employment and seen as a measure for mothers to reconcile work and childcare. The regulation of working-time patterns varies from country to country. In Denmark it is difficult to combine paid employment and care. Full-time employment is the primary route to social benefits and taken as the norm for most social security regulation. Unemployed part-time workers can only receive unemployment benefits when insured part-time and then the replacement rate is significantly lower than for full-time insured workers. Furthermore, it is only possible for full-time workers to take parental leave.

In France the family policy has actively aimed at increasing fertility during the recent decades. Instead of discouraging women from joining the labour force, the solution has been to reduce obstacles for childcare for full-time working women, through maternity/parental leave schemes, day-care institutions and after-school facilities. The result has been that the impact of marriage and motherhood on women's labour market involvement is reduced and fewer mothers leave the labour force after childbirth. This active welfare policy may explain the high level of French mothers who are employed full-time and the comparatively low proportion of part-time workers (Blossfeld 1997). Parental leave can be taken by part-time workers to encourge the reconciliation of care for children and paid work.

In Germany (W) the tax system discriminates against couples with two full-time incomes and rewards the wife's non-work or part-time work. On the other hand, in the recent past German women who leave employment to look after children have gained extended rights to pension entitlements if they leave the labour force immediately after the child is born (Maier *et al.* 1994). These policies act to reinforce women's obligations to care for their children either full-time or part-time. Parental leave can be combined with up to 19 hours of paid work without reductions in benefits. This has encouraged many mothers to continue part-time and the female rate of part-time employment has increased during recent years. It is primarily in the public sector that women have possibilities for working on a part-time basis and here the official policy has been to create jobs which make it possible for married women and women with children to reconcile family obligations and work (Blossfeld and Rohwer 1997).

In Sweden government policy has for a long time been aimed at integrating women who have children into the labour force. The proportion of part-time workers among employed Swedish women has been high for a long time. There are several reasons for this. First, labour force participation has increased most rapidly among women who preferred working part-time, such as married women with pre-school children. Second, Swedish women did not lose their social security benefits by working part-time. Third, a series of reforms have facilitated the employee's opportunities for part-time work and reduced hours. Since 1974 it has been possible to take parental leave on a part-time basis and from 1979 parents of children below 8 years of age have the possibility of working 75 per cent of the full-time average with the statutory right to go back to full-time work later on (Sundström 1997).

In the UK, as in Denmark, full-time employment is the norm and even when care responsibilities might demand part-time work, citizens have to be available for a full-time job when unemployed. This is, however, not the case for lone mothers who have had the opportunity of caring for their children full-time and still receiving social security benefits until the child is 16 years old. Even though almost 45 per cent of British women work part-time (see Table 2.2), the part-timers have few social rights. Until 1995 women who worked fewer than sixteen hours per week had fewer statutory employment rights than the full-time employed. Now the two groups both qualify for social protection including regulation of unfair dismissal, redundancy pay and benefits with maternity leave (Burchell, Dale and Joshi 1997).

Conclusion

The divergence in women's labour market involvement during different periods of their life not only depends on national differences in family policy – parental leave and childcare policy – but also differs within the female labour force between women in different age groups and with different family status. In all five countries considered the relationship between paid work, unpaid work and welfare provision is gendered. This has several consequences. First, women and men enter the labour market on different terms. Women work part-time, take parental leave and interrupt their labour market career in relation to childcaring more frequently than men. Second, the unequal gender positions in the labour market feed back into the private sphere and reinforce men's role as providers of the family income and women's role as providers of care within the family. Third, with the strong link between social citizenship rights and labour market status, employment becomes the key to economic and social independence which again are gendered in men's favour.

A main issue in this chapter has been to clarify how variations in caring arrangements in five European countries influence women's ability to reconcile labour market involvement and childcare responsibilities. To answer this question the focus of the welfare state analysis has to be broadened from the relation between work and welfare provision to the relationship between paid work, unpaid work, and welfare provision. In this respect the link between social citizenship rights and family welfare policy becomes crucial in understanding women's labour market position. Here the five countries differ widely both in their priorities of financial support for families with small children and in their criteria for eligibility for parental leave as well as in access to childcare facilities.

Comparing Denmark and Sweden, which are both characterized by comprehensive family policies, we found that in Denmark parental leave is primarily related to the previous employment experiences of women while it is a citizenship right in Sweden. Furthermore, Sweden has formulated a family policy which improves the situation for women combining care-giving and continuous employment. Extended parental leave with high replacement rates and the right to choose full-time or part-time leave for both parents are crucial elements in this parent-friendly Swedish care policy. In Denmark parental leave can only be taken full-time, and the replacement rates are low after the initial phase. All these elements make time for care-giving gender-biased and imply that it is mainly women who take up parental leave and are the primary care-givers.

In France the right to time for caring is highly diversified between mothers with only one child and those with two or more children. Mothers with one child, which is the usual situation today, have no right to paid parental leave after maternity leave but have access to non-parental childcare, while mothers with two or more children can choose between continuous labour market participation or relatively well-paid parental leave. As a consequence of this, a large group of French mothers take up employment just after maternity leave and for the majority it is full-time employment. Only mothers with more than one child can afford to remain on parental leave for a longer period.

The UK and Germany are both characterized by high rates of employment for women but with markedly different patterns of female labour market behaviour. German women are eligible for a long period of parental leave but with low replacement rates and childcare coverage is scarce. This, combined with tax relief for dependent children and a household-based tax system, discourages women from returning to employment after childbirth and encourages them to become full-time or part-time care-givers. In the UK a combination of maternity leave with low replacement rates, no paid parental leave, and little provision of public childcare forces women to choose between full-time care-giving or an early return to employment. When returning to employment, British women have to choose between part-time jobs which they need to combine with almost full-time care-giving, because of the expense of private childcare, or full-time employment where they earn enough to hire a nanny or to be able to pay for privately provided childcare.

Notes

1   We would like to thank Arnlaug Leira, Janet Gornick, Gudny Eydal, Therese Halskov, Andrea Warman and Ilona Ostner for useful comments and proposals for improvements of earlier versions.
2   The German rate of women's labour market participation includes both the former West and East Germany where women have markedly different rates of labour market participation. In the mid-1990s the rate of labour market participation for West German women (69 per cent) was about 25 per cent lower than for East German women (94 per cent) in the age group 25–54. The differences in rate of employment are not of the same size because of a significantly higher level of unemployment in the New Länder. For women in the age group 24–55 the rate of employment in West Germany was 65 per cent and in East Germany 72 per cent in 1994 (see Maier and Rapp 1995, Table 1.1.2 and Table 1.2.1).
3   Part-time employment and its impact on women's labour market involvement will be discussed later in the chapter.
4   The classification of the countries in strong, modified and weak breadwinner welfare regimes is taken from Lewis (1992) who classifies the welfare systems according to the way in which women are treated in the system as mothers, wives or workers in the taxation, in provision of social benefits, and access to childcare support.
5   This pattern is found in the southern European countries and in Ireland where women's labour market involvement culminates in the late twenties and then a significant group of women permanently leave the labour market in connection with marriage and motherhood. None of the countries included in this analysis has a curtailed pattern of labour market involvement for either men or women.
6   In Denmark the employment rates fell for both men and women in the age group 35–39 in the mid-1990s. This cohort was young and entered the labour market during the serious employment crisis in the years 1978–81. During this period youth unemployment skyrocketed and youngsters had extreme difficulty entering the ordinary labour market. Consequently, a significant proportion of this cohort has never secured employment but has been marginalized and lives on pension or social benefits today.
7   Danes – both men and women – retire much earlier from the active labour market participation than Swedes. In this respect the Danish labour market is more like the continental European countries, France and Germany. A generous early retirement scheme for the core labour force aged 60–66 is the main explanation for the Danish retirement pattern.
8   Most of the empirical data available for this study concern the period 1994–6. Therefore, we have found it – as mentioned above – relevant to distinguish between the former West and East Germany because huge differences can still be observed both in pattern of childcare and in female labour market participation.
9   The number of Swedish women in part-time employment in Figure 2.1 is calculated on the national definition of part-time as less than thirty-five hours a week (see EUROSTAT 1998). According to this definition about 40 per cent of the Swedish women work part-time but most of them work long hours part-time – i.e. between thirty-one and thirty-five hours – which means that the proportion of women in part-time jobs defined as less than thirty hours is significantly lower (see OECD 1999). Defined according to the OECD definition (fewer than thirty hours) the proportion of Swedish women in part-time jobs is similar to Denmark and France

but significantly lower than the UK and Germany where most women work short hours part-time (see Table 2.2).
10   In this analysis of the effects of marriage and motherhood as well as in the following analysis of family policy we do not systematically distinguish between married/cohabiting and single mothers. Doing this would surely reinforce the differences between the different breadwinner regimes.
11   In the national labour force surveys people who are absent from employment because of leave – maternity, parental or sickness – are still counted as in employment. They still have an employment contract but are temporarily absent.
12   Our primary inspiration for this classification is taken from an analysis of gender and care made by Knijn and Kremer (1997) comparing Denmark, the Netherlands and the UK.
13   The Danish parental leave scheme is ten weeks in addition to maternity leave but an extended leave scheme was introduced in 1994. According to this scheme parents were eligible to twenty-six weeks of parental leave in addition to the original ten weeks and this period could be prolonged with another twenty-six weeks depending on the employer's agreement. The leave scheme introduced in 1994 is today badly paid and is therefore only taken up by a small group of (primarily) mothers.
14   The replacement rates for maternity leave in Denmark indicate only the statutory level of benefits. A substantial number of Danish female employees on maternity leave, however, get full income replacement as part of their collective agreements.
15   A flat-rate benefit for fourteen weeks is, as mentioned earlier, available for all women.

References

Almqvist, A.L. and Boje, T.P. (1998) *Women's Labour Market Participation and Family Policy in Different European Welfare Regimes (DK, D, F, S, and UK)*, paper presented at the Annual Conference of the Swedish Sociological Association, Gothenburg, January.

Blossfeld, H.-P. (1997) 'Women's Part-Time Employment and the Family Cycle: A Cross-National Comparison', in H.-P. Blossfeld and C. Hakim (eds) *Between Equalization and Marginalization. Women Working Part-time in Europe and the United States of America*, Oxford: Oxford University Press.

Blossfeld, H.-P. and Rohwer, G (1997) 'Part-Time Work in West Germany' in H.-P. Blossfeld and C. Hakim (eds) *Between Equalization and Marginalization. Women Working Part-time in Europe and the United States of America*, Oxford: Oxford University Press.

Burchell, B.J., Dale, A. and Joshi, H. (1997) 'Part-time Work among British Women' in H-P. Blossfeld and C. Hakim (eds) *Between Equalization and Marginalization. Women Working Part-time in Europe and the United States of America*, Oxford: Oxford University Press.

Esping-Andersen, G. (1990) *The Three Worlds of Welfare Capitalism*, Oxford: Blackwell.

Eydoux, A., Gauvin, A., Granie, C. and Silvera, R. (1996) *Women's Employment in France: Trends and Prospects in the 1990s*, French report for the Women in Employment Network, EU Commission, Manchester, UMIST.

European Commission Network on Childcare (1996) *A Review of Services for Young Children in the European Union 1990–95*, Brussels: European Commission Equal Opportunities Unit.

EUROSTAT (1998) Labour Force Survey. Principal results 1997, *Statistics in Focus* 1998: 5.

Fagan, C. and O'Reilly, J.(1998) 'Conceptualising part-time work: the value of an integrated comparative perspective', in J. O'Reilly and C. Fagan (eds) *Part-Time Prospects. An International Comparison of Part-time Work in Europe, North America and the Pacific Rim*, London: Routledge.

Gornick, J., Meyers, M. and Ross, K. (1996) *Supporting the Employment of Mothers. Policy Variation Across Fourteen Welfare States*, Luxembourg Income Study (LIS) Working Paper 139, New York: Syracuse University.

Halskov, T. (1994) *Liden tue kan vælte stort læs*, Copenhagen: Socialpolitisk Forening & Forlag.

Hansen, H. (1998) *Elements of Social Security. A comparison covering Denmark, Sweden, Finland, Germany, Great Britain, Holland, and Canada*, Copenhagen: The Danish National Institute of Social Research Publ. 98: 4.

Jenson, J. (1997) 'Who Cares? Gender and Welfare Regimes', *Social Politics*, Summer.

Knijn, T. and Kremer, M. (1997) 'Gender and the Caring Dimension of Welfare States: Toward Inclusive Citizenship', *Social Politics*, 4, no. 3: 328–62.

Langan, M. and Ostner, I. (1991) 'Gender and Welfare: Towards a comparative framework', in G. Room (ed.) *Towards a European Welfare State?* Bristol: SAUS Publications.

Leisink P. and Coenen, H. (1993) 'Work and Citizenship in the New Europe', in H. Coenen and P. Leisink (eds) *Work and Citizenship in the New Europe*, Brookfield: Edward Elgar.

Leth-Sørensen, S. and Rohwer, G. (1993) 'Aspects of the Female Life Cycle and Labour Market Participation in Denmark', in H.-P. Blossfeld (ed.) *Between Equalisation and Marginalisation: Part-Time Working Women in Europe and the US*, Oxford: Oxford University Press.

Lewis, J. (1992) 'Gender and the Development of Welfare Regimes', *Journal of European Social Policy*, 2 (3): 159–73.

Lewis, J. (1997) 'Gender and Welfare Regimes: Further Thoughts', *Social Politics*, Summer.

Lister, R. (1997) *Citizenship: Feminist Perspectives*, London: Macmillan.

Löfström, Å. (1995) *Women and the Employment Rate: Causes and Consequences of Variations in Female Activity and Employment Patterns in Sweden*, report for the Equal Opportunities Unit, DGV, EU Commission, UMIST, Manchester.

Maier, H.F *et al.* (1994) *Changing Patterns of Work and Working Times for Men and Women: Towards the Integration or the Segmentation of the Labour Market*, report for the Equal Opportunities Unit, DGV, EU Commission, UMIST, Manchester.

Maier, H.F. and Rapp, Z. (1995) *Women and the Employment Rate: Causes and Consequences of Variations in Female Activity and Employment Patterns in Germany*, report for the Equal Opportunities Unit, DGV, EU Commission, UMIST, Manchester.

Maier, H.F. *et al.* (1996) *Trends and Prospects for Women's Employment in the 1990s*, German Report for the EC Network 'Women and Employment', Berlin: European Commission Equal Opportunities Unit.

Marshall, T.H. and Bottomore, T. (1996) *Citizenship and Social Class*, London: Pluto Press.

O'Connor, J. (1996) 'From Women in the Welfare State to Gendering Welfare State Regimes', *Current Sociology*, 2.

OECD (1994) *The OECD Job Study: Evidence and Explanations. Part I – Labour Market Trends and Underlying Forces of Change*, Paris: OECD.

OECD (1995) *Employment Outlook, July 1995*, Paris: OECD.

OECD (1997) *The Definition of Part-time Work for the Purpose of International Comparisons*, Labour Market and Social policy, Occasional Papers, No. 22, OEDE/GD (97) 121.

OECD (1998) *Employment Outlook, July 1998*, Paris: OECD.

OECD (1999) *Employment Outlook, July 1999*, Paris: OECD.

Orloff, A.S. (1993) 'Gender and the Social Rights of Citizenship: The Comparative Analysis of Gender Relations and Welfare States', *American Sociological Review*, 58: 303–28.

Pateman, C. (1992) 'Equality, Difference, Subordination: the Politics of Motherhood and Women's Citizenship', in G. Bock and S. James (eds) *Beyond Equality and Differences. Citizenship, Feminist Politics and Female Subjectivity*, London/New York: Routledge.

Pitrou, A. and Gaillard, A.-M. (1989) 'Familles de France et de Suède: à la recherche de nouveaux modèles', *Cahiers des Sciences humaines*, 25 (3): 415–28.

Rostgaard, T. and Torben F. (1998) *Caring for Children and Older People – A Comparison of European Policies and Practices*, Copenhagen: The Danish National Institute of Social Research 98: 20.

Rubery, J., Fagan, C. and Smith, M. (1995a) *Changing Patterns of Work and Working-time in the European Union and the Impact of Gender Divisions*, report for the Equal Opportunities Unit, DGV, EU Commission, UMIST, Manchester.

Rubery, J., Smith, M., Fagan, C. and Grimshaw, D. (1995b) *Women and the European Employment Rate: Causes and Consequences of Variations in Female Activity and Employment Rates in The European Union*, report for the Equal Opportunities Unit, DGV, EU Commission, UMIST, Manchester.

Rubery, J., Smith, M. and Fagan, C. (1996) *Trends and Prospects for Women's Employment in the 1990s*, report for the Equal Opportunities Unit, DGV, EU Commission, UMIST, Manchester.

Rubery, J. and Smith, M. (1996) *Factors Influencing the Integration of Women into the Economy*. European Work and Employment Research Centre, UMIST, Manchester.

Rubery, J., Smith, M., Fagan, C. and Grimshaw, D. (1998) *Women and European Employment*, London: Routledge.

Rubery, J. (1998) Part-time Work: a Threat to Labour Standards?, in J. O'Reilly and C. Fagan (eds) *Part-Time prospects. An International Comparison of Part-Time Work in Europe, North America and the Pacific Rim*, London: Routledge.

Sainsbury, D. (1996) *Gender, Equality and Welfare States*, Cambridge: Cambridge University Press.

Statistics Sweden (1995) *Labour Force Survey 1995*, Stockholm.

Sundström, M. (1997) 'Managing Work and Children: Part-time Work and the Family Cycle of Swedish Women', in H.-P. Blossfeld and C. Hakim (eds) *Between Equalization and Marginalization. Women Working Part-time in Europe and the United States of America*, Oxford: Oxford University Press.

Taylor-Gooby, P. (1991) 'Welfare States Regimes and Social Citizenship', *Journal of European Social Policy*, Vol. 1, no. 2.

Van der Veen, R. (1993) 'Citizenship and the Modern Welfare State. Social Integration, Competence and the Reciprocity of Rights and Duties in Social Policy', in H. Coenen and P. Leisink (eds) *Work and Citizenship in the New Europe*, Brookfield: Edward Elgar.

3 Variation within post-Fordist and liberal welfare state countries

Women's work and social rights in Canada and the United States

Cecilia Benoit

(Statistics Canada information is used with the permission of the Ministry of Industry. Information on the availability of the wide range of data from Statistics Canada can be obtained from Statistics Canada regional offices, its World Wide Web site at www.statcan.ca and its toll-free access number 1-800-263-1136.)

Introduction

There is now a substantial literature forecasting the transformation of national markets into 'global economies', with the production of goods and services no longer tied to a particular geopolitical location. The seemingly 'borderless world' (Ohmae 1991) of late twentieth-century capitalism is said to have led to the undermining of secure labour contracts previously hammered out between employers and workers, the demise of labour unions, and a general decline of other Fordist strategies characteristic of industrial capitalist societies during earlier decades of the century (Krahn and Lowe 1998). We have now apparently entered a 'new world of work' (Barley 1996), a post-Fordist era, based on 'flexible accumulation', deregulation of markets, and fluid employment arrangements that include contingent, part-time, and part-year employment, self-employment and structural unemployment (Jessop *et al.* 1987). Some observers of post-Fordism even predict the 'end of work' in the sense of secure employment with job ladders and fringe benefits (Rifkin 1995). The winners in this economic transformation are the small group of privileged 'sky workers' with scarce analytical and technical skills that command high returns on the 'niche markets' of the post-Fordist economy, whereas the losers are the majority of 'ground workers' with few or no marketable skills, who are assigned dead-end jobs with little or no security, and who face the continuous threat of under- and unemployment (Reich 1997).

At the same time, witnesses of post-Fordism also predict a decline in the role of national governments as a negotiating power between employers and workers, and an erosion of welfare state social policies that are seen as outdated and a hindrance in the new flexible employment arrangements. The Fordist welfare state is allegedly being transformed into a post-Fordist 'entrepreneurial state'

(Harvey 1989). Feminist scholars have gendered these predictions and pointed out that post-Fordism threatens to undermine women's hard-won achievements in the postwar period (Jenson *et al.* 1988). Especially worrying, they note, is the threatened demise of social policies upon which women are dependent for income redistribution, public employment, education, health and social services, and social assistance (Armstrong 1993; Oakley and Williams 1994). Recent feminist scholarship points to the 'marketization of the welfare state', including the creation of 'quasi-markets and/or the privatization of core health and social services', as well as the 'individualization of welfare', which involves an incremental movement away from universalism based on welfare state principles of equality and equity, towards provision in the form of targeted services based on criteria of selectivity and prioritization (Popay and Williams 1994; Lewis 1993).

These various developments are said to be especially characteristic of countries that are clustered together under the liberal welfare state regime umbrella – not least Canada and the US (Esping-Andersen 1990). These two North American 'country cousins' are seen as prime candidates for the post-Fordist label, with their borders transparent, not only to each other but to global capital in general. The North American Free Trade Agreement (1994) has been said to 'open Canada for business' in ways not previously possible, and at the same time to reduce the Canadian federal government's ability to influence economic and social matters within the country (Laxer 1989; Armstrong and Armstrong 1988). Even more telling descriptions have been made of the US where the 'invisible hand' of supply and demand has allegedly reduced the federal government's control of market forces, and encouraged less and less social welfare spending (Myles 1996). The post-Fordist economies of the two countries apparently make the liberal welfare state regime label even more apt than previously, both countries are seen as 'laggards' that are willing to provide social support to the disadvantaged only in the final instance of market failure (Kudrle and Marmor 1981). Even feminists, who have challenged the welfare state regime paradigm by arguing that gender cuts across the regime typologies in different ways when attention is paid to women's (and not just men's) employment status, nevertheless tend to share the mainstream view of Canada and the US when it comes to their common welfare state label (Armstrong and Armstrong 1988; Armstrong 1994; O'Connor 1996).

It may be that the concepts of post-Fordism and liberal welfare state regime are beneficial for comparison of a relatively large sample of countries when the focus is on a single variable such as public employment (Gornick and Jacobs 1998). Yet it is argued below that such concepts need to be nunanced when making smaller country comparisons, especially within regime clusters, as others have also argued in regard to the Scandinavian/Nordic states (Leira 1992; Ellingsæter 1998). This chapter presents employment statistics and social policy data on Canada and the US that together suggest the need to nuance the concepts of post-Fordism and the liberal welfare state regime if our goal is to make sense of the complex economic and social realities that these two countries now face at the outset of the twenty-first century. On the one hand, some recent employment trends indicate that, compared with the US, Canada has moved further along the post-Fordist road. Yet other data that focus on women's employment situation and access to social rights show that, compared with Canada, the US more closely fits the 'liberal/entrepreneurial/post' welfare state label.

The chapter is divided into three sections:

- theoretical overview of the concepts of post-Fordism and liberal welfare state regime;
- comparative data on Canada and the US on select economic and social dimensions;
- summary and conclusion.

Although worthy of analysis, space limitations do not allow for discussion of the intra-nation state differences that are particularly apparent in the US but are also visible among the Canadian provinces. Space concerns also prevent examination of variation within the two national populations in regard to race and ethnicity, among other social categories. On the other hand, it should be remembered that both North American countries are ethnically diverse, and they share many historical and cultural features, including a New World heritage and historical ties with Britain.

'Post-Fordism' and 'liberal welfare state regime' as conceptual tools

Market economies around the world are said to be undergoing fundamental restructuring as the new millennium opens. The globalization of finance and application of new information technologies to the production of goods and services are believed to be behind the apparent demise of Fordist capitalism characteristic of earlier decades of the twentieth century that has involved some or all of the following features: industrially based centralized production, national economies supporting domestic mass manufacturing, Keynesian economic policies, collective bargaining, strong unions, full-time employees with job shelters, and welfare state policies such as progressive tax systems, unemployment benefits and pension rights (for description and critique see Reich 1991; Krahn and Lowe 1998; Jenson *et al.* 1988). The argument is that a 'new world of work' has now arrived, a post-Fordist era, characterized by opposite trends that include deindustrialization, corporate linkages, international trade agreements, weakened unions, limited labour contracts, contingent work, increased self-employment and retrenchment of welfare state social policies (Jessop *et al.* 1987; Barley 1996).

Sociologists adopting the post-Fordist thesis have described the emerging economies of industrial capitalist societies as segmented into three distinct employment sectors:

- the innovative sector, a small elite of 'sky workers' in entry port jobs that offer possibilities of further training, career ladders, greater pay and fringe benefits over time, and worker participation (Reich 1997);
- a much larger marginal sector, mainly located in the peripheral/secondary market, occupied by 'ground workers' who are without access to secure employment, performing non-standard jobs that include short-term contracts, self-employment, along with other forms of contingent work accompanied by few if any employment benefits and rarely leading to greater responsibility or higher pay, social security or career ladders (Harrison and Bluestone 1988; Reich 1997);
- an emerging third sector comprising workers doing voluntary/community-based work, which is largely devoid of both pecuniary reward and employment rights (Lewis 1993; Armstrong 1994).

Some sociologists have described these developments in the form of a 'polarization of the labour market' and the 'shrinking of the middle classes', with fewer workers in secure employment, and many occupied in marginal jobs, voluntary activities, or no employment at all (Reich 1991). Economic forecasts for the early decades of the twenty-first century predict entrenchment of this post-Fordist economy – that is, a spiralling down of secure workers, who join the ranks of an enlarged 'disposable workforce' (Moore 1996). The emerging brave new world of virtual companies is predicted to involve trans-national corporations (TNCs) shifting their operations around the globe, irrespective of union contracts and national political boundaries, moving about in a 'borderless world' (Ohmae 1991). Some post-Fordist observers see these developments as a new form of global exploitation:

> TNCs are unencumbered with national baggage. Their profit motives are unconcealed. They travel, communicate, and transfer people and plants, information and technology, money and resources globally. TNCs rationalize and execute the objectives of colonialism with greater efficiency and rationalism.
>
> (Miyoshi 1993: 748)

A possible solution to this ominous prediction announcing the impending demise of secure employment is suggested by Jeremy Rifkin (1995) who calls for public valuation of work now performed outside capitalist markets and state bureaucracies, neither of which, in his view, are likely to offer secure employment for most people in a future society characterized by lean corporations without frontiers and downsized government organizations. Rifkin envisages instead the growing importance of the 'third sector' mentioned above – i.e. voluntary workers providing services to needy individuals, families and communities, perhaps rewarded for their efforts with a minimum monetary payment. What we need, in short, is support for a new 'social economy', as Rifkin (1995: 249–50) explains:

> The globalization of the market sector and the diminishing role of the governmental sector will mean that people will be forced to organize into communities of self-interest to secure their own futures. . . . Today, with the formal economy receding from the social life of the nation and the government retreating from its traditional role of provider as last resort, only a concerted effort spearheaded by the third sector and adequately supported by the public sector will be able to deliver basic social services and begin the process of revitalizing the social economy of every country.

Feminists writing on post-Fordism have argued that it is a gendered process, noting that the demise of the welfare state is directly affecting women in at least three ways (Armstrong and Armstrong 1988; Oakley and Williams 1994). First, it results in a reduction of transfer payments to households and this is especially detrimental to disadvantaged households, among which the most vulnerable are female-headed families. Second, contraction of the welfare state also means an end to secure public sector employment where comparatively large numbers of women workers are located. Third, a leaner public sector results in the loss of important health and social services, including public childcare provision, that make it possible for women to undertake gainful employment in the first instance (Armstrong 1994; Baker 1996). Feminist writers point out that it comes as no surprise that a decline in public sector jobs for women compels a decline in public services for all women (and their families). Nona Glazer (1993: 5–6) has labelled this latter component of post-Fordism the 'work transfer':

> The *work transfer* is the redistribution of labour from paid women service workers to unpaid women family members, but one that maintains a connection between the work. . . . The work transfer exemplifies the capacity of capitalism to shape even the most intimate details of social life, in this case even the tending work that women do as family members. (Emphasis in original.)

The mainstream and feminist scholarship on welfare state regimes to some extent parallels the scholarship on post-Fordism. There is a general tendency by both feminist and mainstream scholars to assume that welfare states at the end of the twentieth century are 'in transition', that nation states are being forced to adapt to global economies, and that the 'golden age' of the welfare state is over

(Esping-Anderson 1996; O'Connor 1996). While this scholarship recognizes that differences due to national institutional traditions between countries will remain, the conclusion – at least in regard to countries like Canada and the US – is that their markets have become increasingly deregulated and the division of labour polarized between core and periphery workers (the latter of which includes a growing voluntary sector), and that their liberal welfare states have reduced public provision even more so in recent decades (Armstrong and Armstrong 1988; Myles 1996). Feminists examining the welfare state regime scholarship have largely accepted these points in the mainstream perspective, but also add that it is women in general, and lone mothers (and their children) in particular (Baker 1996), who are especially vulnerable to this change of events. Feminists point to high dependency rates on social assistance and child poverty rates both in liberal welfare state regimes and in male-breadwinner states (Lewis 1993; O'Connor 1996).

Yet there are critics of the welfare state regime model who argue that the model hides as much as it reveals. Recent scholarship, mentioned above, that highlights differences among the Scandinavian/Nordic countries with regard to public childcare provision and dual-breadwinner families forms part of this scholarship (Leira 1992; Ellingsæter 1998). Diana Sainsbury's (1996) study of significant variations within welfare state regime types along a number of gendered dimensions also challenges the placement of particular countries in clusters with others from which they can be shown to differ in ways that are important for women's economic independence and equality in society. Janet Gornick *et al.* (1997), in their multi-country analysis of social policies promoting employment for mothers, make a similar point about the limitations of the welfare state regime cluster model. In addition, some researchers have highlighted differences between the two North American neighbours by focusing on social services such as healthcare (Olsen 1994). This alternative strategy of investigation – that focuses on highlighting differences as well as similarities between countries that are placed within welfare state regime clusters – is adopted below. The main point is not to suggest that Canada and the US are 'worlds apart', for they are not in many ways. Rather, the aim of the chapter is to attempt to show how they nevertheless differ in key respects, differences that the people of either country are themselves quick to point out, and differences that also explain the relatively economic vulnerability of the Canadian economy compared with its US counterpart, but also the greater support for 'big government' (and hence higher personal taxes) among Canadian than US citizens.[1] The argument made here is also that the two countries differ in regard to women's employment situation and access to social rights, both prerequisites for women's economic independence (Orloff 1993; Polakow 1993).

Some economic and political realities of Canada and the United States

Employment trends

If post-Fordism has indeed arrived and the categorization of Canada and the US as occupying similar welfare worlds is accurate, then it would be expected that the secondary (peripheral) labour market characterized by 'bad jobs' (i.e. those that are non-unionized, low-wage, low-skill, high turnover, few benefits) has expanded in recent decades, and at the same time that government/public employment in the primary (core) sector of the economy has declined over this period. The data, in fact, present a more complex picture than might be expected for either country.

Contrary to the common assumption that the US holds the top place among other OECD nations when it comes to churning out atypical precarious jobs with minimal wages and no job security, a recent study[2] carried out by Statistics Canada comparing the US and Canadian labour force trends over time shows that 70 per cent of the net job creation in the US over the past decade has been in the form of full-time employment and, second, US workers in higher paying jobs over this same period outnumber those with lower earnings by two to one. By contrast, self-employment and part-time jobs[3] have been the main engines of growth in Canada over the past decade, while at the same time the country's unemployment level, though falling in recent years, has remained consistently higher than that of the US (Statistics Canada 1998).

Table 3.1 Employment trends, Canada and the US, 1989–97

	Total employment ('000)	Self-employment (% of total employment)	Part-time employees (% of total employment)	Full-time employment (% of total employment)
Canada				
1989	13,086	13.8	17.5	68.7
1997	13,941	17.8	19.3	62.9
US				
1989	117,342	11.8	14.8	73.4
1997	129,559	11.6	15.3	73.1

Source: Statistics Canada, 1998.

As Table 3.1 shows, self-employment comprised nearly 18 per cent of total Canadian employment in 1997, and almost one-fifth of employees (19 per cent) in Canada work fewer than thirty-five hours per week on average. The comparable figures in 1997 for the US are roughly 12 per cent self-employment, with 15 per cent of employees designated as part-time. Further, the Canadian unemployment rate as of October 1998 (8.1 per cent), even when accounting for different cross-national measurements, remains at nearly double the US rate (4.6 per cent) (Statistics Canada 1998).

On the basis of these initial employment trends, it would seem that Canada is a far better candidate for the post-Fordist label than its country cousin to the south. On other employment and welfare state measures, however, a different picture appears, suggesting the need at least partly to recast this preliminary conclusion. First, let us consider the situation of women's employment in the two countries.

Gender and employment trends

Female labour market participation rates have increased over time in both countries, and the US rate of 71 per cent compares more favourably than the Canadian rate of 67.9 per cent (OECD 1997a). On the other hand, while the unemployment rate for US women had dropped significantly between 1986 and 1996 (from 7.0 per cent to 5.4 per cent), it remains slightly higher than that of their male counterparts (5.3 per cent in 1996). By contrast, Canadian women's unemployment rate, though consistently higher than that of their US female counterparts, nevertheless reversed itself over the decade when compared with that of Canadian men. Thus, today Canadian women experience lower unemployment than Canadian men.

Further, although US women's percentage of part-time employment in 1996 (67.9 per cent) was somewhat lower than that of their Canadian counterparts (69.1 per cent), the US rate increased slightly over the decade (67.4 per cent in 1986), whereas the opposite has been the case for Canadian women in part-time employment (69.7 per cent in 1986) (OECD 1998a). These findings concerning Canadian women's employment (lower unemployment rates compared with men and decline in women's share of part-time employment over time) match those for Sweden and Denmark, and suggest that the concept of post-Fordism may be of limited use in explaining the diverse and complex nature of women's employment in time and across place.[4]

Government service employment

If we examine another post-Fordist prediction – the decline in overall government service employment in the recent period – a similar divergence between the US and Canada emerges. As Table 3.2 shows, this holds true for the US where the drop has been quite significant (a full percentage point between 1989 and 1995). The trend is rather different in Canada, which has seen a very gradual increase in government service employment between 1968 and 1990, and since then a small drop in the size of the public employment sector.[5] At the same time, the percentage of the labour force in the overall service sector (i.e. including both non-government and government service sectors) has increased in both countries, but to a marginally greater extent in the recent decade in the US than in Canada (OECD 1997a).[6]

Table 3.2 Service sector employment, total and government, Canada and the US, 1960–96

	Total service sector			Government services		
			%			
	1960	1990	1996	1968	1990	1995
Canada	54.1	71.2	73.1	18.6	19.7	19.6
US	56.2	70.9	73.3	17.0	14.4*	13.4

* 1989

Source: OECD (1992) and OECD (1998).

Unionization rates

A similar divergence exists between the two countries concerning workers' unionization rates, and this finding is especially the case once gender is taken into account. Whereas US statistics on union decline over the last decade and a half closely fit post-Fordist predictions for both men and women, the prediction does not come true in Canada for either gender, but especially not for women workers. The share of US workers who were members of unions was 20 per cent in 1983, but had declined to 13.9 per cent in 1998 (US Bureau of Labor Statistics 1999). In Canada, however, the rate of unionized workers during this period has remained relatively stable, fluctuating between 31 per cent and 33 per cent between 1983 and 1997. To some extent, Canada's larger public sector explains the differential union rates between the two countries. But over and above this fact, Canadian public employees are also far more likely to be unionized (73.0 per cent) than their US counterparts (37.2 per cent). Further, Canadian part-time workers report higher union rates – in fact, three times the rate (21.8 per cent) – than their counterparts to the south (7.1 per cent) (Statistics Canada 1998).

These differences between the two countries are especially important when women's union membership is taken into account. US female wage and salaried workers have witnessed a decline in union membership over the past fifteen years to a low of 11.4 per cent in 1998 (thus their union membership rate is nearly five percentage points lower than that of their male counterparts at 16.2 per cent). The comparable figure for Canadian women workers was just under 30 per cent, which is a substantial increase over time (the rate in 1966 was a mere 16 per cent) and is today just slightly below that of Canadian unionized male workers (US Bureau of Labor Statistics 1999).

In both countries, unionized workers on average earn more than their non-unionized counterparts. This is especially the case for part-time workers, the majority of whom in both countries are women. In fact, the hourly earnings for unionized part-time workers in Canada in 1998 were nearly double that of their non-unionized part-time counterparts, and a similar picture holds for the US (US Bureau of Labor Statistics 1999; Akyeampong 1998).

Unemployment insurance

In regard to the proportion of workers with access to unemployment insurance in Canada relative to the US, a similar more positive picture can be demonstrated in the Canadian case. Even with recent tightening of federal government eligibility requirements, Canada still spends a much larger share of GDP on unemployment compensation that the US. In fact, the Canadian average is higher than the OECD average (Myles 1996). As has been said about other OECD countries in Europe confronting high unemployment rates, some economists have laid the blame on Canada's relatively generous unemployment insurance system, as well as its higher degree of unionization, as reasons for the 'employment gap' between the two countries. Be that as it may, what is important for the purposes of this chapter is to realize that the two countries vary also in regard to support for those out of work. This finding holds true as well along gender lines: although men in both countries are more likely to be unemployment insurance claimants, Canadian women workers are more likely to have access to these non-means-tested benefits than their US counterparts (Baker 1995).

Healthcare insurance

The two countries stand in stark contrast in regard to access to national healthcare insurance. While in 1996, 14 per cent of the US GDP was spent on healthcare (the highest among OECD countries), only about one-third (6.5 per cent) of the 14 per cent GDP health expenditure in the US was public expenditure. By contrast, the total Canadian GDP expenditure figure was notably lower, at 9.6 per cent, and just under 75 per cent (6.7 per cent) of the total healthcare expenditures in Canada in 1996 were moneys from the public purse (OECD 1997a). What this means for workers is that Canada's universal health insurance plan provides physician and hospital services to all citizens independent of both need and labour force participation (Benoit 1998). In the US, however, employers and employees are forced to make monthly health insurance payments so that workers and their families have access to basic coverage. Healthcare is thus a major 'hidden cost' subtracted from US workers' wages. At the same time, few health insurance plans are comprehensive in nature, most are non-portable from job to job – let alone from state to state – and many employers have no health insurance plans at all (Macionis, Benoit and Jansson 1999). This is especially the case for workers with low earnings, particularly lone mothers but also the 'working poor' two-parent families and minorities, who are often forced to pay out of pocket for their emergency healthcare, or go without any help at all. In 1994 some 40 million Americans (about 15 per cent of the population) were without health insurance, and nearly another 40 million lose their coverage temporarily each year, generally because of layoffs or job changes.

These various differences between the two countries in regard to employment and related issues go some way to explain why the economic gap between advantaged and disadvantaged has widened substantially in the US in recent decades, while the gap has only increased slightly in Canada (World Bank 1998; Macionis, Benoit and Jansson 1999). The fact remains that Canada not only devotes substantially more to public expenditure (42.7 per cent) compared with the US (31.1 per cent) (OECD 1997a); the Canadian welfare state is more progressive than that of its southern neighbour with regard to both taxes on income and transfers such as those above.

It should be pointed out that inequality still exists in Canada, and that particular types of Canadian families have difficulties making ends meet. The point here is rather that the tax and social transfer system in Canada lifts a substantial number of households above the poverty line, though much less so for single-parent families (80 per cent of which are headed by women). By contrast, the US tax and transfer system turns out to be only marginally progressive in the case of all households with children and, in fact, regressive in the case of single-parent households (Baker 1996; Benoit 2000).

Family leave policies

The US is unique among OECD countries in that it has no statutory paid maternity and parental benefits. Some progress was made in 1993 when the federal government passed the Family and Medical Leave Act, which legislates that medium-sized and large firms must grant unpaid parental leave to female and male employees. Businesses with fewer than fifty employees (they employ over 75 per cent of the US labour force) are exempt from this unpaid parental leave law (Reskin and Padavic 1994), although some of these firms nevertheless grant leave in separate contracts with their employees. Further, because there are no benefit requirements attached to the 1993 Act, 'the law is of no value to parents who cannot afford parental leave. According to one study, fewer than 40 per cent of working women have [employer-sponsored] benefits or income protection that would allow them to take a six-week unpaid leave' (Reskin and Padavic 1994: 163).

Although no doubt modest when compared with the Nordic policies in this area (Gornick *et al.* 1997; Sainsbury 1996), Canada's parental leaves policies lend greater support to mothers' employment than new legislation in the US. That is, Canadian laws do not make restrictions on accessing maternity or parental leaves on the basis of size of firm where a worker is located. The actual length of maternity and parental leaves is a matter of provincial/territorial law, and there exists some variation in regard to the latter across the country (Benoit 2000). Yet all provinces and territories have laws mandating at least seventeen weeks of maternity leave, and the vast majority in the past decade have added parental leaves. However, unlike countries such as Sweden and Norway with paternity (father's) leave in place (Branth and Kvande 1998), only the province of Quebec has so far passed legislation in this regard (Benoit 2000).

Canadian legislation also contrasts with that of the US with regard to mandatory benefits while taking family leaves of the two kinds mentioned above. Again, although the wage recovery rate is well below those of the other Nordic countries (Gornick *et al.* 1997), one should not underestimate the qualitatively different situation working mothers (and fathers) in Canada enjoy when compared with their counterparts south of the border in the event of the birth of a child. Both maternity benefits and parental benefits in Canada are federal matters, under the national unemployment insurance system, with the benefit level as of 1997 set at 55 per cent of their previous wage.[7] As of December 2000 the maximum time an individual can draw parental benefits is twelve months.

In brief, although clearly inadequate for many new mothers (and fathers), Canada's family leave policies are substantially more attractive than those of the US where there are no statutory leave benefits for employed parents to access at all. Instead, those American workers with access to 'corporate capital' (employer-sponsored parental benefits) are able to enjoy time with their newborns while the rest must return to work shortly after the birth of their child, or else quit their jobs.

Childcare policies

Although not to the extent found elsewhere (Leira 1992; Tyyskä 1998), both Canada and the US devote some public funds towards childcare, and both have some public policies in this regard. Nevertheless, it can be shown on this measure as well that the Canadian policies are more progressive than those of its neighbour to the south.

On the one hand, neither country has enacted national legislation that guarantees access to public or publicly subsidized childcare (Gornick *et al.* 1997; Benoit 2000).[8] Both countries, on the other hand, provide tax relief to parents to help offset childcare expenses. However, the amount of such tax relief is substantially higher in amount and reaches more families in Canada; tax-free payments were made to 85 per cent of Canadian families with children in 1997 (Finance Canada 1997). By contrast, only 39.9 million people/13.3 million families in the US received an 'earned income tax credit' (child tax credit) in 1992 (Congressional Research Services 1992). Canada also passed National Child Benefit legislation in July 1998, which provides additional federal funds over and above the child tax benefit to families with children to help offset the costs of childcare and related expenses. This new national investment in children (C$850 million in 1998) is available to all families with children across the country, the actual benefit level being determined by the income as declared on the income tax return and being calculated automatically. In addition, the provinces, through their social assistance programmes, offer means-tested benefits (i.e. based on proven need by the client) to needy families to help them meet some of their out-of-pocket childcare expenses.

This latter type of provision is the predominant form of government investment in childcare in the US. One of the most successful US programmes of this type is Head Start, which has provided financial support services and childcare resources for low-income families across the country, although to far fewer than those who are eligible for the programme (Baker 1995). It is also worth noting that the US has recently announced additional funding (US$20 billion) for childcare over the next five years, which involves larger block funding grants to the states for childcare facilities, augmentation of earned income tax credit programme in order to reach more working parents, provision for a new tax credit for businesses to provide on-site childcare to employees, and funds to establish an additional Early Head Start programme (Administration for Children and Families (ACF) Office of Public Affairs 1998).

In short, neither Canada nor the US can be seen to be retracting their welfare states in the past decade with regard to government provision in the childcare area, although it remains the case that neither has implemented legislation for guaranteed childcare coverage for all children, as has been the case in both Finland and Sweden in the past decade (Leira 1992; Tyyskä 1998). Further, Canada and the US differ in their respective levels of public expenditure in this area, and especially concerning the availability of non-means-tested policies and programmes, with Canadians more willing to pay higher taxes for these public expenses than their US counterparts.

These findings are consistent with the other social welfare policies not focused on here due to space limitation (see Benoit 2000 for detail).[9] The final section attempts to relate the overall findings to the two main concepts discussed at the beginning of the chapter, and poses the question as to what explains the different nature of the welfare state in the two countries.

Summary and conclusion

This chapter has presented evidence that calls into question the utility of the concepts of post-Fordism and welfare state regimes in capturing the complicated trends in employment and welfare state policies in Canada and the US over time. Depending upon which dimension (e.g. extent of full-time versus part-time employment, growth of self-employment, quality of new jobs, level of unemployment, etc.) is in focus, the effect of post-Fordism has been more dramatic for marginalized groups in Canada than it has for those of its southern neighbour. Yet, when attention is drawn to other dimensions (comparative size of the government service sector, union rates, national unemployment insurance), the opposite appears to be the case. With regard to the concept of a liberal welfare state regime, the overall evidence presented above shows that this label appears to fit the general organization of welfare policies in the US, although even in that country there have been some welfare state policies (e.g.

1993 parental leave law), as well as recent federal government monetary commitment to enhanced childcare services over the next five years, that caution against the use of the term 'residual' or 'retrenchment' when categorizing the US welfare state in every respect.

It has been argued that such caution is of even greater importance when the focus of attention is on the Canadian welfare state. Although perhaps useful as a tool to initiate research questions, the welfare state regime concept appears of little value in understanding the complex nature of the Canadian welfare state which, in fact, does not seem to fit any welfare state regime box very well. In short, while it may be worthwhile to include the US and Canada under the same welfare state umbrella when broad OECD comparisons are being made along a particular dimension, there is an inherent danger in such a wide-angle approach since it obscures important differences between countries that are likely to emerge only when a more open (non-regime) framework is used to examine the empirical data.

The interesting question remains as to why Canada and the US, so similar in some ways, tend to diverge with regard to public support for the welfare state. This is a research area in its own right, and there is now a substantial literature devoted to explaining the main points of contrast between these two countries that on many other counts are so similar. No doubt the decentralized character of the US federal-state-political system, and the major cleavage along race lines play a role (Skocpol 1988; Polakow 1993; Quadagno 1994). Seymore Martin Lipset (1990: 136) also makes a distinction between the two countries on the basis of communitarianism, maintaining that Canadians are much more supportive of 'the public mobilization of resources to fulfil group objectives'. Of course, Canada too has cleavages of region (province) and ethnicity (two founding nations, in addition to its aboriginal peoples). Yet Canadians look to their welfare state as the glue that holds the country together, not an easy feat given its comparatively large territory and small population, two dominant linguistic groups (French and English), and a mosaic of new immigrants, and a powerful neighbour just south of the border (Jenson 1990; Myles 1996). As Keith Banting (1992) explains:

> [Canadian] Federal welfare programmes, whether delivered directly to individuals or through provincial governments are powerful tools of inter-regional redistribution. They represent one of the few ways in which the federal government can fashion appeals that cut across linguistic and regional divisions.

While there is little doubt that global capitalism will have a further impact on the economies and societies of both countries, the evidence to date compels us to keep our eyes open for continuing differences between the two OECD country cousins.

Notes

1 Canada's total tax load as a percentage of GDP in 1997 was 37.2 per cent, compared with 27.9 per cent for the US (OECD, 1997b).
2 The study, recently released by Statistics Canada (autumn 1998), draws heavily on two national data sources that are very similar in content and methodological approaches: the Canadian Labour Force Survey, and the US Current Population Survey.
3 The US definition of part-time workers was adopted in the report in order to compare trends between the two countries – that is, workers who are employed fewer than thirty-five hours a week in their sole or principal job. This explains the discrepancy in the OECD labour force statistical data which are based on national definitions of employment. Yet it is worth noting that when the Canadian definition of part-time employment is used (usual hours of less than thirty per week at the main or sole job or business), the overall upward trend in part-time employment in Canada compared with the US remains the same, although the cross-national rates drop by several percentage points.
4 See Boje and Almqvist in this volume for a detailed look at the Scandinavian and select other European countries regarding the complex nature of recent employment trends for women and their differential access to family benefits.
5 This decline in the Canadian case has largely been in regard to public administration, defined as workers in federal, provincial and local government (Statistics Canada 1998).
6 The comparable figures of government service employment for Finland were 22.4 in 1990, rising to 25.2 in 1996, and for Sweden 31.7 in 1989 and a slight decline to 31.2 in 1996 (OECD 1992; OECD 1997a). Also see Boje and Almqvist in this volume for a look at Norway and Denmark, where public sector employment over the decade has also held its own.
7 Again, Quebec stands out across the country in this regard as well as in recently increasing the wage replacement rate to 75 per cent (Benoit 2000).
8 However, Quebec passed a provincial law to this effect in 1997, and Hawaii has invested significant funds in this direction as well.
9 As a case in point, Canada not only spends more on education as a percentage of GDP (7.2 per cent in 1997) than the US (6.6 per cent), but a much smaller percentage of the Canadian educational expenditure (7 per cent) is from private sources than the comparable figure of 25 per cent for the US (OECD 1997c).

References

Administration for Children and Families (ACF) Office of Public Affairs (1998) 'President Clinton Announces Childcare Initiative', *White House Fact Sheet*, 7 January. Online. Available HTTP: http://www.acf.dhhs.gov/news/press/980107.htm (14 September 1999).

Akyeampong, E.B. (1998) *The Rise of Unionization Among Women: Special 1998 Labour Day Release*, Ottawa: Statistics Canada. Catalogue no. 75-001-XPE.

Armstrong, P. (1993) 'Women's Healthcare Work: Nursing in Context,' in P. Armstrong, J. Choiniere and E. Day (eds) *Vital Signs, Nursing in Transition*, Toronto: Garamond Press.

Armstrong, P. (1994) 'Caring and Women's Work', *Health and Canadian Society*, 2, 1: 109–18.

Armstrong, P. and Armstrong, H. (1988) 'Taking Women into Account: Redefining and Intensifying Employment in Canada', in Jenson, J., Hagan, E. and Reddy, C. (eds) *Feminization of the Labour Force: Paradoxes and Promises*, pp. 65–84, London: Polity Press.

Baker, M. (1995) *Canadian Family Policies: Cross-National Comparisons*, Toronto: University of Toronto Press.

Baker, M. (1996) 'Social Assistance and the Employability of Mothers: Two Models from Cross-National Research', *Canadian Journal of Sociology*, 21, 4: 483–503.

Banting, K. (1992) 'Neoconservatism in an Open Economy: The Social Role of the Canadian State', *International Political Science Review*, 13: 149–70.

Barley, S.R. (1996) *The New World of Work*, London: British-North American Committee.

Benoit, C. (1998) 'Rediscovering Appropriate Care: Maternity Traditions and Contemporary Issues in Canada', in Coburn, D. *et al.* (eds) *Health and Canadian Society*. Third edition, Toronto: University of Toronto Press.

Benoit, C. (2000) *Women, Work and Social Rights: Canada in Historical and Comparative Perspective*, Scarborough, Ontario: Prentice Hall Canada.

Branth, B. and Kvande, E. (1998) 'Modernity, State Feminism and Flexible Fathers', tabled paper at the ISA conference, Montreal, July.

Canadian Policy Research Network (1998) *Values and Preferences for Canadian Children*, Ottawa: Reneuf Canada.

Castles, F.G. and Mitchell, D. (1992) 'Identifying Welfare States Regimes: The Links Between Politics, Instruments and Outcomes', *Governance*, 5,1: 1–26.

Congressional Research Services (1992) 'Cash and Noncash Benefits for Persons with Limited Income: Eligibility Rules, Recipients and Expenditure Data, FY 1990–92', Washington, DC: Congressional Research Services.

Ellingsæter, A.L. (1998) 'Dual Breadwinner Societies: Provider Models in the Scandinavian Welfare States', *Acta Sociologica*, 41,1: 59–73.

Esping-Andersen, G. (1990) *The Three Worlds of Capitalism*, Princeton: Princeton University Press.

Esping-Andersen, G. (ed.) (1996) *Welfare States in Transition: National Global Economies*, London: Sage Publications.

Esping-Anderson, G. (1989) 'The Three Political Economies of the Welfare State', *Canadian Review of Sociology and Anthropology*, 26: 10–36.

Finance Canada (1997) Budget 1997, 'Towards a National Child Benefit System', Ottawa: Government of Canada. Online. Available HTTP: http://www.fin.gc.ca/budget9/pamphe/childpae.html (14 September 1999).

Glazer, N. (1993) *Women's Paid and Unpaid Labour: The Work Transfer in Healthcare and Retailing*, Philadelphia: Temple University Press.

Gornick, J.C. and Jacobs, J.A. (1998) 'Gender, the Welfare State, and Public Employment: A Comparative Study of Seven Industrialized Countries', *American Sociological Review*, 63, 5: 688–710.

Gornick, J.C., Nyers, M.K. and Ross, K.E. (1997) 'Supporting the Employment of Mothers: Policy Variation across Fourteen Welfare States', *Journal of European Social Policy*, 17,1: 45–70.

Government du Quebec (1997) *New Elements of the Family Policy: Our Children at the Heart of our Decisions*, Montreal: Bibliothèque Nationale du Quebec.

Harrison, B. and Bluestone, B. (1988) *The Great U-Turn: Corporate Restructuring and the Polarising of America*, New York: Basic Books.

Harvey, D. (1989) *The Condition of Postmodernity*, Oxford and Cambridge, MA: Blackwell.

Jenson, J. (1990) 'Representations in Crisis: The Roots of Canada's Permeable Fordism', *Canadian Journal of Political Science*, XXIII, 4: 653–83.

Jenson, J., Hagan, E. and Reddy, C. (eds) (1988) *Feminization of the Labour Force: Paradoxes and Promises*, Cambridge: Polity Press.

Jessop, B., Bonnett, K., Bromley, S. and Ling, T. (1987) 'Popular Capitalism, Flexible Accumulation and Left Strategy', *New Left Review*, 165: 104–23.

Korpi, W. (1985) 'Power Resources Approach vs. Action and Conflict: On Casual and Intentional Explanations in the Study of Power', *Sociological Theory*, 3: 31–45.

Korpi, W. (1989) 'Power, Politics, and State Autonomy in the Development of Social Citizenship', *American Sociological Review*, 54: 309–28.

Krahn, H. and Lowe, G. (1998) *Work, Industry, and Canadian Society*, Third Edition, Scarborough, Ontario: Nelson Canada.

Kudrle, R.T. and Marmor, T.R. (1981) 'The Development of Welfare States in North America', in P. Flora and A. Heidenheimer (eds) *The Development of Welfare States in North America*, London: Transaction Books.

Laxer, G. (1989) *Open For Business: The Roots of Foreign Ownership in Canada*, Don Mills, Ontario: Oxford University Press.

Leira, A. (1992) *Welfare States and Working Mothers: The Scandinavian Experience*, New York: Cambridge University Press.

Lewis, J. (ed.) (1993) *Women and Social Policies in Europe: Work, Family and the State*, Aldershot: Edward Elgar.

Macionis, J.J., Benoit, C.M. and Jansson, S.M. (1999) *Society, the Basics: Canadian Edition*, Prentice Hall Canada.

Lipset, S.M. (1990) *Continental Divide: The Values and Institutions of the United States and Canada*, New York: Routledge.

Miyoshi, M. (1993) 'A Borderless World? From Colonialism to Transnationalism and the Decline of the Nation State', *Critical Inquiry*, 19 (Summer): 726–51.

Moore, T. (1996) *The Disposable Workforce: Worker Displacement and Employment Instability in America*, New York: Aldine de Gruyter.

Myles, J. (1996) 'When Markets Fail: Social Welfare in Canada and the United States', in Esping-Andersen, G. (ed.) *Welfare States in Transition: National Global Economies*, pp. 116–40, London: Sage Publications.

Oakley, A. and Williams, A.S. (eds) (1994) *The Politics of the Welfare State*, London: UCL Press.

O'Connor, J.S. (1993) 'Gender, Class, and Citizenship in the Comparative Analysis of Welfare State Regimes: Theoretical and Methodological Issues', *British Journal of Sociology*, 44, 3: 501–18.

O'Connor, J.S. (1996) 'From Women in the Welfare State to Gendering Welfare State Regimes', *Current Sociology*, 44, 2: 1–125.

O'Connor, J.S. (1998) 'Welfare Expenditure and Policy Orientation in Canada in Comparative Perspective', in O'Connor, J. S. and Olsen, G. M. (eds) *Power Resource Theory and the Welfare State: A Critical Approach*, pp. 154–82, Toronto: University of Toronto Press.

OECD (1992) *Economic Outlook Historical Statistics*, Paris: OECD.

OECD (1997a) *Labour Force Statistics, 1976–1996*, Paris: OECD.

OECD (1997b) *Revenue Statistics, 1965–199,*. Paris: OECD.

OECD (1997c) *Education at a Glance – OECD Indicators 1997,* Paris: OECD.

OECD (1998a) *Labour Force Statistics, 1997–1997*, Paris: OECD.

OECD (1998b) *National Accounts*, Paris: OECD.

Ohmae, K. (1991) *The Borderless World*, London: Fontana.

Orloff, A.S. (1993) 'Gender and the Social Rights of Citizenship: The Comparative Analysis of Gender Relations and Welfare States', *American Sociological Review*, 58: 303–28.

Olsen, G.M. (1994) 'Locating the Canadian Welfare State: Family Policy and Healthcare in Canada, Sweden, and the United States', *Canadian Journal of Sociology*, 19, 3: 303–29.

Polakow, V. (1993) *Lives on the Edge: Single Mothers and Their Children in the Other America*, Chicago: University of Chicago Press.

Popay, J. and Williams, G. (1994) 'Local Voices in the National Health Services: Needs, Effectiveness and Sufficiency', in Oakley, A. and Williams, S. (eds), *The Politics of the Welfare State*, pp. 75–97, London: UCL Press.

Quadagno, J. (1994) *The Color of Welfare: How Racism Undermined the War on Poverty*, New York: Oxford University Press.

Reich, R. (1991) *The Work of Nations: Preparing Ourselves for 21st-Century Capitalism*, New York: Alfred A. Knopf.

Reich, R. (1997) 'Sky and Ground: What the U.P.S. Strike Delivered', *American Sociological Association Organizations, Occupations, and Work Newsletter*, (Fall): 5, 8.

Reskin, B. and Padavic, I. (1994) *Women and Men at Work*, Thousand Oaks, Calif.: Pine Forge Publishers.

Rifkin, R. (1995) *The End of Work*, New York: G.P. Putnam's Sons.

Sainsbury, D. (1996) *Gender, Equality and Welfare States*, Cambridge, Mass.: Cambridge University Press.

Siaroff, A. (1994) 'Work, Welfare and Gender Equality: A New Typology', in Sainsbury, D. (ed.) *Gendering Welfare States*, pp. 82–100, London: Sage Publications.

Skocpol, T. (1988) 'The Limits of the New Deal and the Roots of Contemporary Welfare Dilemmas', in Weir, M., Orloff, A. S. and Skocpol, T. (eds) *The Politics of Social Policy in the United States*, pp. 293–312, Princeton, NJ: Princeton University Press.

Statistics Canada (1998) *Labour Force Update: Canada – US Labour Market Comparison*, Autumn 1998, Ottawa: Minister of Industry. Catalogue no. 71-005-XPB.

Tyyskä, V. (1998) 'Insiders and Outsiders: Women's Movements and Organizational Effectiveness', *Canadian Review of Sociology and Anthropology*, 35, 3: 391–410.

US Bureau of Labor Statistics (1999) 'Union Members in 1998', Washington, DC. Online. Available HTTP: http://stats.bls.gov/news.release/union2.toc.htm (15 September 1999).

World Bank (1998) *World Development Report 1998/99*, New York: Oxford University Press.

4 Welfare states, labour markets and gender relations in transition

The decline of the Scandinavian model?

Anne Lise Ellingsæter

Welfare states under external pressures

That profound restructuring is taking place in economies and labour markets, and that welfare states operate under increasing external constraints, is commonly understood. But the causes, magnitude and direction of labour market and welfare state restructuring are contested. This chapter explores what happens to the configurations of state policies and labour market institutions characteristic of the Scandinavian model in this period of increasing external pressures, and how political-institutional change relates to restructuring of employment and gender relations. Welfare state and labour market structures and processes are gendered, and thus change might affect women and men differently, transforming prevailing gender structures.

Globalization theories are becoming increasingly popular in studies of welfare state and labour market change (see, e.g. Benoit in this book). Globalization processes take place in three areas: the economy, the polity and culture (Waters 1995). The degree of economic globalization and its consequences for the viability of national political strategies are disputed. In an allegedly globalized economy, dominated by uncontrollable market forces and transnational corporations, national economies and domestic political management strategies become increasingly irrelevant (Hirst and Thompson 1996). Thus, declining political autonomy of the nation state is anticipated. Among others, Hirst and Thompson (1996) criticize this 'strong' version of globalization. They argue that although economies are internationalized, and exposure to international product and capital markets render them susceptible to external impacts, they are still regulated nationally.

There are different theories of economic globalization, and some link globalization to transformations of the Fordist production system (Waters 1998). Post-Fordist production is associated with increasing flexibility in both production methods and the use of labour. However, there is considerable disagreement as to whether a shift from Fordist to post-Fordist production is actually taking place or not. Some argue that it implies a structural determinism of a kind similar to the earlier 'industrialism' thesis (Jefferys 1995), that is, the thesis that industrialization would follow the same development in all countries.

In post-Fordist theories the welfare state is seen as moving from a Keynesian full-employment state, with regulation of collective bargaining, to a post-Fordist welfare state, where social policy is becoming increasingly subordinated to the needs of flexibility and international competition (Jessop 1994). National distinctiveness in politics and institutions will give way to convergence, and the international trend is towards a passive, down-scaled state.

Globalization and post-Fordism are related to the idea of deregulation of labour (Lind 1998). The end of Keynesian policies paved the way for a revival of a liberal ideology of market deregulation. Labour market flexibility is the ideal of the deregulated market. State regulations and organized labour inhibit the free functioning of markets. The efficiency of a deregulated labour market has become a dominant international political rhetoric.

How the Scandinavian welfare states fare in an era of pressures from globalized finance and product markets and a neo-liberal ideology is particularly interesting. They are small, open and exporting economies which makes them vulnerable to increasingly internationalized product and capital markets. Their labour market and gender structures, including high female employment rates, have traditionally been explained by their particular political-institutional features, such as active labour market and gender equality policies, unique industrial relations and centralized wage-bargaining systems. The Scandinavian societies have been high work, full-employment oriented, particularly Norway and Sweden

Welfare states, labour markets and gender relations

Once the model state for much welfare state research (Baldwin 1996), and also a model state for gender equality policies, the Scandinavian states, Denmark, Norway and Sweden, have shared several commonalities. The notion of welfare state regimes has become very influential in comparative welfare state research, and the Scandinavian countries are often classified as one type of policy regime, although this is contested. Regime typologies of welfare states and, later, of gender relations, have been important in sensitizing and theorizing the significance of politics and institutions in explaining social structures and practices (Esping-Andersen 1990; Lewis 1992). The main advantage is that policies are seen as clustered in packages, rather than as single issue policies. However, regime models are criticized for a static view of welfare states, oversimplifying questions of change (Daly 1997). Regime models also tend to simplify the complex operation of policy mechanisms, as their nature is to diminish intra-regime differences and augment inter-regime differences (Ellingsæter 1998). For these reasons, 'intra-regime' comparison of change in the Scandinavian countries is likely to be a particularly advantageous approach.

Gender relations in the labour market are shaped in the interplay of economic structures, state policies, cultural ideas and historical traditions. However, there has been a tendency to confine the analysis of the impact of welfare states on gender relations in the labour market to the study of reproductive policies. However, in addition, labour market policies, industrial relations and collective bargaining systems also shape gender relations in crucial ways. What is needed to understand the impact of policies and institutions on gender relations is a multidimensional approach (Orloff 1997).

This chapter examines policy change and restructuring of labour market and gender relations in the Scandinavian countries in the 1990s. The first part explores political-institutional change. Two main questions are addressed:

- are there any trends towards deregulation of labour and decentralization of industrial relations, and do they follow similar patterns?
- are there any common trends towards retrenchments and passivity in state activity, particularly concerning labour market and reproductive policies?

The second part analyses the level and forms of employment generated within the framework of policy change or stability in this period; notably employment and unemployment rates and the prevalence of flexible work forms. The main focus is on the gender relations generated from these patterns. In the final section the relationship between economic globalization, national political-institutional change and restructuring of employment and gender relations is the issue under discussion.

Deregulation of labour?

Economic globalization and neo-liberal political impulses seem to increase the pressure towards labour market deregulation. Theoretically, strict rules for hiring/firing and contracts of limited duration make hiring and firing more costly, but the relationship between regulation and employment/unemployment levels is difficult to establish empirically (Emerson 1988). Employment regulation has been seen as an obstacle to flexible labour markets and employment growth, and as one reason for the high European levels of unemployment compared with that of the US. However, the large variation in unemployment rates in Europe is often overlooked, as well as the differences in employment rates caused by differences in female employment (Nickell 1997; Rubery *et al.* 1998). Moreover, increasing unemployment has been paralleled by increasing female employment. Employment deregulation is assumed to increase the prevalence of non-standard work forms, such as temporary work and part-time work. The gender segregation in such work forms is often neglected (Rubery *et al.* 1998). Labour market deregulation is assumed to increase insecurity of employment among women.

Labour market deregulation must be seen in a historical perspective. Historically, there has been no common Scandinavian employment regulation regime. The OECD's (1994b) ranking of 'strictness' of employment protection legislation shows that the Scandinavian countries are spread across the distribution. Traditionally, Denmark has had the most liberal legislation in certain areas, and only the UK has a legislation more favourable to the employers (OECD 1994b). Lind (1998) argues that the Danish model of employment regulation has traditionally been voluntaristic, and that only moderate change has taken place in the 1990s. Sweden has had the most strict regulation (e.g. regarding dismissals and temporary lay-offs), while Norway has had medium-level protection (Engelund 1992). For example, Norwegian and Swedish companies have a relocation duty, that is, dismissals for reasons of cost-effectiveness are accepted only if it is not possible to find the employee another job within the company. In Norway, courts may also order that the unfairly dismissed workers are to be reinstated (OECD 1994b).

Regulations concerning temporary work and part-time work also vary significantly. Basically there are two types of temporary work: the most common form is that of firms employing individuals directly under fixed-term contract or specific termination date, and there are temporary work agencies, where a worker is contracted out to a firm for a specified period of time (OECD 1993). Concerning the first form of temporary work, Denmark is the most liberal, and there are few restrictions on fixed-term contracts. Sweden is more restrictive, but the Norwegian legislation for fixed-term contracts is the most restrictive. In Norway, temporary contracts are valid only for situations such as replacement of temporarily absent workers and tasks of limited duration (OECD 1994b). A recent revision of the Work Environment Act (1994) actually resulted in some further restrictions on temporary labour in Norway

Legislation on private temporary work agencies has been liberalized in several European countries in recent years, and in Denmark (1990) and Sweden (1993) (Olsen 1997). Despite pressure from employers and an intense public debate, Norway's strict regulations have not yet been lifted. The main rationale of deregulation in Denmark and Sweden was to make the public replacement offices more efficient through increased competition, that is, an ideology subscribing to the idea of deregulation and market efficiency.

In Scandinavia, employment regulation normally also applies to part-time work (Bjurstrøm 1993). However, employment protection and social benefits are reduced significantly for part-time workers in Sweden (working less than twenty-two hours a week) (Ginsburg 1992). Attitudes to part-time work have varied. By the 1970s Sweden had already experienced active reforms in favour of part-time work. In Denmark, by contrast, polices towards part-time work have been deliberately restrictive, strongly influenced by the unions actively opposing part-time work. For example, most collective agreements prohibit part-time work if working hours are below fifteen per week (Bjurstrøm 1993). In Norway, the expansion of part-time work did not occur as a result of public policies, rather it developed as a result of changing firm and worker practices, which were later overtaken by policy regulation.

Decentralization of industrial relations?

One potential consequence of a globalized economy is the weakening of the power of national labour over capital. In neo-liberal thinking, organized labour is seen as a hindrance to job creation. Decentralization and flexibility in industrial relations is, allegedly, the dominant trend towards which countries tend to converge (Scheuer 1992). This might affect women negatively. For example, there is evidence that the form of societal corporatism that has developed in Sweden benefits women; a compressed wage structure implies a smaller gender wage gap (Ruggie 1984). However, while there is no uniform trend towards decentralized bargaining across OECD countries, important changes are taking place. The three Scandinavian countries have had centralized, or national level bargaining systems, and distinctively different developments have taken place in these countries.

The Swedish model of industrial relations has gone through fundamental changes in the 1980s and 1990s, and some even question if the model still exists (Kjellberg 1992). The main drive has been towards decentralized bargaining, flexibility and corporatist decline. However, Sweden still has the highest level of unionization (OECD 1997). A change in political climate is assumed to have contributed to a 'change of system' concerning industrial relations, particularly in the corporatist system. Change has been headed by employers in big firms dominating Sweden (Kjellberg 1992; Stephens 1996). In 1992 the Swedish employers' federation, SAF, advocating privatization and deregulation, withdrew its representation from all government bodies. Later also LO, the main employee federation, decided to withdraw from most government bodies. Unions have accepted the need for increased productivity and a greater spread in wages.

According to the OECD (1997), the Danish system was decentralized in the 1980s, but centralized from 1989 onwards. Somewhat in contrast to this, Scheuer (1992) talks about a 'slow decentralization' in Denmark, which he argues is not a new trend of the 1980s/1990s, but rather a return to the previous traditions of politicized centralization from the 1970s. The Danish development should not be seen as a sign of a crisis or weakening of the Scandinavian model of industrial relations, argues Scheuer (1992). On the contrary, institutionalized bargaining has been strengthened. Decentralization means a move from national, multi-industry bargaining to national single-industry bargaining, and not from national, industry-wide to single-employer bargaining as in many other countries. Scheuer argues that it is rather the Swedish type of model, with 'high-trust relationships between leaders of (social-democratic) governments, LO and the employers' confederations' which has failed. Danish collective bargaining is highly institutionalized and synchronized, and unlike Sweden, major organizations are still represented in public committees.

In Norway bargaining has become more centralized, and it was ranked as the most centralized bargaining system in the mid-1990s (OECD 1997). The revitalization of central bargaining was a response to the increasing unemployment caused by the recession starting in 1988. In 1992 an employment commission was appointed, whose recommendations gained wide support among labour market actors and political parties. The central idea was the launching of the solidaristic alternative, meaning moderation for everyone, particularly for the employed in solidarity with the unemployed (Torp 1995). The support of the labour market actors was manifested in the moderation line followed in the collective wage-bargaining processes. Wage moderation contributed to keeping inflation down, which has been seen as a major key to economic recovery and strong employment growth since 1993.

Employment policies: a passive state?

In a globalized economy national management strategies seemingly become less relevant and viable, implying less state intervention. Employment policies have been at the centre of the debate over labour market flexibility and employment growth. A distinction is generally drawn between passive and active policies. Passive policies are directed at replacing some of the income loss connected with unemployment, by various forms of unemployment benefits. In a neo-liberal ideology, generous benefits are assumed to lower the unemployed's incentive to find a new job, thus creating rigidities in the labour market. Stricter eligibility conditions affect the share receiving unemployment benefits. In particular, groups which do not fit the full-time continuous labour market participant model get less protection against the costs of unemployment: this affects women more than men in most countries (Rubery *et al.* 1998). Active policies are directed at increasing the employability of the unemployed through various labour market programmes. If eligibility to benefits defines access to programmes, women will often be worse off than men.

Generous unemployment benefits and active labour market policies have been a characteristic particularly of the Scandinavian welfare states. The general policy trend in most European countries has been tightening of access to unemployment benefits. However, apart from Sweden, the Scandinavian response has been expansion (Daly 1997). In Denmark, a new transitional benefit for older workers was introduced in 1992. It was tied in to active measures of job activity or training. However, others argue that there have been reductions in access to unemployment benefits, accompanied by stricter obligations to participate in employment or other activation schemes in the 1990s (Lind 1998). Changes in unemployment insurance have made part-time work less attractive (ibid.).

In Norway, qualifying conditions for unemployment compensation have been liberalized since 1990 (Daly 1997). Unlike in Denmark and Sweden, unemployment benefit is not tied to union membership in Norway, where the only eligibility criterion is previous income. But, in contrast with most countries, the income criteria are so low that even marginal part-time workers can easily fulfil them (Maier 1991). However, the income threshold was raised slightly in 1996. Unemployed persons accepting a part-time job are eligible for unemployment benefits for the hours they work below the level of full-time employment. This is also the case for Denmark and Sweden, but benefits have limited duration and have become increasingly restricted. For Scandinavian women, however, eligibility problems are losing significance, because of their increasingly continuous labour market patterns. Yet, in Sweden labour market policies have been monitored for their gender perspective since 1994 (Gonäs and Spånt 1997).

The membership criterion has been a central element in the Swedish system, but it is contested. The conservative government suspended this criterion in a system introduced in 1994. However, the old system was reintroduced shortly after the Social Democrats regained power (Gonäs and Spånt 1997). The level of compensation has, over time, been reduced from 90 per cent to the current 80 per cent, but the Swedish replacement level is still the highest in Scandinavia.

Active labour market policy has formed an important element in the Swedish model. The extent of Swedish labour market policy has not changed, except for the composition of various measures, and training measures have been given precedence over job-creation measures (Auer and Riegler 1994). Auer and Riegler find it paradoxical that the conservative government in the early 1990s, which was initially critical of labour market policies, has expanded the measures beyond the level which the public placement service found effective. There is now a political consensus that there is no alternative to active labour market policies. However, further extensions of the active labour market policy have not been able to stop employment decline and rising unemployment. The policy seems to have lost its impact.

Labour market schemes have played a significant role in Norwegian labour market policy during the recession (1988–93), reflecting a political strategy in which investments in education are seen as preferable to open unemployment. This strategy was implemented mainly through the labour market qualifying programmes, but also through the expansion of the number of places in the educational system. For example, from 1988 to 1993 the number of places in universities was increased from 103,000 to 160,000 (Torp 1994).

Historically, Denmark has been less oriented towards active policies than Sweden and Norway (Furåker *et al.* 1990). But, in the 1990s, labour market programmes have played an important part in Denmark's strategy to fight unemployment. Leave schemes, aimed at the redistribution of work and thus the reduction of the insider–outsider problem, have been the main new strategy. In 1994 leave programmes for educational purposes, for parental and sabbatical leaves, were introduced. Interestingly, work–family reforms in Denmark thus emerged as a labour market policy issue, and not as a family policy issue as in the two other Scandinavian countries.

Public employment and reproductive policies: less state?

Economic globalization and neo-liberal policies are associated with a down-scaled state. Some anticipate that 'less state' means more market and more family, with adverse consequences for women's employment (e.g. Siim 1993), as women are more dependent on the welfare state as employer and provider of services. A high demand for workers in the public sector combined with highly developed public care services has formed particularly favourable conditions for Scandinavian women. Also the extension of the work contract to encompass care responsibilities, providing flexibility and decommodification through paid leaves of absence, has been important.

Sweden, Denmark and Norway, in that order, still have the largest public sectors in the OECD area, accounting for more than one-third of all employees in the mid-1990s (SOU 1996). The extent of down-scaling policies varies between the three countries. To reduce public expenditure, Denmark experienced a freeze in the growth of public employment during the 1980s, increasing the number of private sector service jobs much faster than that in the public sector (Boje 1995). This encouraged women to enter the labour market via jobs in the private sector. There have been strong political efforts to reduce the public sector and to encourage employment growth in private services (Boje 1995). In Norway, women's employment stability was cushioned by welfare state expansion during the recession (1988–93), when significant expansions in local welfare services took place. The number of people employed in government services increased by 14 per cent. Traditional Keynesian policies were made feasible by the country's oil revenues, which increased the state's freedom of action in a situation of external pressures. The oil economy means fewer economic constraints, which made room for more social investments and public employment. Less economic pressure may also influence the internal power balance between labour and capital. Nevertheless, Norway's particular economic foundation should be seen as one of several factors interplaying in complex ways. In Sweden, by contrast, welfare state retrenchments in the 1990s have involved significant public sector down-scaling. From 1990 to 1995 the number of people employed in the public sector declined by nearly 300,000. Privatization of telecommunication and postal services is part of this decline, but rationalization has also been important in the restructuring of the public sector (SOU 1996).

Concerning the organization of public childcare and other reproductive policies there has been no homogeneous Scandinavian approach. There have been important variations in terms of coverage of childcare services, the extent of care leave arrangements and how family childcare is compensated. Sweden and Denmark have had considerably higher coverage rates in services than Norway. Swedish parents have had the most generous leave arrangements. A decisive line in policy 'packaging' has been the balancing of the gender 'equality-difference' dimension (Ellingsæter 1998). Swedish and Danish policy models have been more oriented towards the individual than the Norwegian model. Moreover, Sweden and Norway have had a stronger leaning towards gender difference in the organization of care and time than Denmark. Policies particularly in Sweden, but also in Norway, have encouraged family care by enabling women to stay at home on paid leave with their children, and have institutionalized the right to reduced working hours. Danish policies have encouraged public care by the strong emphasis on public childcare services for the youngest children, enabling women to stay at work.

In the 1990s policy reforms there are some trends of convergence, but also of divergence. Whether Swedish reproductive policies are characterized by less state intervention is difficult to say. On the one hand, cutbacks in replacement levels in parental leaves and privatization of childcare have been among the most prominent policy changes. On the other hand, parents' reproductive rights have been strengthened through the introduction of a new requirement that local authorities have to provide childcare when parents are working or studying. Moreover, cutbacks have occurred on previously high replacement levels, and the privatization efforts in the care sector have yielded modest results; the number of private employees in the care sector was only 6 per cent in the mid-1990s (Sainsbury 1996). By comparison, Norway has a much higher share of privately run childcare institutions.

In Norway the 1990s have undoubtedly been a period of 'more state' in reproductive policies. The number of places in public childcare schemes increased considerably. Parental leave schemes have also been significantly improved, and parents now enjoy the most generous economic compensation in Europe. A 'forced' father's quota has been introduced, with great success; fathers have to take one month's leave, and if they do not, this time will be lost to the parents. Such a 'daddy's month' has also been introduced in Sweden. However, subsidized public childcare is contested in Norway. New policies in this area were introduced in 1998. The new Centre coalition minority government reached a majority for an extensive cash benefit reform, the 'cash support'. Parents with small children who do not use public childcare will be paid in cash the amount equivalent to the state subsidy for a place in the services. The aim is to make parents spend more time with their children, to increase parents' freedom of choice regarding childcare, and to equalize the distribution of state subsidies independent of the form of childcare parents prefer. A similar reform was introduced by the Conservative government in Sweden in 1994, but was withdrawn when the Social Democrats came to power shortly after. By contrast to this extension of pay for care, the 'work line' has been strengthened for other groups of parents; restrictions in the duration of transitional benefits for single providers came into effect in 1998.

Danish policies in the 1990s also imply 'more state'. While Denmark has had the highest service coverage for the youngest children, parental statutory rights to leave for care have been significantly less extensive compared with those of Sweden and Norway. However, the broad labour market reforms in 1994 have resulted in better leave opportunities for parents. This case demonstrates a different national legacy concerning reproductive policies in Denmark: parental leave reform was motivated by labour market concerns, in contrast with the family orientation of similar arrangements in Norway and Sweden.

Labour market transformations: employment and unemployment

The following two sections examine the restructuring of employment and gender relations in the context of the political-institutional change discussed above. Thus the focus is on the level and forms of employment generated in the 1990s, notably employment and unemployment rates, the prevalence of flexible work forms and the gender relations generated from these patterns.

The Scandinavian 'high employment' societies are still among the countries that integrate the highest share of their population in the labour market. Norway, in particular, but also Denmark, has been able to increase its employment ratios into the late 1990s (Table 4.1). In Denmark this at least in part reflects the active labour market policy. In 1997 Norway had the highest employment ratio in the OECD area, after Iceland. Sweden, on the other hand, has experienced a dramatic fall. The employment ratio is now level with that of the UK. Thus the highest employment levels were achieved in Norway, in the context of a combination of continued employment regulation and a strengthening of centralized collective bargaining.

Table 4.1 Employment/population ratios, 1983, 1990 and 1993–7

	1983	1990	1993	1994	1995	1996	1997
				%			
Denmark	72	75 |	72	72	74	74	75
Norway	77	73	71	72	68 |	75	77
Sweden	80	83 |	73	72	72	72	71

Note: | indicates breaks in time series.

Source: For 1983: OECD 1997, Table B. Other years: OECD 1998, Table B.

Female employment is still at very high levels in Scandinavia. However, women in other countries are approaching the Scandinavian level, demonstrating that high female employment rates are not a unique characteristic of an interventionist welfare state. For example, in the US and the UK, an expanding private service sector combined with a decline in real wages has increased women's labour supply. The Scandinavian development is not uniform, but women's employment reflects the overall country trends: in Sweden women's employment ratios have declined considerably in the 1990s, by more than 10 per cent, while a modest increase took place in Norway and Denmark, towards the end of the 1990s (Table 4.2). However, Sweden still has the smallest gender differences in employment, only 3 per cent in 1997, suggesting that economic recession did not disadvantage women in particular. The largest drop in employment in Sweden has occurred among people under 25 years old, which might be one of the reasons behind a dramatic fall in fertility. Women in general have fewer children, but an increasing proportion of women with little education in the most vulnerable labour market situation are postponing having children (Möller and Hoem 1997). In Norway both women and men have benefited from the economic recovery since 1993. Norwegian women's employment exceeds that of Sweden and Denmark for the first time in the postwar period. In Denmark employment growth has benefited men somewhat more than women.

Table 4.2 Employment/population ratios, 1983, 1990 and 1993–7, by gender

		1983	1990	1993	1994	1995	1996	1997
					%			
Denmark	Women	65	71 |	69	67	67	67	69
	Men	78	80 |	76	78	81	81	81
Norway	Women	70	67 |	67	68	68 |	70	72
	Men	88	79 |	76	77	78 |	80	82
Sweden	Women	76	81 |	72	71	71	70	69
	Men	85	85 |	73	72	74	73	72

Note: | indicates breaks in time series.

Source: For 1983: OECD 1997, Table B. Other years: OECD 1998, Table B.

The recession of the early 1990s led to an increase in unemployment levels in most countries, including Scandinavia. Norway and Sweden experienced the highest unemployment levels in the postwar period (Table 4.3). While Swedish unemployment has continued at a high level, about 8 per cent, Norway has recovered and unemployment has fallen to about 4 per cent. Unemployment in Denmark has traditionally been much higher than in Sweden and Norway, but Denmark has experienced a notable decline in recent years. Thus, the increasing inclusion of women in the Scandinavian labour market has taken place under quite different national economic conditions. Unemployment rates vary considerably between the countries, and fluctuate over time.

Table 4.3 Unemployment rates 1983, 1990 and 1993–7

	1983	1990	1993	1994	1995	1996	1997
				%			
Denmark	9.7	8.5	10.9	8.1	7.0	6.9	5.4
Norway	2.5	5.3	6.1	5.4	4.8	4.9	4.1
Sweden	3.5	1.7	8.2	8.0	7.7	8.1	8.0

Source: For 1983: OECD 1997, Table B. Other years: OECD 1998, Table B.

The duration of unemployment is generally seen as a manifestation of the flexibility of labour markets; the longer the duration, the less flexible the market. In the late 1990s, the Scandinavian countries had the lowest rates of long-term

Table 4.4 Incidence of long-term unemployment, twelve months and over, as percentage of unemployment, 1983, 1990 and 1994–7

		1983	1990	1994	1995	1996	1997
Denmark	Men	39	28 |	32	32	28	26
	Women	50	32 |	32	25	25	28
	Total	44	30 |	32	28	27	27
Norway	Men	6	19	28	29	16	14
	Women	7	20	30	17	12	11
	Total	6	19	28	27	14	13
Sweden	Men	11	5	19	17	19	32
	Women	10	4	14	14	15	27
	Total	10	5	17	16	17	30

Note: | indicates breaks in time series

Source: For 1983: OECD 1997, Table I. Other years: OECD 1998, Table I.

unemployment in the OECD area (Table 4.4). Norway and Denmark experienced a declining trend, while there has been an increase in Sweden.

The level of unemployment is determined not only by the flexibility of the market or the demand for workers, but also by the flexibility of the labour force to do other things than be employed or register as unemployed. An important characteristic of the Norwegian workforce is that it is one of the most flexible in the OECD area, in terms of labour supply (Larsen 1992). When employment opportunities decrease, the number offering their labour supply in the market also declines, reducing the total labour force. A contrasting example is Denmark, where the labour force has been continuously growing despite high unemployment rates. The high levels of unemployment in Norway in the 1990s generated a relatively higher proportion of a 'silent reserve' among women than among men; but this is concentrated among young women, who were more flexible than young men in such matters as education and other non-employment activities. Thus, in economic recession, the state serves as a 'buffer' to young women.

In periods of poor job prospects, some individuals leave the labour force, and others do not enter. These are defined as discouraged workers: people excluded from the labour force because they fail the job search criterion (OECD 1993). Low unemployment rates have been associated with higher discouraged worker ratios, especially in Sweden and Norway. Unemployment rate differentials between countries would be narrowed if discouraged workers were included. Women typically make up a larger share of discouraged workers, but the share is diminishing.

The general gender pattern in unemployment in Europe has been that women's unemployment rates exceed those of men, but the long-term trend is a narrowing of the gender gap (Rubery *et al.* 1998). In Scandinavia gender differences in the 1990s vary both in magnitude and in direction. In Denmark women have consistently suffered higher unemployment than men, and the gender gap has increased with improved labour market conditions. In Norway the recession has led to relatively higher unemployment rates among men, but in the economic recovery the gender gap again has been reversed. In Sweden men had significantly higher unemployment rates than women in the early 1990s, but the gap is narrowing (Table 4.5). Long-term unemployment also varies with gender. The gender differences are generally small in the Scandinavian countries, but vary over time (Table 4.4). In both Norway and Sweden women have lower proportions of long-term unemployment than men in the late 1990s.

Table 4.5 Unemployment rates, 1983, 1990 and 1993–97, by gender

		1983	*1990*	*1993*	*1994*	*1995*	*1996*	*1997*
				%				
Denmark	Women	10.4	9.0 |	11.2	9.0	8.6	8.4	6.5
	Men	9.2	8.0 |	10.6	7.3	5.7	5.6	4.6
Norway	Women	2.8	4.9	5.3	4.8	5.2 |	4.9	4.3
	Men	2.3	5.8	6.7	6.0	5.2 |	4.8	4.0
Sweden	Women	3.6	1.6 |	6.6	6.7	6.9	7.5	7.5
	Men	3.4	1.7 |	9.7	9.1	8.5	8.5	8.5

Note: | indicates breaks in time series.

Source: For 1983: OECD 1997, Table B. Other years: OECD 1998, Table B.

In the Scandinavian countries there are hardly any gender differences in the proportion of the unemployed who received unemployment compensation, constituting about 84 per cent for both women and men in Denmark, and respectively 67 per cent and 69 per cent of the unemployed in Sweden (Rubery *et al.* 1998). Moving from a returner pattern to continuous labour market participation makes questions of eligibility to benefits based on a 'male' continuous pattern less disadvantageous to women. However, the access to partial unemployment benefit for part-time workers in permanent work contracts was restricted in Sweden in 1995, which made some (women) leave a permanent part-time job for a temporary one (Gonäs and Spånt 1997).

Neither do labour market programmes exclude women. In Norway women are over-represented in labour market programmes, which has to do with the type of places offered (Torp 1994). As a consequence, women's registered unemployment would have increased more than men's if labour market programme participants had been included. Thus, the gender differential in the extent of exclusion from the ordinary labour market is less when employment programmes are included. This would also be the case in Sweden. In 1993, 6.5 per cent of the workforce was involved in active labour market policy measures (Auer and Riegler 1994). Thus, a total of about 15 per cent of the labour force was not in regular employment. In Denmark there is an increasing number of unemployed who take up the vacancies formed by the leave schemes, which have been a great success (Boje 1995). The number of people on leave peaked in 1996, when about 55 per cent were on parental leave. The number of leave-takers has since been substantially reduced as the level of economic compensation has been gradually cut. Sabbatical leave has virtually disappeared. About 90 per cent of those taking leave are women, and about 50 per cent of the women were formerly unemployed (Madsen 1995). Leave benefits are lower than unemployment benefits, but those on leave are not required to be available to take jobs offered by the labour exchange office. As in Sweden, those on leave are counted as employed if they were working previous to the leave period. This has an impact on both employment and unemployment figures.

The problem of women returners has, to a large degree, disappeared. For example, comparing the situation of job-seekers immediately before starting to seek work, only 3 per cent of women came from a status of 'domestic work' in Denmark, compared with 38 per cent in the UK (Rubery *et al*. 1998). However, in Denmark a new type of re-entry problem among women is appearing. The new leave schemes have some undesirable impacts on gender equality. An increasing number of mothers are caught in the 'leave trap' after taking long care leaves (Ligestillingsrådet 1998). The recent decline in unemployment has had only marginal effects among women in the 25–39 age group, which is likely to be related to the leave arrangement. Women caught in the leave trap have spent a long time on leave, and many have little or outdated education or brief work experience prior to the leave. While on extended leave, neither seniority nor pension rights are accumulated, and the women are treated as newly unemployed because the leave period is not included in the unemployment duration. This has created the need for re-entry programmes arranged by the employment offices. This case illustrates the dilemma that work–family reforms, which aim at improving the work–family balance, might have adverse gender-equality effects.

Labour market transformations: flexible forms of work

Temporary work and part-time work are the most common forms of flexible work, forms which have traditionally been dominated by women. The relationship between regulation and flexibility is more complex than is often assumed, however. Grubb and Wells (1993) argue that where standard full-time workers are strongly protected this status is always viewed as the ideal. For example, concerning temporary work, they conclude that the incidence of fixed-term contract work is increased by restrictions on dismissal of regular workers, and is reduced by restrictions on fixed-term contracting itself. They suggest that 'regulation of various kinds reduces the regulated form of employment and increases forms of employment to which the regulation does not apply' (Grubb and Wells 1993: 34). Flexible work forms, thus, are often prominent in regulated systems with strong protection.

There has been no general tendency for temporary work to increase over time (OECD 1996). It is argued that the need for temporary hiring is greatest in countries where conditions of permanent employment are most restricted

(Engelund 1992). In Norway and Sweden, with strict regulation on hiring/ firing and on temporary work, high incidences of temporary work are found (Table 4.6). Sweden experienced an increase towards the end of the 1980s, but a decline in the 1990s (SOU 1996). In comparison, in the UK, where there are few regulations for normal full-time work and no restriction on temporary work, the share of temporary work is much lower, 7 per cent in 1994 (OECD 1996). However, Denmark also has few regulations but here relatively high incidences of temporary work are found. As a general trend, women make up a somewhat higher share of temporary workers than men. Gender differences are partly explained by the higher proportion of women on parental leave, who are replaced by temporary workers.

Table 4.6 Incidence of temporary employment, 1983 and 1994

	1983			1994		
			%			
	All	*Men*	*Women*	*All*	*Men*	*Women*
Denmark	13	12	13	12	11	13
Norway[1]				12	10	15
Sweden	12	10	14	14	12	15

Note: 1 1993 (Torp 1998).

Source: OECD 1996: 8.

The relationship between strictness of legislation and the size of temporary work agencies is also ambiguous. The liberalization of temporary work agencies in Sweden was followed by a significant increase in the number of people employed temporarily through work agencies. However, the share of the total workforce is still insignificant, only 0.2 per cent. In Denmark, in contrast, there has been no noticeable growth. Interestingly, an increase was found in Norway, where the legislation remained unchanged. Also in Norway the share of employees in temporary work agencies in the total labour force is low, 0.5 per cent, albeit a little higher than in the two other liberalized Scandinavian countries (0.1 per cent in Denmark). Olsen (1997) maintains that these different developments illustrate that it is difficult to separate the policy impact of liberalization from the period effect of increasing labour demand, and that there are probably limits to firms' benefits from hiring this type of worker.

Flexibilization of labour implies a loosening of the employer–employee relationship, and temporary work contracts are often used as an indication of this. On the other hand, increasing the duration of employment is taken as an indication of growing internal labour markets, that is, a strengthening of the employee–firm relationship. Longer employment durations are evidenced in both Sweden and Denmark (Engelund 1992). However, the Danish trend is partly explained by the changing age composition of the labour force.

The increasing importance of part-time work in Europe is often associated with greater labour market flexibility in work arrangements (OECD 1994a). Growth in part-time work in some countries accounted for almost all of the employment growth in the 1980s, e.g. in Germany and the UK (OECD 1994a). In the Scandinavian countries, where the highest shares of part-time work have traditionally been found, part-time work has declined slightly since the 1980s (Table 4.7). Among women there has been a significant decline, particularly in Sweden and Norway, while there has been a modest increase among men in Sweden and Denmark. Historically, Norway has had the highest share of part-time work. Among mothers, there has been an increase in the proportion working full-time in all three countries in the past decade. Norwegian mothers have had the highest levels of part-time work, and Danish mothers the lowest (Ellingsæter 1998).

Table 4.7 Incidence and composition of part-time work, 1983 and 1993–6

		1983	1993	1994	1995	1996
Denmark	% of total employment	24	23	21	22	22
	Women	45	37	34	36	35
	Men	7	11	10	10	11
Norway	% of total employment	30	27	27	27	27
	Women	55	48	47	47	46
	Men	12	10	9	9	10
Sweden	% of total employment	25	25	25	24	24
	Women	46	41	41	40	39
	Men	6	9	10	9	9

Source: OECD 1996, Table E and OECD 1997, Table E.

The nature of part-time work or temporary work cannot be seen as uniformly marginal (Ellingsæter 1992; OECD 1994a), but some segments of Scandinavian part-time workers are marginalized, for instance the underemployed, of whom a majority are women. There are significant differences in the prevalence of underemployment among part-time workers, and its significance in the total unemployment picture. First, underemployment is highest in Sweden, where one in three part-time workers seeks more work. In Denmark and Norway the prevalence is much lower, at about 15 per cent (Nilsen and Try 1998). However, as part of the total unemployment problem (underemployment among part-time workers as a percentage of those fully unemployed), it is highly significant in Norway. It is less so in Sweden, while the problem is negligible in Denmark. However, as a percentage of the total labour force, the underemployed have the highest share in Sweden, closely followed by Norway. The different national arrangements concerning unemployment benefits for this group might be a partial explanation of the large variations, as there is evidence that the duration of unemployment benefits tends to influence the duration of unemployment (Nilsen and Try 1998).

Decline of the Scandinavian model?

Three main conclusions can be drawn from this analysis. First, that the configurations of state policies, labour market institutions, employment structures and gender relations characteristic of the Scandinavian model are not static entities, but do change. Second, that while global economic integration and increasing openness of economies might pose similar problems to advanced capitalist welfare states, change is characterized by differences in national adjustments, grounded in their historical legacies (see also Benoit in this volume). Third, that the causal relationships between policies and employment levels, employment forms and gender relations, are complex to disentangle, but evidence repeatedly contradicts neo-liberal arguments.

Scandinavian transformations in the 1990s are coloured by the countries' historical legacies. This analysis emphasizes country differences: there is no common employment regulation regime. Trends in bargaining systems differ, as do labour market policies and reproductive policies (see also Ellingsæter 1998). In each country there are trends of continuity in both policies, labour market structures and gender relations. However, there are also new elements which indicate change, although there is no fundamental dismantling of the societal models of the Scandinavian countries, at least in the medium term. Concerning the countries' political-institutional models, there is no common trend towards deregulation of labour or decentralization of bargaining, neither is there any uniform trend towards retrenchment and passivity in state activity. However, elements of some of these are found in each country.

Denmark has traditionally been more liberal and market-oriented than Norway and Sweden, and only modest deregulation has taken place, e.g. the liberalization of temporary-work agencies. Collective bargaining is mostly centralized, and is highly institutionalized and synchronized. Active labour market policies were significantly strengthened through broad labour market reform in the mid-1990s and, as part of that, reproductive rights were improved through new parental leave arrangements.

Relatively speaking, the institutional features of the Norwegian welfare state have been strengthened. There is little evidence of deregulation of labour, and centralized bargaining has been revitalized and strengthened. Active labour market policies expanded particularly during the recession of 1988–93. Family policy has been an area of considerable expansion, but here new policies demonstrate that the social-democratic model for public childcare is challenged.

There are only modest changes in the Swedish welfare state concerning deregulation of labour, but the bargaining system has been seriously weakened. Moreover, state activities and social benefits have been subject to retrenchments. However, the active labour market policies have continued, and although the previously generous reproductive rights have been reduced, they were also improved in some areas. There are several studies arguing that welfare state restructuring in Sweden is, first of all, of a quantitative nature rather than a qualitative break with the past (e.g. Sainsbury 1996). Welfare state cutbacks in

Sweden should be seen in the light of the much more extensive welfare state developed there than in either Denmark or Norway.

One of the main differences between the three countries was the degree of institutional stability in the 1990s. Esping-Andersen (1996) has argued that a major reason for Sweden's dramatic economic slide was the erosion of its consensus-building institutions. Others would argue that institutions have eroded as a consequence of economic crisis. The reason for Sweden's current problems is contested. Some argue that it is the very 'Swedish model' that has damaged its competitive position, others argue that it was the shift in economic policies in the early 1990s, from full employment to fighting inflation (Auer and Riegler 1994). Whatever the reason, change in Swedish industrial relations is interesting because it probably reflects particularities in the institutional past. Compared with Norway, for example, Swedish employers have had a more autonomous position, and relations between capital and labour have been more in conflict over the years. Moreover, the role of the state has been less prominent in Sweden.

Considering the restructuring of employment levels and forms, there are complex patterns over time in the three countries, manifesting both growth and decline in employment, unemployment, and in flexible work forms. The Scandinavian welfare states are still the ones which integrate the largest share of the population into the labour market, and have the lowest levels of permanent labour market exclusion. The effects on gender relations differ between the countries. In contrast to Denmark, the Norwegian and the Swedish labour market model has tended to be slightly more exclusionary for men than for women in the 1990s. The Scandinavian countries still generate the highest employment rates among women, but they do not hold the supreme position as they used to. Flexible forms of work are not new phenomena in the Scandinavian labour markets. These work forms are clearly gendered, but there is no general tendency of increase. Part-time work in general is slowly declining; among women there has been a substantial decline. Temporary work has been fairly stable in Norway and Denmark, but somewhat less so in Sweden.

A remarkable feature of the Scandinavian societies in the 1980s was the combination of high employment and high fertility among women, particularly in Sweden. The significant drop in Swedish women's fertility in the 1990s suggests that evaluation of policy impacts on women's employment should also include an assessment of their impacts on fertility. If one is concerned about women's, and increasingly men's, opportunities to combine work and family, change in societal conditions which in effect make it less desirable to have children needs to be taken seriously.

Clearly, change in Scandinavian state policies, labour market institutions, employment structures and gender relations cannot be subsumed under any simplistic model of deregulation of labour markets and down-scaling states. Following Waters (1998), this might not be so surprising, as he argues that economic globalization is likely to be most advanced in areas of financial markets and organizational ideologies, and least advanced in the labour market. The main 'globalizing' mechanism is the extent to which exchange is symbolically mediated. Symbolic goods are less constrained within geographical and temporal boundaries than material items; labour is material and largely controllable. Thus, deregulation is expected to be more prominent in political rhetoric than in labour market structures.

However, there are signs that neo-liberal rhetorics are weakening in Europe in the late 1990s. In some policy areas, such as labour market and family policies, there is evidence that several European countries are moving in a more interventionist direction. There has been a general policy shift throughout the European Union from passive to active labour market policies (Daly 1997; OECD 1993), thus favouring increased state intervention. However, this is paralleled by a strengthening of disincentives for remaining on unemployment benefit. Moreover, family policies in Europe have been an area of expansion: there is 'more state'. Maternity/parental benefits have generally been more deeply institutionalized and improved in generosity and conditions (Daly 1997). The employment effects of reproductive policies may be ambiguous, however. Pay for care might pull women out of the labour market; more state intervention may mean more family in effect.

This study suggests complex relationships between policies, labour market structures and gender relations. This is particularly evident in the relationship between labour market regulation and labour market flexibility. Labour market regulation needs to be understood in the light of other social and economic institutions which underpin variations in employment and unemployment rates (Rubery *et al.* 1998). Deregulation and decentralization are not the obvious political solutions to unemployment. The Norwegian case supports Nickell's (1997) conclusion that strict employment protection, high levels of unionization and generous unemployment benefits do not have serious implications for average unemployment, if combined with high levels of co-ordination in wage bargaining and pressures on the unemployed to take jobs. Moreover, OECD (1997) shows that countries which moved towards decentralization or less co-ordination over the past decade, one such case being Sweden, experienced larger declines in the employment rates than countries which did not experience such decentralization. The present study also supports those who argue that deregulation and flexibility should be treated as separate factors (Dex and McCulloch 1997). Flexible forms of work are not structural trends inherent in a certain mode of regulation. There is an increasing recognition of the existence of different sources of flexibility. Sources of flexibility in the Scandinavian labour markets, such as parental leave arrangements, have tended to be undervalued because they have counted only as 'costs'.

Acknowledgements

This research was supported by a grant from the Norwegian Research Council's research programme 'Labour Market and Regional Research'.

108 *Anne Lise Ellingsæter*

References

Auer, P. and Riegler, C.H. (1994) 'Sweden: The End of Full Employment', *Employment Observatory Policies*, no. 46: pp. 16–23.

Baldwin, P. (1996) 'Can We Define a European Welfare State Model?', in B. Greve (ed.) *Comparative Welfare Systems. The Scandinavian Model in a Period of Change*, London: Macmillan.

Bjurstrøm, H. (1993) *Deltidsansattes rettigheter. En komparativ studie av Danmark, England, Norge og Tyskland,* Oslo: Institute for Social Research.

Boje, T.P. (1995) *Women and the European Employment Rate. National Report for Denmark,* EU Network on the Situation of Women in the Labour Market.

Daly, M. (1997) 'Welfare States under Pressure: Cash Benefits in European Welfare States Over the Last Ten Years', *Journal of European Social Policy*, 7: 129–46.

Dex, S. and McCulloch, A. (1997) *Flexible Employment: The Future of Britain's Jobs,* Basingstoke: Macmillan.

Ellingsæter, A.L. (1992) *Part-time Work in European Welfare States,* Oslo: Institute for Social Research.

Ellingsæter, A.L. (1998) 'Dual Breadwinner Societies: Provider Models in the Scandinavian Welfare States', *Acta Sociologica*, 41: 59–73.

Emerson, M. (1988) 'Regulation or Deregulation of the Labour Market: Policy Regimes for the Recruitment and Dismissal of Employees in the Industrialised Countries', *European Economic Review* 32: 775–817.

Engelund, H. (1992) *Fleksibilitet på arbejdsmarkedet i Norden,* Copenhagen: Socialforskningsinstituttet.

Esping-Andersen, G. (1990) *The Three Worlds of Welfare Capitalism,* Cambridge: Polity Press.

Esping-Andersen, G. (1996) 'After the Golden Age? Welfare State Dilemmas in a Global Economy', in G. Esping-Andersen (ed.) *Welfare States in Transition. National Adaptations in Global Economies*, pp. 1–31, London: Sage.

Furåker, B., Johansson, L. and Lind, J. (1990) 'Unemployment and Labour Market Policies in the Scandinavian Countries', *Acta Sociologica*, 33: 141–64.

Ginsburg, N. (1992) *Divisions of Welfare. A Critical Introduction to Comparative Social Policy,* London: Sage

Gonäs, L. and Spånt, A. (1997) *Trends and Prospects for Women's Employment in the 1990s,* Solna: National Institute for Working Life.

Grubb, D. and Wells, W. (1993) 'Economic Regulation and Patterns of Work in EC Countries', *OECD Economic Studies*, no. 21: 7–58.

Hirst, P. and Thompson, G. (1996) *Globalization in Question,* Cambridge: Polity Press.

Jefferys, S. (1995) 'European Industrial Relations and Welfare States', *European Journal of Industrial Relations*, 1: 317–340.

Jessop, B. (1994) 'The Transition to Post-Fordism and the Schumpeterian Workfare State', in R. Burrows and B. Loader (eds) *Towards a Post-Fordist Welfare State?*, pp. 13–37, London: Routledge, .

Kjellberg, A. (1992) 'Sweden: Can the Model Survive?', in A. Ferner and R. Hyman (eds) *Industrial Relations in the New Europe*, Oxford: Blackwell.

Larsen, K.A. (1992) 'Arbeidsstyrkens konjunkturfølsomhet', *Søkelys på arbeidsmarkedet*, 9: 93–98.

Lewis, J. (1992) 'Gender and the Development of Welfare Regimes', *Journal of European Social Policy*, 2: 159–73.

Ligestillingsrådet (1998) 'Ud af orlovsfælden'. *Lige nu*, no. 6, April, Copenhagen.

Lind, J. (1998) 'Trends in the Regulation of Employment Relations in Denmark', *International Journal of Employment Studies*, 6: 1–16.

Madsen, P.K. (1995) *Working Time Policy and Leave Arrangements. The Danish Experience in the 1990s*, paper presented at the Conference on Working Time Policy, Center for European Labour Market Studies, Gothenburg, 20 October.

Maier, F. (1991) 'Part-time Work, Social Security Protection and Labour Law: An International Comparison', *Policy and Politics*, 19: 1–12.

Möller, E.L. and Hoem, B. (1997) 'Lågutbildade väntar med barnen', *VälfärdsBulletinen*, no. 2: 18–19.

Nickell, S. (1997) 'Unemployment and Labor Market Rigidities: Europe versus North America', *Journal of Economic Perspectives*, 11: 55–74.

Nilsen, A.K. and Try, S. (1998) 'Delvis sysselsatte arbeidssøkere i Norden'. *Arbetsliv i Norden*, 12: 15–17 (March).

OECD (1993) *Employment Outlook*, Paris.

OECD (1994a) *The OECD Jobs Study. Evidence and Explanations. Part I – Labour Market Trends and Underlying Forces of Change*, Paris.

OECD (1994b) *The OECD Jobs Study. Evidence and Explanations. Part II – The Adjustment Potential of the Labour Market*, Paris.

OECD (1996) *Employment Outlook*, Paris.

OECD (1997) *Employment Outlook*, Paris.

OECD (1998) *Employment Outlook*, Paris.

Olsen, K.M. (1997) *Vikarbyråer i vekst*, Oslo: Institute for Social Research.

Orloff, A.S. (1997) 'Comment on Jane Lewis's "Gender and Welfare Regimes: Further Thoughts" ', *Social Politics*, 2: 189–201.

Rubery, J., Smith, M., Fagan, C. and Grimshaw, D. (1998) *Women and European Employment*, London: Routledge.

Ruggie, M. (1984) *The State and Working Women: a Comparative Study of Britain and Sweden*, Princeton: Princeton University Press.

Sainsbury, D. (1996) *Gender, Equality and Welfare States*, Cambridge: Cambridge University Press.

Scheuer, S. (1992) 'Denmark: Return to Decentralization', in A. Ferner and R. Hyman (eds) *Industrial Relations in the New Europe*, pp. 168–97, Oxford: Blackwell.

Siim, B. (1993) 'The Gendered Scandinavian Welfare States: The Interplay Between Women's Roles as Mothers, Workers and Citizens in Denmark', in J. Lewis (ed.) *Women and Social Policies in Europe. Work, Family and the State*, pp. 25–48, London: Edward Elgar.

SOU (1996) *Hälften vore nog – om kvinnor och män på 90-talets arbetsmarknad*, SOU 1996: 56, Stockholm: Arbetsmarknadsdepartementet.

Stephens, J. (1996) 'The Scandinavian Welfare States: Achievements, Crisis, and Prospects', in G. Esping-Andersen (ed.) *Welfare States in Transition. National Adaptations in Global Economies*, pp. 32–65, London: Sage.

Torp, H. (1994) 'Arbeidsløsheten og kvinners yrkesaktivitet', *Søkelys på arbeidsmarkedet*, 11: 29–31.

Torp, H. (1995) *Labour Market Institutions and Development. Norway Baseline Study*, Oslo: Institute for Social Research.

Torp, H. (1998) 'Midlertidige ansatte: Hvor arbeider de?', *Søkelys på arbeidsmarkedet*, 15: 11–118.

Waters, M. (1995) *Globalization*, London: Routledge.
Waters, M. (1998) *PostFordism and the Globalization Thesis: Myth and Reality*, keynote address to Work Employment and Society Conference, Cambridge University, 14–16 September.

5 Family policy and mothers' employment

Cross-national variations

Janet C. Gornick

Gendering welfare state comparisons

The publication of Esping-Andersen's *The Three Worlds of Welfare Capitalism* (1990) gave birth to an extensive critical literature. Some critics focused on Esping-Andersen's core theoretical contribution – his overall framework for conceptualizing welfare state variation – while others questioned the empirical results, either the resultant typology, or the classification of particular countries, or both. The strand in this critical literature that has been the most sustained concentrates on Esping-Andersen's inadequate treatment of gender – and, by extension, the lack of attention paid to family policy.

Some have described Esping-Andersen's work, rooted in class theory, as fundamentally omitting gender as an important analytic factor (Sainsbury 1994). Lewis (1992) noted that 'women disappear from the analysis'; Orloff (1993) argued that 'gender relations and their effects are ignored'. Others saw the core of a gender analysis, but found it inadequate; Langan and Ostner (1991) argued that women 'remain an elusive presence in Esping-Andersen's work'. Some feminist scholars observed that central elements of family policy – for example, policies that support mothers' employment – are omitted entirely from Esping-Andersen's underlying empirical construction (Gornick, Meyers and Ross 1997).

Feminist critics of mainstream welfare state theory, typified by Esping-Andersen, have concluded that a core dimension along which welfare states are compared, that of decommodification – the extent to which social rights eliminate dependence on the labour market – applies poorly to women's social circumstances and needs (O'Connor 1992; Orloff 1993). These critics have countered that decommodification is not emancipatory for those with restricted ties to paid work in the first place; persons must be commodified before they benefit from a loosening of their commodity status.

Since 1990 feminists have substantially reshaped conceptions of welfare state variation. Orloff (1993) argues that access to paid work should constitute an independent dimension in any model of welfare state variability. O'Connor (1992, 1996) suggests supplementing, or even replacing, the concept of decommodification with that of autonomy, or insulation from dependence more broadly, including dependence on family members. Hobson (1990), and Bianchi,

Casper, and Peltola (1996), recast earnings differentials between spouses as economic dependency within marriage, and argue that dependency in this form is embedded in gender differentials in labour market engagement; Hobson thus calls for 'bringing economic dependency into welfare state research' (1990: 247). Pateman (1988), Lister (1990) and others contend, furthermore, that freedom from economic dependency is a prerequisite for full citizenship status.

Despite remaining conceptual disagreements, much recent scholarship on gender and the welfare state concludes that public policies that support gender equality in the labour market form the core of the 'woman-friendly' welfare state. Comparisons of welfare states that reflect the reality of women's lives must highlight the extent to which state policies – such as childcare and family leave laws – promote women's opportunities to engage, and advance, in paid work to the same extent that men do.

Supporting mothers' employment: cross-national variation in public policy

Many studies have documented dramatic cross-national variation in existing family policies in the industrialized countries – including family policies that support maternal employment, such as publicly supported childcare and family leave benefits (Hofferth and Deich 1994; Gustafsson and Stafford 1995; Kamerman 1991; Kamerman and Kahn 1991, 1998). The origins and development of programmes that aid parents in combining employment and family are rooted in a diverse set of overlapping and frequently shifting concerns; these have included aiding child development, providing income maintenance for families, and enabling women's employment.

Gornick, Meyers and Ross (1997) studied supports for maternal employment – focusing on childcare and family leave – across fourteen countries, in the mid- to late 1980s. They found that all fourteen countries dedicated some public expenditure to childcare; however, the form and magnitude of public expenditure varied markedly. Although reasonably comparable data on direct childcare expenditure were available for only six countries, marked variation was evident. At the high end, Sweden spent $1,885 (in 1987 US dollars) a year per child under 15 and Finland spent $1,212. At the low end, the US and Canada each invested less than $50 per child. Tax relief – indirect spending that aims at offsetting the cost of private household expenditures on childcare – was available in eight of the fourteen countries; the generosity of these provisions varied from a high of $1,118 in Belgium to a low of $198 annually for one child in Finland (in 1987 US dollars).

Gornick, Meyers and Ross argued that an important indicator of government commitment to the provision of childcare is the adoption of national legislation that explicitly guarantees access to public or publicly subsidized care. By the late 1980s, only three of the fourteen countries – Denmark, Finland, and Sweden – had adopted legislation that established childcare as a right for all (or nearly all) children under the age of 6. France guaranteed childcare to all children aged

2 to 5; Belgium had extended the promise of universal coverage to younger children (birth to age 2) but not to older pre-school children.[1]

Presumably, the adoption of childcare guarantees has two effects. First, it sends a signal to mothers that the state is committed to assisting them in balancing employment and family responsibilities. Second, the correspondence between childcare entitlements and high levels of enrolment in publicly supported care suggests that childcare guarantees increase the supply of childcare. In the provision of childcare for infants, Denmark was the clear leader with 48 per cent of children under the age of 3 in publicly supported care. Four additional countries (Belgium, Finland, France and Sweden) also had relatively high rates of public provision, with 20–32 per cent of children under the age of 3 in care. Provision for children under the age of 3 was substantially less in the remaining countries, with 12 per cent of children in Norway and fewer than 5 per cent of children in the remaining countries enrolled in public or publicly funded care.

Overall, public childcare provisions were more highly developed for pre-school children. In four countries (Belgium, Denmark, France and Italy), over 85 per cent of children were in public day-care or pre-schools. At the other end of the spectrum, four countries (Australia, Canada, Norway and the UK) enrolled only 25–40 per cent of pre-school children in publicly supported care. The US again stood out as the exceptional case. Although use of all forms of non-parental care was relatively high in the US, the heavy reliance on private arrangements and narrowly targeted means-testing for public benefits was evident in the enrolment in publicly supported care of fewer than 15 per cent of pre-schoolers.

Maternity and parental leave schemes also varied markedly. As of the mid- to late 1980s, all of the countries, with three notable exceptions, made near-universal provisions for job protection and wage replacement for women in the months following the birth of a child. The US and Australia were the most prominent exceptions. The US had no national law providing job protection at the time of childbirth; in Australia, federal law guaranteed up to 12 months of job protection but provided no wage replacement. The UK also fell short relative to other countries, primarily because eligibility restrictions (e.g. on minimum earnings and job tenure) were such that only approximately 60 per cent of employed women had access to both job protection and wage replacement.

In the other countries, all or nearly all employed women were covered by national job protection and wage replacement benefits. The length of protection and adequacy of wage replacement varied substantially. On the high end, generous, universal systems in three Nordic countries (Sweden, Finland and Norway) provided full, or nearly full, wage replacement for six months to one year. In Finland, generous paid leave was supplemented with over two years of extended, job-protected leave; in Sweden, parents had a right to unpaid leave until the child was 18 months old.

In about half of the countries studied, paternal involvement in early childcare was facilitated by the extension of some form of paid or unpaid leave to fathers.

In general, countries with more extensive maternity benefits were more likely to provide benefits to fathers. Some exceptions are notable. Australia, with very limited benefits for women, did extend limited benefits to fathers as well. At the same time, a few countries with relatively generous policies for mothers had made no provisions for fathers – including Belgium, Luxembourg and the Netherlands.

Gornick, Meyers and Ross integrated and reduced these findings by combining multiple indicators of public provision of childcare and family leave into two composite indices that capture the provision of supports for the employment of mothers with children under the age of 3, and 3 to school age, respectively. The composite findings indicate that the six highest performing countries, with respect to mothers with children below school age, included France and three Nordic countries – Finland, Denmark and Sweden – followed by Belgium and Italy. Each of these countries combined generous maternity benefits with high levels of publicly provided or financed childcare. A middle tier included a heterogeneous group of five countries – Luxembourg, Germany, Canada, the Netherlands and Norway. These countries were characterized by moderate to generous maternity leave policies but limited paternity benefits and much lower levels of public childcare. Policies in three English-speaking countries – Australia, the UK and the US – were the least supportive of maternal employment.

The Gornick/Meyers/Ross indices reveal wide variation across the industrialized countries in family policies that support women's employment. This variation is of substantive interest, because the adequacy of these policies has implications for the extent and continuity of women's employment and for families' economic wellbeing. Policies that increase women's employment options have implications for mothers' employment and economic opportunities in both the short and long term. They also have important and frequently overlooked implications for the economic wellbeing of families. With the growing importance of women's earnings in household income – in both dual- and single-earner families – policies affecting mothers' employment are increasingly important. They not only foster gender equality in and out of the labour market, they constitute an increasingly important component of national policy packages aimed at securing family income and preventing poverty.

Gender equality in the labour market: cross-national variation in women's employment

Characterizing gender equality in the labour market

The study of women's employment patterns raises the question of optimal outcome(s): does the 'woman-friendly' welfare state produce, or encourage, high rates of female employment and full-time hours for all? Most feminist scholars sidestep this problem by arguing that the ideal outcome is one in which the labour market is characterized by gender equality. Nevertheless, defining and measuring gender equality in the labour market remains a surprisingly thorny problem.

One substantial challenge is offered by traditional economists who place little significance on observed gender differences in labour market outcomes. Neoclassical economists have attributed differences in outcomes to the fact that women's 'tastes' for paid work lag men's, albeit to varying degrees in different places and at various times (Becker 1985; Mincer and Polachek 1974; Polachek 1995). The traditional claim is that women simply prefer time spent outside paid work more than men do, or readily accept the advantages of specializing in unpaid work at home. As a result, women accumulate less education and fewer skills (Becker 1981), and they are less likely to seek paid work, especially full-time; some argue that women prefer a subset of occupations and jobs (Polachek 1995; Hakim 1997), which explains workplace segregation. Thus, substantial gender differences in employment outcomes are seen as reflecting women's underlying tastes, rather than indicating the presence of social or institutional constraints on women's labour market involvement.

However, women's 'tastes' in the absence of existing social expectations and institutional limitations constitute a classic counterfactual; they cannot be measured. It is clear that much gender differentiation, particularly in activity rates and hours, is located on the supply-side of the labour market; in other words, women *are* less likely to seek employment, especially full-time employment, than are men. However, feminist labour market scholars have challenged the premise that women's underlying tastes for time spent in market work are distinct from men's (Bergmann 1986; Folbre and Hartmann 1988; Reskin and Padavic 1994), and/or have argued that women's tastes 'are undoubtedly influenced by social attitudes and norms' (Blau and Ferber 1992: 87). Given the methodological difficulties of explaining gendered outcomes by gender-differentiated tastes or preferences, the optimal approach is, arguably, simply to equate 'gender inequality in the labour market' with observed gender differences in all labour market outcomes.

A second complication in the conceptualization of gender equality in the world of work comes from feminists. Fraser (1994) suggests that the convergence of women's and men's involvement in paid work, if achieved, would not constitute full gender equality if it were not accompanied by a breakdown of the sexual division in care-giving that persists in all western countries. Concomitantly, promoters of women's employment – those envisaging what Fraser calls a 'universal breadwinner model' – must bear in mind possible disadvantages for women, such as the potential for increasing their time spent in paid work without any reduction in their duties on the 'second shift'.

Fraser is clearly correct that fully realized gender equality with respect to work must include gender equality in care-giving and other unpaid work, and that an integrated picture of *paid* and unpaid work would be ideal. Unfortunately, cross-nationally comparable data on the sexual division of unpaid work are very imited. At the same time, there is no clear evidence that the achievement of gender equality in paid work in the shorter term will do other than accelerate the breakdown of the sexual division of labour in unpaid work in the longer term. As

US economist Heidi Hartmann has observed (personal communication), when women come closer to achieving parity in the labour market, many will reduce their disproportionate responsibilities in the home by 'voting with their feet'; meaning, they will go to their jobs, leaving more unpaid work to the men with whom they live. Nevertheless, the potential costs of increasing and strengthening women's labour market ties – without achieving gender parity in unpaid work – must be considered.

The changing labour market

Since the end of the Second World War, the industrialized countries have seen a dramatic increase in the participation of women, especially of married women with children, in the paid labour market. Yet, despite the rapid increase in women's employment, substantial gender gaps persist in all industrialized labour markets. As of the late 1990s, throughout the industrialized countries (OECD 1998; OECD 1999):

- women are still less likely to be employed than are men;
- employed women are less likely to hold full-time jobs than are employed men;
- women and men are employed in different industries and in different occupations and, within those, in different jobs, i.e. substantial segregation pervades the workplace;
- women receive lower hourly wages than do men, even after a host of worker and job characteristics are controlled for; combined with women's fewer hours, the gender gap in annual earnings is even greater;
- women contribute the majority of household labour and maintain primary responsibility for child-rearing; the sexual divisions in the paid labour market are paralleled in unpaid work.

The last four decades have been a time of uneven change with respect to these critical indicators. Between 1960 and the late 1990s, women's *labour-force participation* increased in every OECD country, with the sharpest rise seen among mothers; in some countries, women's participation rates more than doubled. Because male participation rates fell steadily throughout the same period – although from much higher base levels – the female share of the labour force increased sharply (OECD 1992; OECD 1998; OECD 1999).

Change in the percentage of women *employed part-time* showed more variation. Between 1960 and 1990, the percentage of employed women employed part-time increased, sometimes dramatically, in two-thirds of the OECD countries, and decreased, usually modestly, in about one-third; growth was particularly rapid in the 1980s. At the same time, the percentage of employed men in part-time jobs also increased – although from much lower base levels – in all of the industrialized countries (OECD 1994; OECD 1999; Smith *et al.* 1998). As a result of the two trends, the female share in part-time employment has remained fairly stable during this period. Currently, women's share in part-time work averages about 80 per cent in the European/OECD countries (OECD 1999), establishing that part-time work, for the most part, remains 'women's work' across the western industrialized countries.[2]

Change with respect to *occupational and industrial segregation* by gender presents a mixed picture. Cross-national data are not widely available, and methodological difficulties limit comparability across countries. Nevertheless, between 1960 and the mid-1980s, occupational segregation by gender appears to have declined in most countries (OECD 1984; Jacobs and Lim 1992). However, the decline is slow and levels of segregation remain high; in most countries, women remain concentrated in a few occupations. Industrial segregation by gender, while less pronounced, shows no clear pattern of change since the early 1970s. Structural effects – i.e. changes in the size of female-dominated sectors – appear to play little part in the moderate decline of occupational segregation. There is, however, some evidence that structural shifts are working in the direction of increasing industrial segregation, possibly explaining the overall absence of decline (OECD 1985).

Considerable empirical research in recent years has been carried out on the *gender earnings gap*, and a substantial cross-national literature exists (Blau and Kahn 1992; Gornick 1999; Rosenfeld and Kalleberg 1990, 1991; Treiman and Roos 1983). Gross (unadjusted) female–male hourly earnings differentials in the OECD countries averaged between 15 per cent and 45 per cent in the late 1980s, with an overall trend in the industrialized countries towards a narrowing of the gap during the preceding two decades (OECD 1988). Single- and multi-country studies which have attempted to adjust for worker characteristics, job characteristics, or both, typically report smaller but always positive unexplained wage differentials. The factors that drive the gender earnings gap are complex and varied. Nevertheless, a consensus has emerged that, in most countries, a primary factor underlying the persistent earnings gap is the high level of occupational segregation (Gunderson 1989; Reskin and Padavic 1994), specifically, women's continued over-representation in low-wage occupations. Until substantial desegregation of the labour force takes place, the goal of equal earnings for men and women will remain elusive.

Variation across welfare states: a cross-national portrait

How much variation currently exists in women's employment patterns? And what role does parenting play in gender differences in employment patterns throughout the industrialized countries? Table 5.1 reveals, first, that across fifteen diverse welfare states women's overall employment rates in the early 1990s varied considerably, ranging from 85 per cent in Sweden down to 31 per cent in Spain, a spread of over 50 percentage points.[3] Men's overall employment rates varied much less, falling within a ten percentage point range (89 per cent to 79 per cent); Canada was an exception, with somewhat lower male employment rates reported (74 per cent). The near uniformity in men's employment rates suggests that the sources of the variation in women's outcomes are gender-specific. Cross-national variation in women's employment rates is not simply traceable to fundamental differences – for example, demand-side factors – in the overall labour markets in these countries. The relatively invariant male rates also mean that the cross-national picture of women's overall employment rates parallels the portrait indicated by the ratios, and thus the two indicators can be used fairly interchangeably (compare the first and third columns).

That care-giving responsibilities are a powerful source of gender differentiation in employment can be seen in the comparison of persons in all family types with the subgroup of married parents. Table 5.1 reveals that mothers of young children are less likely to work for pay than are women overall in nearly all countries; the exceptions are Belgium, Italy, Denmark, and Sweden.[4] By contrast, Table 5.1 indicates that fathers of young children – i.e. the husbands of these mothers – are more likely to be employed than are men overall, in all fifteen countries. While mothers in only two countries (Denmark and Sweden) have employment rates exceeding 70 per cent, fathers' employment rates are 80 per cent or higher in all fifteen countries, and 90 per cent or higher in twelve. The general pattern of reduced employment among mothers and greater employment among fathers combines to produce the result that female/male employment ratios are substantially lower – i.e. the gender differences are larger – among parents. In twelve countries (Belgium, Denmark, and Sweden are exceptions), the female/male employment ratios fall by ten or more points as we shift from the population that includes all family types to the parents subgroup; in Germany, the female/male employment ratio falls by over thirty points. Clearly, the presence of young children is a powerful source of gender differentiation, and more so in some countries than in others.

Do different 'types' of welfare states produce distinct employment patterns? Esping-Andersen (1990) posited that three welfare state models exist and that each is associated with a distinct labour market trajectory for women – in particular, that regime types shape female employment levels. He argued that women's employment rates would be highest in the social-democratic countries, where both supply and demand are increased by the extensive provision of public services. Moderate levels of female employment were predicted in the liberal countries, where workers – including women – are less decommodified and alternatives to labour market income are limited. The lowest levels of women's employment would be expected in the conservative countries, as a result of a slow-growth service sector and policies that encourage mothers to remain in the home.

The results in Table 5.1 largely conform to these predictions. Cross-national variation in gender equality in activity rates can be seen both within and across the dominant welfare state clusters; however, by and large, the clusters do have corresponding employment levels. Women's overall employment rates, relative to men's, are highest in the social-democratic countries (0.93 to 0.98), with the exception of Norway. Slightly lower employment ratios are reported in Norway and in the four liberal countries (0.80 to 0.89, with Australia lagging at 0.73).[5] Women's employment rates are most different from men's, consistently, in the conservative countries. Variation among the conservative countries, however,

Table 5.1 Employment rates and employment ratios, early 1990s
(Luxembourg Income Study data)

	Persons in all family types			Married persons with a child under age 6		
	Female	Male	Female/ male	Female	Male	Female/ male
	%		ratio	%		ratio
Sweden (1992)	85	87	0.98	86	92	0.93
Finland (1991)	77	83	0.93	68	94	0.72
Denmark (1992)	74	80	0.93	77	89	0.87
UK (1991)	68	82	0.83	53	87	0.61
US (1991)	68	83	0.82	55	90	0.61
Norway (1991)	67	84	0.80	62	95	0.65
Canada (1991)	66	74	0.89	61	83	0.73
Australia (1989)	63	86	0.73	49	91	0.54
Germany (1989)	61	88	0.69	38	96	0.40
France (1989)	60	83	0.72	55	94	0.59
Belgium (1992)	57	83	0.69	62	95	0.65
Netherlands (1991)	51	83	0.61	37	90	0.41
Luxembourg (1991)	49	89	0.55	42	95	0.44
Italy (1991)	42	79	0.53	42	97	0.43
Spain (1990)	31	79	0.39	26	90	0.29

Note: Results refer to persons aged 20–59; employment rates include the self-employed; the countries are ordered in relation to the first column of the table.

Source: Luxembourg Income Study (LIS).

is substantial; whereas ratios approaching those in the liberal countries are seen in Belgium, France, and Germany (0.69 to 0.72), women in Spain are only 39 per cent as likely as men to be employed.

When attention is focused on parents, gender differences are sharper everywhere, but the cross-national comparative portrait is largely upheld. Among adults raising young children, women's employment patterns most resemble men's in three social-democratic countries (Denmark, Finland, and Sweden) and in Canada, where mothers are more than 70 per cent as likely to be employed as the fathers of these young children. The remaining liberal countries follow, joined by Belgium and France, with employment ratios ranging from 0.54 to 0.65. The countries in which mothers' and fathers' employment rates are most sharply differentiated include the remaining conservative countries – Germany, Italy, Luxembourg, the Netherlands, and Spain – in which mothers of young children are less than half as likely as their husbands to work for pay.

120   *Janet C. Gornick*

Women's employment rates indicate the likelihood that they are engaged in paid work, but they mask the intensity of that engagement.[6] Many women in these countries – especially those with young children – are employed part-time, most of them 'voluntarily' (OECD 1999), meaning that they have sought part-time hours.[7] Table 5.2 indicates the percentage of employed women and men whose employment is part-time (defined as fewer than thirty-five hours per week), and the female/male ratios in part-time rates; again, results are presented separately for people in all family types and for the subgroup of parents.

Table 5.2 reveals that part-time employment as a share of women's employment varied widely in the early 1990s, ranging from a high of 59 per cent in the Netherlands, to a low of 10 per cent in Finland and Italy. As with their overall employment rates, the share of men's employment that is part-time varied much less, nowhere reaching as high as 12 per cent. Clearly, part-time work remains female-dominated throughout the welfare states of the 1990s.

Table 5.2 Part-time employment as a proportion of employment, early 1990s (Luxembourg Income Study data*)

	Persons in all family types			Married persons with a child under age 6		
	Female %	*Male*	*Female/ male ratio*	*Female* %	*Male*	*Female/ male ratio*
Netherlands (1991)	59	9	6.6	89	8	11.1
Norway (1991)	48	9	5.3	–	–	–
UK (1991)	45	4	11.3	74	3	24.7
Sweden (1992)	40	5	8.0	54	5	10.8
Australia (1989)	39	5	7.8	63	3	21.0
Denmark (1992)	38	11	3.5	–	–	–
Belgium (1992)	36	6	6.0	47	6	7.8
Germany (1989)	36	3	12.0	81	1	81.0
Canada (1991)	30	9	3.3	38	5	7.6
Luxembourg (1991)	30	2	15.0	57	1	57.0
France (1989)	24	4	6.0	–	–	–
US (1991)	22	7	3.1	32	2	16.0
Spain (1990)	12	2	6.0	–	–	–
Finland (1991)	10	4	2.5	16	3	5.3
Italy (1991)	10	3	3.3	–	–	–

Note: Data are for persons aged 20–59; employment rates include the self-employed; the countries are ordered in relation to the first column of the table; part-time employment based on the LIS data is defined as fewer than thirty-five hours per week.
* Exceptions: rates for France, Italy, Spain, Denmark, and Norway are from OECD (1994).

Sources: Rates are based on data from the Luxembourg Income Study (LIS).

As with activity rates, the strong effect of care-giving responsibilities can be seen when we shift our attention to the married parents of young children. In all countries, employed women's likelihood of part-time employment increases, in many cases dramatically; by contrast, in none of the ten countries for which we have data are fathers more likely to work part-time than are men as a whole. With three exceptions (Finland, Canada and the US), approximately half or more of employed mothers with young children hold part-time jobs; remarkably, in two countries, Germany and the Netherlands, more than four out of five employed mothers are employed part-time.

Table 5.2 reveals that high levels of female part-time work cut across the three welfare state models and that the regime types show substantial variation within. While a large share of employed women (38–48 per cent) in three Nordic countries (Denmark, Norway and Sweden) hold part-time jobs, the pattern in Finland (10 per cent) is sharply different. Rates of female part-time work in the UK (45 per cent) are double what they are in the US (22 per cent), and part-time work in Australia and the UK is as common as it is in the Scandinavian countries. Among the conservative countries, while women in the Netherlands report the highest rates of part-time employment (59 per cent), part-time employment in Italy and Spain (10–12 per cent) is as rare as it is in Finland.

With the exception of the relatively homogeneous results seen in Denmark, Norway and Sweden, the extent to which women engage in part-time employment (using the 35-hour cut-off) does not vary clearly by welfare state model. That is not surprising, in part because there is little correlation between rates of female part-time work and overall employment rates. The relationship between the two indicators is positive, but weak – across these fifteen countries, r = +0.29 – a finding that counters a widespread perception that high rates of part-time work among women, as seen in the Scandinavian countries, are necessary for high rates of employment.

One crucial explanation for the lack of correlation between employment rates and part-time rates rests on cross-national variation in demand-side factors. For example, in high female-employment Finland, while public institutions have encouraged both the supply of, and the demand for, women's employment, neither the state nor the private sector has actively sought the expansion of part-time jobs (Pfau-Effinger 1998). By contrast is the UK, where there is no cohesive public commitment to women's employment overall, the state has a long history of encouraging the development of part-time jobs. Briar (1992) argues that in the UK, since the 1940s, state policies have actively promoted part-time work for women, ostensibly to meet temporary labour shortages and to increase labour market flexibility.

Table 5.3 presents further results on women's part-time employment in eighteen countries, for the same period, i.e. 1990 (OECD 1999). Part-time rates in Table 5.3 are based on a 30-hour cut-off, rather than a 35-hour cut-off (as in Table 5.2) and, as a result, reported rates of part-time employment are systematically lower.[8] Table 5.3 reveals at least two interesting results. First, we

Table 5.3 Women's part-time employment rates and shares, 1990
(OECD data)

	Part-time employment as a proportion of employment (women)	Women's share in part-time employment
	%	
Netherlands	52.5	70.4
Switzerland	42.6	82.4
UK	39.5	85.1
Norway	39.1	82.7
Australia	38.5	70.8
Japan	33.2	70.5
Belgium	29.8	79.9
Germany	29.8	89.7
Denmark	29.6	71.5
Canada	26.8	70.1
Sweden	24.5	81.1
France	21.7	79.8
Ireland	20.5	71.8
US	20.0	68.2
Luxembourg	19.1	86.5
Portugal	11.8	74.0
Spain	11.5	79.5
Finland	10.6	66.8

Note: Part-time employment refers to persons who usually work fewer than thirty hours per week in their main job; the countries are ordered in relation to the first column of the table.

Source: OECD (1999).

see that, using the lower cut-off, overall cross-national variation in part-time employment rates is less than in Table 5.2 because the part-time employment rates fall more (between Table 5.2 and Table 5.3) in the countries with higher part-time employment at the 35-hour cut-off. Second, some of the countries' rankings change considerably; most notably, Denmark and Sweden join the group of countries with moderate rates of part-time employment, alongside three conservative countries (Belgium, France and Germany), and Canada as well. Clearly, cross-national comparisons of part-time employment rates must be interpreted with care, at least in part because the results are so sensitive to the definition used.

Linking policy to employment outcomes: theoretical and empirical results

One of the most challenging problems facing scholars of family policy and women's employment concerns the question of causality. To what extent does cross-national variation in public policies that support mothers' employment (i.e. the variation in supply-side policies, as described earlier) explain cross-national patterns (above) in maternal employment? Is the policy pattern shaping the employment outcomes, or is the employment pattern shaping the policy outcomes?

While the question ultimately remains an open one, economic theory provides a useful framework for assessing the impact of government policies on women's employment decisions. Extending the basic consumption model from micro-economics, women's labour supply – that is, a woman's decision as to how to allocate her time between paid work and other activities, including childcare-giving – is viewed as a consumption choice between two commodities: market income, derived from paid work, versus time spent outside paid work.

A large body of empirical literature demonstrates that the labour supply (participation and hours worked) of individual women is, in fact, influenced by family-related factors, which interact as well with market forces and policy configurations (Berndt 1991; Killingsworth and Heckman 1986). For women, choosing to seek employment is particularly sensitive to the presence of dependent children and to government policies that offset the associated care-giving demands. The economic model predicts that the presence of children in the home will have an impact on women's employment decisions by changing the value that they place on their time outside paid work. The cost of alternative childcare arrangements will also lower women's effective market wages. Several empirical studies confirm that – in most countries, especially those with minimal public investments in childcare – the greater are a woman's child-rearing responsibilities, the less likely it is that she will choose to participate in paid work; for women who are labour force participants, greater child-rearing responsibilities reduce hours in paid work (Connelly 1991; Gornick, Meyers and Ross 1998; Leibowitz, Klerman and Waite 1992).

Economic theory is also helpful for understanding the effects of childcare on women's employment; two theoretical approaches have been taken. The first depicts childcare conditions as affecting the value that a woman places on her time at home (Blau and Ferber 1992). In the second approach, the cost of childcare is viewed as a tax levied on mothers' wages so that higher-priced care would have the same effect as lower net wages – decreasing employment and hours of paid work (Connelly 1992; Michalopoulos, Robins and Garfinkel 1992). Both approaches predict that improvements in women's childcare options will be associated with increases in their labour supply and a large body of empirical work supports this prediction (Blau and Robins 1988; Connelly 1991, 1992; Leibowitz, Klerman and Waite 1992; Michalopoulos, Robins and Garfinkel 1992).

The relationship between maternal employment and family leave policies is understood differently by economists. Generous maternity leave provisions are generally believed to increase women's attachment to paid work in the short term. In addition to offering income support, many maternity policies are explicitly designed to prevent women from leaving employment following childbirth (Trzcinski 1991). A small empirical literature has examined the impact of maternity leave in the short term. Joesch (1995) and O'Connell (1990) report that the availability of leave increases labour force attachment and the likelihood of an early return to work after first childbirth. Klerman and Leibowitz (1996) find only weak evidence of a relationship between state maternity leave statutes and employment, but Waldfogel (1996) reports an increase in job-guaranteed leaves and a small positive net employment effect after the passage of the US Family and Medical Leave Act. More research is needed to establish the longer-term impact of leave policies – especially of extended leave policies – on women's employment and earnings.

One recent cross-national study (Gornick, Meyers and Ross 1998) aimed to focus more sharply on the question of causality, i.e. on the nature of the linkage between policy and maternal employment outcomes. In the study, the independent variable was national policy performance, as captured in two comparative indices that included measures of childcare and family leave policy. The dependent variable was the country-specific (regression-adjusted) estimate of the decrease in mothers' employment probability given the presence of young children at home, rather than the maternal employment level itself. The author's term for this dependent variable is the child penalty. The use of this dependent variable – which correlates only weakly with maternal employment levels – has the advantage of isolating the effect of children on employment, exactly what policy factors would be expected to affect. The results suggest a strong association between policy configurations and the effects of children on maternal employment patterns. These child penalties are greatest in those countries with the weakest policy on childcare and family leave provision, and non-existent in countries with extensive provision.

As noted above, cross-national variation in the provision of childcare and family leave benefits is dramatic, and patterns of maternal employment also vary markedly across the industrialized countries. While there is a rich literature describing cross-national differences in policy as well as variation in employment patterns, comparative scholars have yet to specify fully the association between the two. Empirical studies using cross-national data to link variations in childcare and maternity leave directly to patterns of maternal employment are also very limited, although a handful of recent studies suggest that this is a fruitful direction for research (Bradshaw *et al.* 1996; Gornick, Meyers and Ross 1998; Gustafsson and Stafford 1995; Schmidt 1993; Ruhm and Teague 1996). Progress has been limited, however, by the lack of a model that specifies the association between the 'package' of national policies affecting women's employment decisions and the country-specific pattern of maternal employment and, even more importantly, by the lack of comparable cross-national data. Further research that aims to tease out these causal links between policy and outcomes is clearly crucial.

The state of the literature: recent contributions

As Daly observes, in this volume, in recent years there has been an outpouring of feminist scholarship on the welfare state. Daly notes that feminist analyses of the welfare state have generally proceeded along two lines: while some feminist critics have offered wholly new concepts and approaches to welfare state scholarship, more commonly, scholars concerned with gender have struggled to render existing frameworks more capable of incorporating gendered factors and processes. Substantively, feminist work has focused, variously, on the concept of care, the gendered nature of citizenship, or on the characterization of welfare states using the breadwinner/housewife typology.

Daly's aim is to lend a critical eye to this now substantial body of feminist welfare state scholarship, an exercise that she argues – persuasively – is now overdue. Among her recommendations is the call for a reorientation of methods, arguing in particular that 'typologizing should be set aside in favour of few countries/many factors type of work. In other words, the many countries/few variables approach has reached its limits in the welfare state field.' In the end, Daly calls for the adoption of a diverse set of methods that will take comparative research in a new direction, one that more successfully accounts for the rich detail of welfare state features considered in their national contexts.

In the subsequent chapter in this volume, Boje and Almquist aim to assess the impact of family policy on women's labour market involvement in five diverse welfare states – Sweden, Denmark, France, Germany and the UK. One of the main contributions in Boje and Almquist's work is the distinction they make, when comparing welfare states, between the 'right to receive care' and the 'right to time for care'. The 'right to receive care', in this context, reflects the extent to which public policies support or provide childcare services. The 'right to time for care' is generated by family leave schemes, as well as what the authors term 'the possibilities for part-time work'. The possibilities for part-time work are shaped both by market conditions and by public policies that regulate working time, in the public and private sectors, as well as by income transfer rules.

The distinction between the 'right to receive care' and the 'right to time for care' mirrors, to a large extent, the commonly drawn contrast between childcare policies (which provide or subsidize out-of-home non-parental care) versus paid family leave schemes (which support in-home parental care). While both childcare policy and paid family leave allow some reconciliation for mothers between employment and care responsibilities, and both approaches have a direct or indirect income transfer component, their effects on mothers' labour market attachment differ. In general, publicly supported childcare schemes increase mothers' time spent on the job, strengthening their labour market attachment, while paid leave schemes can have more mixed effects. While short-term leaves appear to increase job retention and reduce turnover, long periods of supported leave (even if formal employment is maintained) can reduce workers' accumulation of skills and experience and, in turn, suppress job advancement and wages, leaving women caught in what has been called the 'leave trap'. Similarly, policies (both supply-side and demand-side) that provide incentives for part-time work may benefit women in the short-term by increasing their options. At the same time, in many countries – some Nordic countries are arguably an exception – the costs of part-time work for women can be considerable in both the short and long term; part-time employment often brings lower hourly pay, limited access to public and occupational benefits, and a restricted choice of occupations.

While the 'right to receive care' – here, in the form of childcare – is clearly advantageous to women in relation to their integration into the labour market, a social protection system that leans toward shoring up the 'right to time for care' may produce a more complex and ambiguous set of gendered consequences. Thus, while Boje and Almquist's 'right to time for care' dimension is useful for characterizing and comparing welfare states, the dimension ought to be reshaped in two ways. First, it should incorporate public recognition of the costs to the carer of taking time away from paid work. In the service of women's labour market gains, it is crucial, for example, that public and private support for time to care be accompanied by various protections such as working time regulations that guarantee pay equity (in relation to full-time employment) in cash wages and benefits as well as access to a full range of occupations. Second, if the 'right to time for care' dimension is to be associated with gender equality, it should explicitly recognize the entrenched gendered nature of caring and, in response, incorporate policy elements that urge a more egalitarian division of labour in care-giving for children between mothers and fathers – at a minimum, the extension of all care rights to both parents and, ideally, components in the policy design that provide incentives for men to take time to care as well (e.g. the provision of 'use-or-lose daddy leave', as has been implemented in Norway).

In another contribution in this volume, Benoit (Chapter 3) compares the Canadian and US cases to explore the gendered nature of the 'new world of work', referring to a post-Fordist era characterized by the deregulation of markets, the rise of new and less stable forms of employment, and an array of social welfare reversals. She illuminates the differences between these two relatively similar liberal welfare states in the ways in which women have access to diverse social welfare policies that shape, and are shaped by, their relationship to the labour market. Her cross-country comparison covers multiple policy arenas – government service employment, unemployment and healthcare insurance, family leaves and benefits, and childcare services – all of which are facing the possibility of substantial reform in the current era of welfare state and labour market change.

The strength of Benoit's analysis is that she responds squarely to the calls by Orloff and others to incorporate gender into welfare state research and to craft analyses that are explicitly comparative. As Orloff (1996) notes, the first generation of feminist analyses focused on identifying universal welfare state features, generally those that were detrimental to women's interests, rather than exploring variation in the gendered effects of public policies across countries. Thus, the early feminist work on the welfare state was not comparative in focus. In recent years the complaint has been raised that '[m]ainstream comparative research has neglected gender, while most feminist research on the welfare state has not been systematically comparative' (Orloff 1993:303). Sainsbury (1994) argues persuasively that variation across countries should be the focal point for research, because some systems are more 'woman-friendly', to use Hernes's (1987) term, than others. Benoit's analysis responds to these calls for new lines of work, in that it stresses cross-national differentiation during a time of change; she also responds, arguably, to Daly's call for more work in the tradition of 'few countries/many factors'.

Finally, in Chapter 4, Ellingsæter focuses on the Scandinavian countries – making contrasts with Germany and the UK – in an attempt to assess and disentangle three current and inter-related trends: changing welfare states, restructuring labour markets, and shifting gender relations in work and employment. Ellingsæter argues, persuasively, that three general trends are under way. First, in many countries, welfare states are retrenching and restructuring, and collective bargaining systems and a range of employment protections are weakening in the name of increasing labour market flexibility. Second, many labour markets are undergoing rapid structural change, with one critical result being increasing inequality in employment rates and remuneration by skill level. Third, gender relations in employment are shifting in a multitude of ways, partly as a result of state and labour market shifts. While Ellingsæter speculates on some of the causal linkages among these inter-related trends, she refrains from an extensive analysis of the underlying mechanisms or direction of causality – thus setting up a crucial research agenda for comparative scholars interested in the effects of ongoing state and market transformations.

Ellingsæter's focus on labour markets has another advantage when conceptualizing gender relations in employment: it brings into relief the role that labour market structures play in shaping gender equality. As Blau and Kahn (1992) and others have reported, a highly unequal overall wage distribution means that all low-paid workers fall further from the middle and upper ends of the wage distribution. Since women are over-represented everywhere among lower paid workers, overall wage inequality increases the gender wage gap. One somewhat counter-intuitive implication of this conclusion is that government policies that narrow the distribution of wages throughout the economy are, in many cases, more fruitful avenues for promoting economic equality for women in the labour market – in particular, women's wages relative to men's – than are programmes and policies specifically targeted on women's advancement.

Conclusions

Much recent scholarship concludes that policies that support maternal employment vary markedly across the industrialized countries. Furthermore, both theory and recent empirical research indicate that this inter-country policy variation goes a long way in explaining cross-national variation in women's employment patterns. In particular, policies that increase the provision of childcare and/or family leave offset some of the downward pressure that parenting responsibilities place on mother's labour market attachment. The results are higher levels of labour market attachment among women who are combining parenting and employment, which in turn increase both gender equality in the labour market and the economic security of families with children.

These findings lead us to consider two unanswered questions that ought to be placed at the top of the research agenda on the relationship between public policy and women's labour market integration. The first concerns the direction and magnitude of policy shifts over the next decade and beyond, as the post-industrial transformation continues. The combination of ongoing labour market restructuring, persistently high male unemployment rates (especially in some European countries), and selected welfare state retrenchment suggests that policy supports for women's labour market integration will face heightened scrutiny. It remains to be seen whether demands for men's employment opportunities and/or welfare state reversals will overwhelm the economic, social, and political imperatives of women's labour market integration.

So far, the evidence suggests that, during the 1980s and 1990s, national policies that support maternal employment – especially public childcare, maternity benefits, and parental leave policies – have in general held steady and in some countries been expanded significantly (Gornick and Meyers 1999; Kamerman 1998). The apparent resilience, thus far, of family policies that support maternal employment is particularly remarkable, given that cutbacks in other programme areas – e.g. old age pensions, unemployment insurance and disability benefits – have been enacted in several countries during the same period. Whether the maintenance and growth of these crucial family policies continues remains an open question.

A second question concerns the possibility of policy expansion in the direction of measures aimed directly at reducing the sexual division of labour in unpaid care work; so far, those waters are largely uncharted. Fraser (1994) suggests that an ideal outcome, in the long term, is one of convergence of women's and men's work patterns; she envisages an arrangement in which both women and men work for pay and care for their families. Yet the progress towards gender equality in the labour market may level off, limited by the intransigence of gendered patterns in care-giving. Unfortunately, there is little consensus among welfare state scholars as to what kinds of policies would encourage gender parity at home – the exception perhaps being 'use-or-lose daddy leave', which increased men's parental leave take-up rate by nearly twenty-fold in the two years following its 1993 enactment in Norway (Bruning and Plantenga 1999). Nevertheless, there is considerable agreement that unpaid work is the next frontier; thus, policy development aimed at altering gender inequalities in unpaid work may constitute the next wave of 'woman-friendly' welfare state development.

Notes

1 Several countries have added or expanded childcare guarantees since then. In the 1990s Denmark adopted a childcare guarantee for children aged 1 to 5, Germany implemented a universal right to nursery school, and both Sweden and Spain enacted new childcare guarantees (see Gornick and Meyers 1999).

2 See Table 5.3 for women's shares in part-time employment in 1990 in eighteen countries Note that women's average share in part-time employment in the European/OECD countries was the same in 1998 as it was in 1990 (OECD 1999).

3 Results are based on data from the Luxembourg Income Study (LIS) See Gornick (1999) for a detailed discussion of the LIS data and of these employment indicators.

4 Note that the differences in employment rates between the two groups – persons in all family types versus the subset of married parents with young children – are not adjusted for intergroup differences in any other characteristics, such as age. Thus, the generally lower employment rates among the mothers of young children are found despite the likelihood that women in this subgroup are younger, on average, than women in the larger sample; in general, younger women would be expected to report higher rates of employment.

5 Canada's employment ratio indicates a relatively high level of gender equality within this group of countries, but it is the relatively low male employment rate that drives that result.

6 While this discussion is limited to cross-country comparisons of engagement in part-time work, there is another dimension related to employment intensity that varies across countries: the rate of work absence among employed women. Rubery *et al.* (1998) report rates of absence from work for reasons of maternity leave and for other reasons, including personal/family reasons, among women aged 15–49, for 1983 and 1992, in nine EU countries. Their data indicate both that rates of weekly work absence rose nearly everywhere between the two points in time, and also that work absences vary substantially across countries. In 1993 the highest rates of absence among employed women were reported in Denmark and Germany (where parental leaves are paid) and the lowest rates were reported in the Netherlands, Portugal and Spain (where parental leaves are unpaid).

7 To describe all women who seek part-time employment as 'voluntary' part-time workers is somewhat misleading in that many women face employment constraints on the supply side. A mother who cannnot arrange suitable childcare, for example, and who seeks part-time employment as a result, is a 'voluntary' part-time worker according to this standard economic definition.

8 Comparing results between Tables 5.2 and 5.3 must be done with caution due to the difference in sources, in addition to the different cut-offs used. The LIS-based part-time employment rates (Table 5.2) are primarily based on responses to income surveys while the OECD-based rates (Table 5.3) come from labour force surveys.

References

Becker, G. (1981) *A Treatise on the Family*, Cambridge, MA, Harvard University Press.

Becker, G. (1985) 'Human Capital, Effort, and the Sexual Division of Labour', *Journal of Labour Economics*, 3: 33–58.

Bergmann, B.R. (1986) *The Economic Emergence of Women*, New York: Basic Books Inc.

Berndt, E.R. (1991) *The Practice of Econometrics: Classic and Contemporary*, Reading, MA: Addison-Wesley.

Bianchi, S., Casper, L. and Peltola, P.K. (1996) 'A Cross-National Look at Married Women's Economic Dependency. Luxembourg Income Study Working Paper, no. 143, Luxembourg: Luxembourg Income Study.

Blau, D.M. and Robins, P.K. (1988) 'Childcare Costs and Family Labour Supply', *The Review of Economics and Statistics*, 70: 374–381.

Blau, F.D. and Ferber, M.A. (1992) 'Women's Work, Women's Lives: A Comparative Economic Perspective', in H. Kahne and J.Z. Giele (eds) *Women's Work and Women's Lives: The Continuing Struggle Worldwide*, pp. 28–44, Boulder, San Francisco, Oakland: Westview Press.

Blau, F.D. and Kahn, L.M. (1992) 'The Gender Earnings Gap: Learning from International Comparisons', *The American Economic Review*, 82: 533–38.

Blau, F.D. and Ferber, M.A. (1992) *The Economics of Women, Men, and Work*, 2nd edition, Englewood Cliffs: Prentice-Hall.

Bradshaw, J. *et al.* (1996) *Policy and the Employment of Lone Parents in 20 Countries*, York: University of York.

Briar, C. (1992) 'Part-Time Work and the State in Britain, 1941–1987', in B Warme, K. Lundy and L. Lundy (eds) *Working Part-Time: Risks and Opportunities*, pp. 75–86, New York: Praeger.

Bruning, G. and Plantenga, J. (1999) 'Parental Leave and Equal Opportunities: Experiences in Eight European Countries', *Journal of European Social Policy*, 9, 3: 195–209.

Connelly, R. (1991) 'The Importance of Childcare Costs to Women's Decision Making', in D. Blau (ed.) *The Economics of Childcare*, pp. 87–117, New York: Russell Sage Foundation.

Connelly, R. (1992) 'The Effect of Childcare Costs on Married Women's Labour Force Participation', *Review of Economics and Statistics*, 74: 83–90.

Esping-Andersen, G. (1990) *The Three Worlds of Welfare Capitalism*, Princeton: Princeton University Press.

Fraser, N. (1994) 'After the Family Wage: Gender Equity and the Welfare State', *Political Theory*, 22, 4: 591–618.

Folbre, N. and Hartmann. H. (1988) 'The Rhetoric of Self-Interest and the Ideology of Gender', in A. Klamer *et al.* (eds) *The Consequences of Economic Rhetoric*, pp. 184–203, New York: Cambridge University Press.

Gornick, J.C. and Meyers, M.K. (1999) 'Cross-National Family Policy Developments During Economic Hard Times: Retrenchment or Resilience?', paper presented at the Annual Meeting of the Association for Policy Analysis and Management, Washington, DC, 6 November.

Gornick, J.C. (1999) 'Gender Equality in the Labour Market', in D. Sainsbury (ed.) *Gender Policy Regimes and Welfare States*, pp. 210–42, Oxford: Oxford University Press.

Gornick, J.C., Meyers, M.K. and Ross, K.E. (1997) 'Supporting the Employment of Mothers: Policy Variation Across Fourteen Welfare States', *Journal of European Social Policy*, 7, 1: 45–70.

Gornick, J.C., Meyers, M.K. and Ross, K.E. (1998) 'Public Policies and the Employment of Mothers: A Cross-National Study', *Social Science Quarterly*, 79, 1: 35–54.

Gunderson, M. (1989) 'Male-Female Wage Differentials and Policy Responses', *Journal of Economic Literature*, 27: 46–72.

Gustafsson, S. and Stafford, F.P. (1995) 'Links between Early Childhood Programs and Maternal Employment in Three Countries', *The Future of Children*, 5: 161–74.

Hakim, C. (1997) 'A Sociological Perspective on Part-Time Work', in H. Blossfeld and C. Hakim (eds) *Between Equalization and Marginalization: Women Working Part-Time in Europe and The United States of America*, pp. 22–70, Oxford: Oxford University Press.

Hernes, H. (1987) *Welfare State and Woman Power: Essays in State Feminism*, Oslo, Norway: Norwegian University Press.

Hobson, B. (1990) 'No Exit, No Voice: Women's Economic Dependency and the Welfare State', *Acta Sociologica*, 33: 235–50.

Hofferth, S. and Deich, S. (1994) 'Recent US Childcare and Family Legislation in Comparative Perspective', *Journal of Family Issues*, 15: 424–48.

Jacobs, J.A. and Lim, S.T. (1992) 'Trends in Occupational and Industrial Sex Segregation in 56 Countries, 1960–1980', *Work and Occupations*, 19: 450–86.

Joesch, J.M. (1995) 'Paid Leave and the Timing of Women's Employment Surrounding Birth', paper prepared for the Annual Meeting of the Population Association of America, San Francisco, April.

Kamerman, S.B. (1998) 'Does Global Retrenchment and Restructuring Doom the Children's Cause?', University lecture, 30 November, Columbia University.

Kamerman, S.B. (1991) 'Childcare Policies and Programs: An International Overview', *Journal of Social Issues*, 47: 179–96.

Kamerman, S.B. (1991) 'Parental Leave and Infant Care: United States and International Trends and Issues, 1978–1988', in J.S. Hyde and M.J. Essex (eds) *Parental Leave and Childcare: Setting a Research and Policy Agenda*, pp. 11–23, Philadelphia: Temple University Press.

Kamerman, S.B. and Kahn, A.J. (1991) *Childcare, Parental Leave, and the Under-3s: Policy Innovation in Europe*, New York: Auburn House.

Kamerman, S.B. and Kahn, A.J. (1991) *Government Expenditures for Children and Their Families in Advanced Industrialized Countries, 1960–85*, Florence, Italy: UNICEF Economic Policy Series.

Killingsworth, M.R. and Heckman J.J. (1986) 'Female Labour Supply: A Survey', in O.C. Ashenfelter and R. Layard (eds) *Handbook of Labour Economics* (Volume 1), 1st edition, pp. 103–204, New York: North-Holland.

Klerman, J.A. and Leibowitz, A. (1996) 'Labour Supply Effects of State Maternity Leave Legislation', in F. Blau and R. Ehrenberg (eds) *Gender and Family Issues in the Workplace*, pp. 65–91, New York: Russell Sage Press.

Langan, M. and Ostner, I. (1991) 'Gender and Welfare: Toward a Comparative Framework', unpublished paper: Bath, England.

Leibowitz, A., Klerman, J.A. and Waite, L.J. (1992) 'Employment of New Mothers and Childcare Choice: Differences by Children's Age', *The Journal of Human Resources*, 27: 112–33.

Lewis, J. (1992) 'Gender and the Development of Welfare Regimes', *Journal of European Social Policy*, 2: 159–73.

Lister, R. (1990) 'Women, Economic Dependency and Citizenship', *Journal of Social Policy*, 19: 445–67.

Michalopoulos, C., Robins, P.K. and Garfinkel I. (1992) 'A Structural Model of Labour Supply and Childcare Demand', *The Journal of Human Resources*, 27: 166–203.

Mincer, J. and Polachek S. (1974) 'Family Investments in Human Capital: Earnings of Women', *Journal of Political Economy*, 82: 79–108.

O'Connell, M. (1990) 'Maternity Leave Arrangements: 1961–85'. Work and Family Patterns of American Women, Current Population Reports, Special Studies Series P-23: 11–27.

O'Connor, J.S. (1992) 'Citizenship, Class, Gender, and the Labour Market: Issues of Decommodification and Personal Autonomy', paper presented at the International Sociological Association Conference on Comparative Studies of Welfare State Development, University of Bremen, Bremen, Germany, September.

O'Connor, J.S. (1996) 'From Women in the Welfare State to the Gendering Welfare State Regimes', *Current Sociology*, 44: 1–130.

OECD (1984) *The Employment and Unemployment of Women in OECD Countries*, Paris: OECD.

OECD (1985) *The Integration of Women into the Economy*, Paris: OECD.

OECD (1994) *Women and Structural Change: New Perspectives*, Paris: OECD.

OECD (1988) *Employment Outlook*, Paris: OECD.

OECD (1991) *Employment Outlook*, Paris: OECD.

OECD (1992) *Employment Outlook*, Paris: OECD.

OECD (1998) *Employment Outlook*, Paris: OECD.

OECD (1999) *Employment Outlook*, Paris: OECD.

Orloff, A.S. (1993) 'Gender and the Social Rights of Citizenship: The Comparative Analysis of Gender Relations and Welfare States', *American Sociological Review*, 58: 303–328.

Orloff, A.S. (1996)'Gender in the Welfare State', *Annual Review of Sociology*, 22: 51–78.

Pateman, C. (1988) 'The Patriarchal Welfare State', in A. Gutman (ed.) *Democracy and the Welfare State*, pp. 231–60, Princeton: Princeton University Press.

Pfau-Effinger, B. (1998) 'Culture or Structure as Explanations for Differences in Part-Time Work in Germany, Finland, and the Netherlands', in J. O'Reilly and C. Fagan (eds) *Part-Time Prospects: An International Comparison of Part-Time Work in Europe, North America, and the Pacific Rim*, pp. 57–76, London: Routledge.

Polachek, S. (1995) 'Human Capital and the Gender Earnings Gap: A Response to Feminist Critiques', in E. Kuiper and J. Sap (eds) *Out of the Margin: Feminist Perspectives on Economics*, pp. 61–79, New York: Routledge.

Reskin, B. and Padavic I. (1994) *Women and Men at Work*, 1st edition, Thousand Oaks, London, New Delhi: Pine Forge Press.

Rosenfeld, R.A. and Kalleberg A.L. (1990) 'A Cross-National Comparison of the Gender Gap in Income', *American Journal of Sociology* 96: 69–106.

Rosenfeld, R.A. and Kalleberg, A.L. (1991) 'Gender Inequality in the Labour Market: A Cross-National Perspective', *Acta Sociologica*, 34: 207–25.

Rubery, J., Smith, M., Fagan, C. and Grimshaw, D. (1998) *Women and European Employment*, London: Routledge.

Ruhm, C.J. and Teague, J.L. (1996) 'Parental Leave Policies in Europe and North America', in F. Beau and R. Ehrenberg (eds) *Gender and Family Issues in the Workplace*, pp. 133–65, New York: Russell Sage Press.

Sainsbury, D. (1994) 'Women's and Men's Social Rights: Gendering Dimensions of Welfare States', in D. Sainsbury (ed.) *Gendering Welfare States*, pp. 150–69, London, Thousand Oaks, New Delhi: Sage Publications.

Schmidt, M.G. (1993) 'Gendered Labour Force Participation', in F. Castles (ed.) *Families of Nations: Patterns of Public Policy in Western Democracies*, pp. 179–237, Aldershot: Edward Elgar.

Smith, M., Fagan, C. and Rubery, J. (1998) 'Where and Why is Part-Time Work Growing in Europe?', in J. O'Reilly and C. Fagan (eds) *Part-Time Prospects: An International Comparison of Part-Time Work in Europe, North America, and the Pacific Rim*, pp. 35–56, London: Routledge.

Treiman, D.J. and Roos, P.A. (1983) 'Sex and Earnings in Industrial Society: A Nine-Nation Comparison', *American Journal of Sociology*, 89: 612–650.

Trzcinski, E. (1991) 'Employers' Parental Leave Policies: Does the Labour Market Provide Parental Leave?', in J.S. Hyde and M.J. Essex (eds) *Parental Leave and Childcare: Setting a Research and Policy Agenda*, pp. 209–28, Philadelphia, PA: Temple University Press.

Waldfogel, J.(1996) 'Working Mothers Then and Now: A Cross-Cohort Analysis of the Effects of Maternity Leave on Women's Pay', in F. Blau and R. Ehrenberg (eds) *Gender and Family Issues in the Workplace*, pp. 92–129, New York: Russell Sage Press.

Part II

Family policy – work and care in different welfare systems

6 Gendered policies

Family obligations and social policies in Europe

Chiara Saraceno

Social policies as means to regulate gender and household relations

At the beginning of the twentieth century the first items of social legislation were introduced in most European countries. They have developed along three lines, the timing and weight of which differed in the various countries. First, the labour market participation of women and children was regulated. Second, insurance measures against loss of work income (due to unemployment, old age and sickness) were introduced. Third, some family dependencies were acknowledged, as in the case of family allowances, the extension of the coverage of health services to family dependents and the introduction of survivors' pensions.

In regulating labour relations and conditions, and in defining which needs might be socially acknowledged and (at least partly) supported, social legislation and then social policies have implicitly regulated, or at least interfered with, family and household formation models: redefining the relationships of dependence and interdependence between gender and generations, modifying the conditions and costs of reproduction, rewarding, or discouraging, particular family patterns. An example of this is the introduction of old age pensions at the beginning of the century: having a pension, in fact, allowed the elderly not only to look with a degree of security to their future out of work; it also allowed them not to depend too exclusively on their families', particularly children's, solidarity. On the contrary, restrictions on child and women's labour, together with the introduction of compulsory schooling, de facto, constituted a means of regulating workers' households, with regard to gender and intergenerational relations: first of all by distinguishing between 'workers' and 'family dependents' among household members.[1]

During the twentieth century the means and criteria of social policies' interference in the conditions for family formation and everyday living and organization have changed, due to changes in behaviour and in family relations themselves, and to the emerging of a new awareness of the diversity of needs and interests among families, but also within families: between genders as well as between generations. The direction taken by these developments has further differentiated the various European countries, intertwining and overlapping national differences in social protection packages targeted at workers as such. As a consequence, at present, variations between countries in assumptions concerning gender relations and intergenerational solidarity – therefore concerning family organization and family obligations – that are implied in the different social arrangements and in national welfare regimes are clearer and more explicit than in the past. Their roots, however, lie as much in the specific gender and intergenerational relationships acknowledged and shaped by turn of the century legislation as in the nation-specific trends and conditions of more recent changes in gender and household relations and behaviours.

At the same time, the new awareness of the assumptions concerning family organization and responsibilities contributes to a better delineation and understanding of the 'families of nations'. As a matter of fact, attention to the different ways in which gender relations and intergenerational obligations are supported, expected or promoted by social policies has contributed not only to the enlargement of the scope and dimensions of welfare state research, but to the creation of a whole new family of welfare state typologies. Thus, on the one hand we have – conflicting – typologies proposed by scholars mainly interested in how gender relations are framed within social policies and welfare mixes; on the other hand we have typologies proposed by scholars who focus on how intergenerational relations and obligations are framed by and within social policies. From the former perspective at least two typologies have been developed. One is based on the degree to which a policy regime is committed to the male breadwinner–female housewife model (e.g. Lewis 1993, 1997; Langan and Ostner 1991; Sainsbury 1994, 1996); the other is based on the degree to which it is possible for women, as well as for men, to form an autonomous household (e.g. Hobson 1990, 1994; Orloff 1993; O'Connor, Orloff and Shaver 1999). Connected to these are typologies based on 'models of motherhood' (Leira 1992). From the latter perspective (intergenerational obligations) also different typologies have been developed on the basis not only of the extension and duration of normative obligations (e.g. Millar and Warman 1996), but also of what specific intergenerational link and obligation is focused on: e.g. parents–children (e.g. Gauthier 1996; Ditch *et al.* 1998; Hantrais and Letablier 1996; Bradshaw *et al.* 1996) or children–elderly parents (e.g. Leseman and Martin 1993). The need to distinguish between these two directions of intergenerational family obligations in comparative social policy analysis, and therefore in constructing typologies, has become particularly evident in comparative analyses of social care services addressed to children and to the elderly (Anttonen and Sipilä 1996; Lewis 1998).

Thus, introducing the factor of family relations – from a gender, but also from an intergenerational perspective – has not only enriched, but complicated social policy analysis and comparison, reducing the explanatory power of, albeit useful, typologies. If these vary as soon as we introduce a new dimension/indicator, or change one, we must either rethink the whole set of dimensions and indicators deemed crucial, or question the degree of generalization of typologies themselves. Since this is a relatively new field and yet to be fully explored, maybe we should be satisfied with partial exercises in generalization and in typology construction, without aiming – yet at least – at grand theories and fully coherent and encompassing typologies.[2]

In this chapter I will analyse differences in perceiving and framing gender and intergenerational relations within the family with regard to the degree to which social security and social assistance regulations assume intra-household and intra-kin economic solidarity, to patterns of defining parenting responsibilities and responsibilities towards frail elderly kin. I will use existing typologies more as a way of presenting specific sets of arrangements with regard to a given set of problems than as a way of identifying overall mixes, or regimes.

Excursus: the design of social security systems and the gender risks of means-testing

The degree to which social security systems are linked not only to status in the labour force, but also to family status may influence both women's economic autonomy and their strategies in relation to the labour market. In countries such as Belgium, the Netherlands, Italy (until the 1995 pension reform) and the UK different statutory retirement ages for men and women are based upon assumptions about marriage and the 'normal' age differential between husband and wife. Due to an average of shorter and more interrupted careers for women and to average lower wages, this age differential produces substantially lower pension returns for women, although on average they benefit from them longer. To this it should be added that more women than men are employed in the irregular labour force and, therefore, are not entitled to any occupational pension. Since in most EU countries there is no universal flat rate state pension, many women in old age can rely only on a social assistance pension, which is usually very low (as in Italy), or on a survivor's pension. Given the increasing instability of marriages, however, the latter can no longer be viewed as a viable solution for women in old age

Means-tested income support measures particularly addressed to lone mothers are almost totally lacking in southern European countries which rely heavily on extended family solidarity and on a strongly gendered division of labour in the family. They are also lacking in (mostly Scandinavian) countries where the focus on individual rights and on gender equality in the public sphere supports women's and mothers' participation in the labour market while providing resources for children. On the contrary those measures are present and relatively generous in the countries (e.g. Germany and the UK) where support for the male breadwinner model must deal with the consequences of the lack of a male breadwinner.[3] In these same countries, particularly in the Netherlands and the UK where mothers' caring obligations were assumed to last longer than in any other countries, in so far as they were exempted from the requirement to be available for work well beyond their children's school age, in recent years these policies have been subjected to criticism and reform. The official reason for reform was the poverty trap and welfare dependency which such a policy created for women; yet, the incentives and obligations to be available for paid work were put in place more quickly and easily than the support systems (childcare services, extended school hours, training, good paying jobs) which are needed in order adequately to manage caring and income providing obligations (e.g. Knijn 1994). That of the worker with caring obligations is still far from being a fully acknowledged social figure – in these, but not only in these, countries.

Other means-tested measures may also act as disincentives to women, particularly in lower income brackets, to enter the labour market. This is the case with family allowances in Italy: targeted to lower income families of wage workers on the basis of household income and household size, they are fairly generous for large families belonging to the lowest income bracket.[4] Working for (probably modest) official wages would be cost inefficient for mothers in dual-parent families in these cases. However, as their children come of age, the value of the allowance declines, irrespective of the household income. Since the chances to enter the official labour market decline for unskilled mature women as well, these, and their families, are exposed to the risk of falling into poverty. Other examples concern the use of means-testing to define childcare fees or charges in the national health system.

Generally, means-testing on a household basis without taking into account the household size and the number of workers,[5] is likely not only to reinforce the breadwinner model, but to produce poverty traps for women, and also for households. Since means-testing is increasingly resorted to in many countries in the context of shrinking budgets and the rethinking of the welfare state, introducing a gender perspective in the way household income is conceptualized appears to be crucially necessary.

Defining obligations to provide for children

In all countries parents are perceived and defined as the main, and natural, responsible actors towards their children. Yet, the specific boundaries and contents of these obligations may vary quite widely not only at the level of shared values, but also in legislation. And there is a great variation in the degree to which the state may enforce, as well as surrogate, parents' obligations

Of course, values and opinions may differ on how to interpret the presence or absence of a public responsibility towards children. Someone might interpret the offer of public childcare services as an interference in, or weakening of, family autonomy and responsibility; while others might interpret the absence of these same services as an indicator of social irresponsibility towards children and their parents and of neglect of the individual rights of the former. These different evaluations, in turn, reflect different ideas and priorities concerning not only family/parents' responsibilities, but the existence of autonomous rights of children, on the one hand, and the degree and manner in which the principle of subsidiarity is conceptualized and enforced in a given country.

As a matter of fact, the idea of subsidiarity, which has become standard European jargon, is highly culturally and country-specific. It is more easily recognized and used in public discourse in continental European countries, with a strong presence of Catholic and Protestant social organizations and/or deeply rooted ethnic divisions; while in culturally and socially more homogeneous groups, with a high emphasis on the state as 'the common house' – such as the Scandinavian ones – it may sound foreign and useless. However, where the concept is part of the common language and is used to explain what the role of the state should be in relation to other communities – local governments, ethnic groups, religious institutions, volunteer and non-profit institutions and families – it might mean quite different things in policy terms. Thus, in the case of state–family relations, it might mean that the state does not intervene except in extreme cases in which families are not able to solve problems on their own – that is, when they are for some reason inadequate or unfit; but it might also mean that the state has some kind of obligation to provide support for families to enable them to fulfil their obligations. In the latter meaning, it can in turn motivate different policies on the basis of what kind of support is provided (e.g. to enable women to stay at home with their children or to enable them to reconcile family and work responsibilities, or to enable parents to share childcare responsibilities).

Two main issues are involved here: who should care for the children and who should bear the costs of raising a child. In both cases, the issue is two-fold, in so far as it addresses responsibilities within the household, first of all between parents, but also the division of responsibilities between families and community, and families and the state.

If one considers the degree to which policies support the reconciliation of family responsibilities and paid work either for mothers only or for mothers and fathers (i.e. the kind and duration of maternity and parental leave, the kind and degree of coverage of childcare services, and so on)[6] one might group the countries into four categories. This grouping differs from the most popular typologies in welfare state analysis:

- the Scandinavian countries, but also France and Belgium, in which the state and local governments actively support mothers in reconciling paid work and family responsibilities through both a flexible and generous (in terms of income replacement) leave policy and good availability of childcare services. In all these countries there is also the possibility of parental leave. In addition, in Sweden and Norway a portion of the leave may be taken only by fathers, or it must go unused. In these countries women's activity rate is high even among mothers; the incidence of part-time work is high among women, and also among men, compared with other countries, although to a much lower degree than among women;
- the countries which support a strong division of labour between fathers and mothers and at the same time encourage a 'sequential' investment by women in family and paid work. Germany, Austria, the Netherlands and Luxembourg belong to this group. Maternity leave is comparatively long and income replacement generous; but childcare services, particularly for children under 3 years old, are scarce and school hours do not favour families where both parents are in paid work. As a consequence, women's

activity rate is lower than in the first group, although increasing; mothers of very young children tend to remain at home, and to work part-time afterwards;

- the UK is a category of its own, since reconciling family and paid work responsibilities is mostly considered a private affair, with little or no support from the state, either in the form of maternity leave or in the form of childcare services. Many working women work too few hours to be covered by social security guarantees, in particular to be entitled to paid maternity leave. Working women who are covered by social security have comparatively reduced rights in a social security system which is still strongly slanted towards the male breadwinner model: although the maternity leave may last for up to forty weeks, it is only partially paid; job maintenance is granted during the leave, but with no social security (pension benefits) attached. Women's activity rate is quite high, but it follows a sequential or alternate pattern: 75 per cent of women are in the labour market, but only 50 per cent of mothers. Also the incidence of part-time work is high and it concerns mainly women;

- the southern countries share a cultural emphasis on the gender division of labour within the family, on the crucial role of mothers' presence and care in the early childhood years, and a high reliance on family for supporting individual and household needs, including childcare needs. Women's official activity rate in these countries is the lowest in Europe (with the partial exception of Portugal), although women mostly work full time, since the availability of social security covered part-time jobs is scarce. At the same time there is an estimated high quota of women working in the informal labour market. These countries, with the exception of Greece, also share the lowest, and fastest declining, fertility rates in Europe and in the world. Italy is a particular case among these countries, in so far as it has one of the longest maternity leave systems, with generous income replacement, as well as a relatively long parental leave system, which might be taken by fathers, on condition that the mother is entitled to it. The offer of childcare services for children between 3 and 6 years old is high, covering more than 80 per cent of all children in this age bracket, while the coverage for children under the age of 3 is less than 5 per cent at the national level.[7]

The activity rate of lone mothers appears to depend even more than that of married mothers both on cultural assumptions and on social policy provisions. Although data are variable depending on their source (possibly due both to definitions of the category 'lone mother', and also 'lone parent', and to data sets),[8] a clear pattern seems to emerge. Lone mothers' activity and occupation rates are lower in those countries, such as Germany and, until very recently, the Netherlands, and the UK, where cultural values stress the priority of the motherhood role (and its potential of conflict with the working role), and income support policies suggest that it is legitimate for mothers to stay at home to take care of their children and to receive economic support when in need. It is higher where either there are policies which support dual roles for mothers, such as in

Sweden and Denmark and, to some extent, Norway, or there are no ad hoc policies targeted to lone mothers as such, as in Italy. Italy has, in fact, the highest percentage of working women among lone mothers compared with mothers living in couples. This does not depend, as in the Scandinavian countries, on a consensus on the normalcy of dual roles for mothers and the existence of supportive services. It rather stems from the lack of policies addressing lone mothers and their children in a situation in which the strong gender division of labour within the family has a severe impact on women and children when the marriage breaks up (Barbagli and Saraceno 1998). The fact that in recent years changes in policies in some of the countries (the Netherlands, the UK, Norway) which, to some degree, discouraged lone mothers from working have produced increasing activity and occupation rates within this group indirectly confirms the role of policies in supporting (and sometime enforcing) changes in behaviour (e.g. Knijn 1994; Waerness 1998).

These differences point to national variations in assumptions concerning not only gender and parental roles, but also the state's responsibilities towards regulating, or supporting, specific patterns of gender relations, parental obligations and children's individual rights. Within these differences, it is worth noticing that the same kind of policy may be motivated by a different set of goals. Particularly with regard to childcare services, their provision may be grounded on a child-centred approach, focusing on child development and on equalization of chances among children, as in France and Italy with regard to kindergartens, or on the need to support working women in their effort of reconciling family and work responsibilities, as in the Scandinavian countries (Norway excepted) in the 1970s (Leira 1992, 1993, 1996; Lewis and Åström 1992) and, more recently, in the UK and in the Netherlands. The latter goal is the most prevalent – and at the same time less legitimate than the former – in the case of care services for children under 3 years old in most countries.

In an overview of the institutional framework of family obligations in the European Union, Millar and Warman (1996, see also Millar in this volume) suggest, however, that, mostly as a cost-containment measure and also in countries where both the presence and quality of child-care services are high and the services are oriented not only to help working mothers but also to provide children with precious educational resources, there has been a recent shift to home care rather than care in centres. In Denmark a complex leave scheme was introduced to allow parents to care for their children as an alternative to sending them to day-care centres. In Norway and Finland a home care allowance has also been made the subject of legislation, with some controversy. These moves, which imply the offer both of time off work and of an allowance instead of a place in a childcare service, are explained in the language of opening options for parents and of granting all children the same degree of resources (which would not be the case if only services for children of working parents were offered). Yet, since it is mostly women who take up this opportunity, particularly within the least skilled groups, concern has developed about the gender implications of such a measure. As often happens with measures supporting mothers, it may in fact be read as a measure enabling women to deal more flexibly with their work and family obligations or, alternatively, as a measure encouraging women to remain at home (Fagnani 1994; Fagnani and Rassat 1997; Waerness 1998; Leira 1998). The prevalence of one or other meaning depends not only on explicit intentions, but on context: if the labour demand is abundant and favours women, the choice and opportunity dimension is clearer, although differentiated across social stratification; if labour demand is scarce and unfavourable, and women's unemployment high, the incentive to full-time motherhood becomes stronger. Also, as Leira points out in contrasting the Norwegian with the Finnish scheme, it makes a difference if the alternative between using a childcare service and receiving money is real. This is apparently the case in Finland, where if the mother chooses to send her child to a childcare service this must be provided, but not in Norway, where the provision is not assured, therefore greatly reducing the meaning of 'choice' left to (particularly low income) mothers.

With regard to the obligation to provide for children, in all countries parents' duties of guardianship and care generally cease at the age of 18–19, when children become 'adults', and in some cases even before. However, while in some countries (such as the Scandinavian countries and the UK) this also involves the end of any legally enforced financial obligation, in others, parents' legal financial obligations continue until the child is 'self-supporting', and in some countries may continue indefinitely (Millar and Warman 1996). In Germany, Italy, Spain, Austria, Belgium and Luxembourg, for instance, a child unable to support him/herself, even if able-bodied, can claim support from his parents throughout his/her life. This means that if adult children claim social assistance parents may be legally required to contribute.[9] On the other hand, in Sweden, Denmark and Finland students are entitled to financial support in their own right and without any account taken of parental income at 18–20 years of age – when their parents lose entitlement to child allowance.

At the same time, there are countries in which parents' financial obligations are actively supported by the state, while in others they are only expected and enforced. Thus, in the majority of EU countries, the state shoulders a part of the cost of a child up to a certain age (coming of age, or end of study) not only through the offer of free education, health services and so forth, but also through child allowances or child benefit schemes and/or child-related tax allowances.[10] In others, such as in Italy, Greece, Spain and Portugal, parents' financial obligations do not receive any state support in the form of child allowance and very little in the form of tax allowances. Only selected economically deprived groups receive some kind of allowance, as in the case of the Italian *assegno al nucleo familiare*, paid to low-income wage workers' households (Saraceno 1998).

A comparative analysis by Bradshaw *et al.* (1993) ranked OECD countries on the basis of the overall income support they offer to families with children (child allowances, housing allowances, medical costs, etc.), indicating that countries may be clustered in easily identifiable groups. These, once again, do not often correspond to those identified in prevalent welfare state analyses and comparisons. Thus, France, Luxembourg and Belgium cluster together with the Scandinavian countries, Germany and the Netherlands with the UK and Australia, Spain, Portugal, Ireland, Greece and Italy with the US and Japan. It is worth noticing that the countries in which the subsidiarity principle seems most to be enforced in terms of 'non-policy' are also those in which, at present, both women's activity rates and fertility (with the exception of Ireland) are lowest.

Of course, legally prolonged financial obligations towards one's own children may be purely symbolic if entrance to the labour market is not difficult and/or if the cost of higher education is low (that is, it is subsidized by the collectivity/the state). But when both youth unemployment and school costs are high, this obligation may substantially raise the cost of children. This is the case, for instance, in Italy, Spain, Portugal, Austria, and Ireland.

Another indicator of the degree to which the state assumes direct responsibility towards children is the regulation of child support when one parent, particularly the father, is absent. It is a particularly crucial issue, given the increasing fragility of marriage, with its consequences for the father–child relationship and for the children's economic wellbeing (OECD 1990; Kurz 1995; Jensen 1999; Sørensen 1999). Policies from this point of view seem to develop along two, sometimes alternative, sometimes integrated directions: the strengthening and enforcing of fathers' responsibilities and the partial substitution of a father's responsibilities with the state's.

On the one hand, legislation as well as juridical and social practice in many countries tends not only to encourage but to enforce fathers' responsibilities towards their children irrespective of their relationship with the mothers. Thus, in the case of separation and divorce, joint custody is preferred, or even enforced (e.g. in France) rather than custody by one parent. This policy is supported by the need to sustain continuing relationships between fathers and children, and by the belief that if fathers are given direct responsibility for their children they are more likely to contribute to support them. Research in the United States (e.g. Seltzer 1991) generally confirms this, indicating that joint legal custody encourages similarities between the way divorced fathers and fathers in two-parent households invest in their children. Qualitative research also finds that sometimes fathers with joint custody fail to contribute to the child's support above what they spend for their children on 'their' share of custody, irrespective either of the children's needs or of their mothers' economic situation (Seltzer 1991; Arendell 1995; Martin 1997), as well as of the actual time children spend with them.[11]

A different way to enforce fathers' responsibility is that recently pursued by the UK, where legislation strongly enforces fathers' obligation to support all their children economically, irrespective of the formers' relationship with the mother (see, e.g. Scheiwe 1994). This has been criticized as well, not on principle, but because it seems to be more focused on obliging fathers to do their duty (and mothers to denounce failing fathers), than on providing support when fathers do not.

The second policy line does not, on principle, deny parents'/fathers' responsibility, but it tries to distinguish it from the personal relationships between parents; at the same time it focuses on the children's need for support, rather than on the ideal supporter. Therefore, in countries like France and the Scandinavian countries, the state offers support in case a father does not, or cannot support his children. The collection of non-cohabitant parents' support is – always, or in particularly conflictual cases – a state's responsibility. This dual approach first of all grants a support basis to the child; second, it avoids the issue that the payment or non-payment of child support be used as a weapon by either parent in dealing with issues of access to children. From this point of view, we might contrast the present British and French approaches to who has responsibility for supporting a child when the parents do not live together: the former focuses almost exclusively on parents', and particularly absent fathers', responsibility, with the state granting only coercive support; the latter focuses rather on the state's responsibility that the child receive support in the first place, thus granting both positive (to children) and coercive (against failing parents) support (Martin 1995, 1997).[12]

Care for disabled and frail elderly people

A similar analysis might be developed with regard to the provision of care for the handicapped or for frail elderly people. Within the persistent gendered nature of caring at this level (Höllinger and Haller 1990; Leseman and Martin 1993; Facchini and Scortegagna 1993; Twigg 1993; OECD 1994), the presence of the state's obligations may differ quite substantially, therefore having an impact both on the resources and rights of those needing care and on the conditions and constraints of women as family carers. Moreover, with the exception of the Scandinavian countries, there is no clear overlapping between countries which are generous in providing childcare and countries generous in providing care for the frail elderly (Anttonen and Sipilä 1996). For instance, the Netherlands, Norway and the UK, which have low provision for pre-school children,[13] have a good public coverage for the frail elderly. The reverse is true for France and Belgium. This, again, points to differences in definitions of intergenerational obligations, in this case towards the elderly, within family and extended networks.

From this perspective, Millar and Warman (1996) group countries in four main categories on the basis of how their policies implicitly or explicitly conceptualize family obligations to care for disabled adults and frail elderly relatives.

In the first group, which includes Italy, Spain and Portugal, there are legal obligations between family members to support each other not only in economic terms, but in terms of caring. Family includes spouses, children, siblings and children-in-law. Thus, for instance, in Italy help at home is provided by the municipality under a dual test of means: only low income disabled or frail individuals with no family, particularly with no female family available, may receive it. The family may be called upon to contribute to the (non-hospital) cost of an old people's home, if the elderly person him/herself cannot provide for it.[14]

In the second group, which comprises Austria, Belgium, France, Germany, Greece and Luxembourg, legal obligations are restricted to children. The costs of non-hospital long-term care which are not covered by health insurance, however, are paid through local social assistance if the individual cannot meet these costs him/herself. Children are not expected to shoulder them. In Germany and Austria social insurance systems now include compulsory 'care insurance' precisely to face the growing needs of long-term care by an ageing population.

In the third group (the UK and Ireland) there are no legal obligations to provide or pay for care of frail or disabled adults. Yet, as happened in the UK after the passing of the 1990 Community Care Act, in reaction to financial pressures, local governments have started to assess the means not only of spouses but of adult children when providing long-term care. As Millar and Warman observe, however, as opposed to what occurs in most southern European countries, 'discontent expressed through the carers organizations suggests that paying for the care of even elderly parents is not generally accepted as being "natural" in the UK'.

The fourth group comprises the countries – such as the Scandinavian countries and partly the Netherlands[15] – in which state obligations to adults with care needs are made explicit and where support is directed to the individual, not to the family. Although even in these countries adult children, and particularly daughters, are the primary care-givers for many frail elderly, older people consider access to public services as an entitlement, independent of their family situation, while help received from children or family is perceived as an extra deriving from choice.

Only in this last group of countries, therefore, are services provided to grant individual rights to care recipients, irrespective of their family situation. In other countries, the offer of services may range from scarce and based on the unavailability of family, as in Italy, Spain and Portugal, to higher availability (and clearer regulation) with a consideration of the family-kin situation not so much in order to ration access, as in order to collect contributions.

Only in the fourth group of countries is the state neutral with regard both to gender and to family obligations respectively to care and to support. In the first group it is neutral neither with regard to gender obligations to care nor with regard to family financial obligations. In the second and third groups the state is formally neutral with regard to gender obligations to care, but not with regard to family financial obligations. Of course, neutrality may mean both that policies do not positively enforce a specific gender pattern, but de facto accept, and use, that which is culturally enforced, or it may mean that policies positively encourage rebalancing or renegotiating gender patterns in care-giving. Apparently, active neutrality in the second meaning occurs only, and even then partially, when the state provides a degree of non-family resources and services as a matter of social right.

Things have become further complicated in recent years due to two distinct phenomena. The first is the increasing introduction of market regulations within public social services, particularly for the elderly, together with an increasing recourse to contracting out and delegation to some non-state body. (Le Grand and Bartlett 1993; Evers and Svetlik 1993; OECD 1996; Lewis 1998). The second is the widespread introduction of some payment for care (Evers, Pijl and Ungerson 1993; Ungerson 1997; Lewis 1998). Both these phenomena occur in all social services, but are particularly visible in services and activities concerning the frail elderly and the handicapped.[16] They have no univocal meaning in principle or in the reasons which prompted them and in their consequences. As such, they are subject to highly controversial and contested analyses.

With regard to the former phenomenon, the issues at stake are those of quality, of choice, but also of the status and rights both of those cared for and of professional carers. As the debate and the national case indicate, since reasons and context differ, outcomes may also differ. In particular, as Daly and Lewis (1998) observe, in some countries, although there has been a substantial change in the way services are provided, the nature of the reforms has been characterized more by continuity than by change; while in other countries changes greatly affect the way care is provided in terms of quality and sometimes even quantity. Moreover, processes of contracting out may have quite different meanings, as well as outcomes, depending on the strength of the third sector in a given country, on its internal composition, and on its relative importance in relation to both the market and the state in providing services. In particular, it is well known that there are quite distinct traditions within European countries with regard not only to the relative importance of markets, but also to the relative importance of the third sector (an item not adequately taken into account in most welfare state typologies, including that of Esping-Andersen). This, in turn, gives a distinctive content to the concept and practice of subsidiarity. To simplify, we go from the extreme of Scandinavian countries with little space either for the market or the third sector to that of the Netherlands, Belgium and Germany where the third sector has been historically institutionalized as a partner of the welfare state. France has a much less institutionalized third sector than Italy, where the growing trend towards explicitly creating partnerships with the third sector in social services provision is premised on its having been an implicit, and even subsidized, partner for a long time. In the UK as well, the third sector, there more specifically indicated in the voluntary organizations, has a well-rooted history, although its partnership with the welfare state is institutionally much weaker than in the Netherlands and it is less linked to ethnic or religious institutions than in Germany or Italy (Kramer 1992; James 1989).

The redrawing of boundaries between the different social actors in the restructuring of welfare states, therefore, involves not only state and family boundaries, or centre–periphery responsibilities, but also state/market/third sector responsibilities and boundaries. Thus, one might expect that the assuming of public responsibilities by non-public bodies affects the way these different actors and the providers of care within them perceive themselves. Usually this is looked at mainly from the point of view of the increasing presence of 'market rules' within the public sector itself (with the multiple meanings this process may assume depending on the point of view, or on the particular aspect being looked at). However, it can also be viewed from the point of view of what happens to markets (and professionals within them) which have public responsibility for providing care. As for third sector institutions and agencies, observers usually point to the risk of bureaucratization and secularization they incur when they are called to take up public responsibilities. Less reflected upon are two other issues. The first concerns the diverse distribution of third sector institutions within a country, which might further geographical differences in the provision of services, developing what elsewhere (Saraceno 1994) I have defined as 'local systems of citizenship'. The second is the highly ideological or value-laden perspective of many third sector institutions (and of their workers). This may certainly be viewed as an added value to their work, in terms of motivation; but it may also be viewed as a constraint for users, particularly if they cannot opt out because of lack of alternatives

With regard to the phenomenon of the introduction of payments for care the reasons for apparently similar measures may differ quite substantially: they may aim at substituting for other kinds of (more expensive) services, as in the case of payments made to family care-givers in the UK and in certain Italian regions on the condition that they look after a frail elderly relative; or they may aim at enlarging options for care recipients, as in the case of benefits paid to the invalid elderly in Germany, Austria and France in order for them to be able to pay for care; or they may aim at granting more rights both to care-givers and care-recipients while promoting more family involvement. This is the case in the Swedish and Norwegian schemes, where family care-givers are not only paid, but also are acknowledged, receive pension contributions and sick leave and where this recruitment of family members creates a generally good service provision. Yet, in all these schemes, although the family/state boundaries may be affected quite differently depending on the overall package they contribute to, it is certainly clear that it is mostly women who are called upon as – more or less paid – care-givers. Therefore, this form of support might help recreate, or reproduce, the traditional gender structure of family caring obligations precisely when there are fewer daughters available for this kind of work. From this perspective it is worth mentioning that recently in Finland elderly spouses actually lost entitlement to caring allowances due to the introduction of an age threshold to be acknowledged as carers: as if implicitly care given by a spouse were defined as a natural obligation, to be expected and not acknowledged or supported.

Beyond the refamilialization/defamilialization opposition?

Family-relevant policies may draw boundaries between families, between individuals and families, between state and families, as well as between state, family, market and third sector in a different manner. Thus, in Italy, Spain and Portugal, legally enforced obligations cross household boundaries to comprise a substantial number of kin and semi-kin (in-laws), while in Germany or France they involve only the nuclear family, with the partial exception of parents and adult children whose reciprocal obligations may last all through life; and in the Scandinavian countries most reciprocal family obligations cease once reaching adulthood and even children are perceived as having rights of their own, irrespective of their family membership (Therborn 1993).

The role of the state/goverment in all these different situations is far from standardized. It may positively enforce obligations through legal and constrictive means, or just by not providing alternatives, or by offering positive incentives. To read institutional frameworks and social expectations as merely reflecting deeply rooted values risks ignoring the conflicts, negotiations, power struggles and imbalances which underlie them and the context-specific conditions which allowed their development

At present all countries seem to be faced, although to different degrees, by the task of redrawing these arrangements under the three-fold pressure of changing values (e.g. with regard to gender relations, and to intergenerational obligations), of the increasing fragility of traditional forms of support, be it the social security system or marriage/family arrangements, and budgetary constraints.

Countries approach this task from different viewpoints not only with regard to their position in the international division of labour and the state of their economy, but with regard to their political history and culture, including the conceptions of what a family is about, what the contents of gender roles and relationships are, what the shared and 'socially legitimate' intergenerational obligations (Finch and Mason 1993) are, as well as the characteristics, role and degree of institutionalization of third sector institutions (e.g. Gidron, Kramer, Salamon 1992; Kramer 1992).[17] Thus, it is not surprising that the countries which have up to now most relied on extended family solidarity and obligations and on the gender division of labour (such as in Italy or Spain), and which experience both severe budgetary constraints and high unemployment rates, find an apparently easy solution to the growing imbalance between needs and resources in appealing on the one hand to an increased role of third sector (mostly Catholic) institutions in providing services, and on the other hand to a strengthened family solidarity, possibly supported by some kind of payment for care, although these two trends might heighten some of the problems which affect Italian society. The explicit recourse to a subsidized highly ideological third sector, in fact, may reinforce both geographical differences and inequalities in the provision of services and introduce an unbalanced 'pillarization' (in so far as only the Catholic third sector has a strong institutional backing) in the Italian welfare system. At the same time, the newly explicit familialization of caring and support duties may result in a further constraint on families', and particularly women's, options, therefore also constraining fertility, with the consequence of further aggravating the demographic imbalance. Yet, given the institutional and cultural framework and the budgetary constraints, alternative solutions/visions appear difficult to articulate in a way which may gain the consensus needed to redesign the social policy framework and its implicit pacts.

Straightforward refamilialization is a less readily available solution in countries where extended family obligations are not legitimized and supported by institutional policies, where the third sector is either weaker or more culturally diversified, and where gender relations are less asymmetrical. Certainly there are risks of a (gendered) refamilialization of obligations, as we pointed out in the case of payments for care. However, the strong culture of individual social rights and of gender equality requires that the redefinition of boundaries and obligations be carefully negotiated. At the same time, the risks of ideological pillarization or of ruthless marketization involved in the redrawing of boundaries between state and market and in the incentives given to third sector actors may be perceived differently, with the dimensions of choice and of the new role of civil society having greater play.

The discourses concerning these trends have common concerns and are framed often in the same language across very different countries. Thus concerns over choice and civil society are clearly present in Italy and concerns over marketization are present in Scandinavia. This testifies to the existence of underlying common dilemmas in these trends, as well as to the power of international discourses, sometime even promoted by international institutions such as the EU (see, e.g. its push towards subsidiarity, which is certainly neither a concept nor a practice which stems from the Scandinavian or British experience). Yet, this commonality must not hide strong internal cultural, institutional and political histories.

With this in mind the discourse itself concerning the issue of defamilialization or refamilialization of needs and entitlements needs to be reconsidered. Various authors (Hobson 1990, 1994; Orloff 1993; O'Connor, Orloff and Shaver 1999; McLaughlin and Glendinning 1994) have suggested that a useful indicator in constructing welfare state typologies might be the degree to which economic and social rights are granted to individuals of all ages and family conditions or are, alternatively, contingent on family circumstances. From this viewpoint 'defamilialization' would indicate 'the terms and conditions under which people engage in families, and the extent to which they can uphold an acceptable standard of living independently of the (patriarchal) family' (McLaughlin and Glendinning 1994: 65). In a situation, common to all industrialized countries, where family obligations rest on a smaller circle of family members, and on more fragile family ties, the extent of defamilialization might be as crucial to the welfare of individuals and families as is the strength of family obligations themselves. Defamilialization does not imply a breaking of family bonds. The issue is not whether people are completely defamilialized but rather the extent to which packages of legal and social provisions have altered the balance of power between men and women, between dependents and non-dependents and, hence, the terms and conditions under which people engage in familial caring relationships.

As a matter of fact, both the concepts of familialization and defamilialization appear less set in meaning than at a first glance. As we have seen above, both culturally and institutionally family obligations may differ in intensity and in the range of relationships involved. These are two quite distinct dimensions. Thus, while the intensity of parent–children obligations is about the same, from the legal point of view, in Germany and Italy, it is not so for the full range of institutionally defined family obligations. This in turn implies that individuals living in countries where institutional and cultural obligations cover a wider range of relationships may, on the one hand, count on a substantial source of differentiated informal resources; on the other hand, they may find themselves in competition with each other for family resources and family networks may suffer from a wider range of competing demands than in other countries.[18]

Things are even more complicated with regard to defamilialization. First, defamilialization may be the extreme consequence of lack of economic and social resources, the best exemplar being that of the slaves in the US. In more contemporary or non-slave societies, international emigrants may be a case in point, in so far as many of them cannot bring their families with them and, because of residence rules and economic constraints, have difficulties in forming a family of their own. Many Filippino or Latin-American women doing paid work in Italian households, particularly for the frail elderly, have husbands and children in their own country.[19] In other words, defamilialization may be the more or less unintended consequence of the functioning of the economy, of the labour market, as well as of rules concerning the right of immigrants. To a less dramatic degree this is apparent also in the impact of working time schedules in the possibility of participating in family life. Usually this phenomenon is seen as visible when wives and mothers enter the labour market, in so far as they have less (or no) time for daily family life: caring for children, preparing meals, catering to their husbands, caring for relatives. But the defamilialization of men (as well as the familialization of women and children) was the main principle on which the 'traditional' family was constructed in modern times. This means that policies oriented to re-familialize or defamilialize might have a quite different meaning for men and women, for different class and ethnic groups, as well as for countries in which these processes have a different history and have reached a different point. Thus, while payments for care in the form of substitution of income benefits for social services in the case of small children may encourage the persistence of a strong gender division of labour within the family, particularly within the low income strata, policies providing incentives for fathers to take leave to care for their children may be read as an attempt at refamilializing men in a more gender-equal framework (see also Leira 1998). In general the introduction of family-linked paid leaves of absence for men and women may be interpreted as a way of acknowledging family obligations in a context characterized by strong work attachments and participation, therefore in acknowledging that the social rights of citizens should not concern only their rights as (paid) workers. Finally, defamilialization in the sense of allocating part of traditional duties and responsibilities to actors other than the family may occur in different ways and directions: through the allocation to the public sphere, but also to the third sector and to the market. These are not neutral moves, but neither are they unambiguous in their meaning, depending rather on national and local cultures and circumstances, the resources of specific social groups and so forth (see also O'Connor, Orloff and Shaver 1999).

This focuses on the question of what supporting the family might mean. If it means enabling the family and its members to take care of each other, to shoulder the obligations they freely choose to enter into, without, at the same time, creating power imbalances, overdependencies and no-exit loops, a degree of defamilialization both of women's obligations and of dependent family members' needs and rights might become the basis on which new individual–family–state contracts may be negotiated. At the same time, however, the right to care – as well as to be cared for – should be acknowledged as a part of social, citizenship rights, for men as well as for women (Knijn and Kremer 1997). On the contrary, over-familialization, or forced refamilialization of responsibilities and of individual rights, may result either in an overburdening of the family which might in turn cause further social problems (e.g. poverty, social exclusion), or in a refusal to assume family obligations at all – be it through (un)reproductive behaviour, or through a refusal to fulfil one's obligations towards adult family members needing support. Abandonment and institutionalization of the handicapped and the frail elderly may be the, still rare, reaction to obligations framed in exclusively familial terms, with the state intervening only as a last resort, not as a strong, and 'normal' partner.

Another possible perverse effect of overfamilialization in the provision of resources and services and in the definition of interpersonal obligations, is tax revolt and tax evasion. One might reflect on the fact that those countries where the degree of defamilialization is lowest are also those where tax revolt is more vocal and sometimes tax evasion higher: overfamilialization might mean also an inability to create the basis for social responsibility, in a contemporary re-edition of the perverse social effects of 'amoral familialism'. The recourse to self-help, volunteer, non-profit groups from this point of view, in the absence of a clear framework of social, citizenship rights and obligations, is no solution. First, in fact, it may increase the discretionary use and offer of resources, therefore increasing local and social differences and inequalities between individuals and between families; second, analogously to intra-family solidarity, it may easily stand side by side with a low degree of social integration and solidarity beyond that of the small, chosen group. Actually, in cultural and political contexts in which the institutional and symbolic framework of citizenship is weak, volunteer associations and activities may act in two, opposite, directions: as a means of activating a civic culture of rights and obligations and as a means of offering self-righteous excuses for not developing such a culture, remaining instead among one's own 'chosen', or peers. It may even represent a way of strengthening family power relations and family dependencies. This is particularly clear in the case of childcare services and of the school: in so far as the state and the public sector, in the name of 'family (actually parents') choice' move from directly providing services to financing private – market or third sector – ones, or to offering families a voucher to buy what they prefer, this means acknowledging parents' absolute right to decide which education to offer to their children well beyond the first years of life and over the rights of children themselves. At the same time it strengthens cultural rifts and class and geographical differences

To be sure, social and policy trends are not spontaneously generated. Rather they are the outcome and the context of interactions and sometimes conflict between various social actors, as well as of individual behaviour at the micro level. In these interactions new actors, as well as new meanings may be shaped. What is clear is that what the family is or should be and what obligations should be expected in gender and intergenerational relations within it, are increasingly at the core of social policy and of the process of drawing, and redrawing, boundaries between social spheres and actors, of acknowledging needs and rights and of allocating responsibilities and resources.

Notes

1 I have developed this historical account in *Politiche sociali e famiglie*, to be published in the final volume of *The History of European Families* edited by M. Barbagli and D. Kertzer (forthcoming) and jointly published by Laterza and Yale University Press. Parts of the information collected for this chapter have been developed for a paper presented at the OECD High level conference on 'Beyond 2000. The social policy agenda'. See Saraceno 1997.

2 Even Esping-Andersen (1999) in his last book sounds more ambivalent with regard not only to his own typologies, but to the degree to which these are useful in understanding the working of specific welfare states, and at times seems to suggest the need to go back to detailed case studies.

3 See e.g. Ostner 1994. The case of France is possibly an exception, since the generous support given through the allocation to the *parent isolée* is mainly motivated by a focus on children's needs and welfare. The time mothers receiving it are allowed not to be available for work is also shorter than in the UK or the Netherlands: until the youngest child is 3.

4 At the same time they do not provide any support for poor households whose income does not derive primarily from wages or who have no income, even if there are children.

5 i.e. taking into account that the same overall household income costs more if it is earned by two rather than one worker; and that if the second earner is the wife-mother, there is an additional cost in terms of reduced availability of non-commodified goods produced through family work. On the gender-specific risks of means-testing on the basis of household income see also Holland 1993; Gambardella 1998; Saraceno 1998.

6 See Gornick *et al.* 1997; Hantrais and Mangen 1994; Hantrais and Letablier 1996.

7 In any case it should be kept in mind that in Italy there is a wide geographical variation both in fertility rates and in women's labour force participation: the fertility rate is lowest, and the labour force participation is highest in the centre-north, where childcare services are also more numerous.

8 Bradshaw *et al.*'s (1996) figures, based on OECD data, are in fact different from those offered by Esping-Andersen (1999: 152), based on LIS data. On mothers' and lone mothers' labour-market participation see also the chapters by Boje and Almqvist, Gornick, and Larsen in this book.

9 In Italy, but also in Spain, legally enforced financial obligations extend to adult children, parents, parents in law, siblings (including adult siblings). See also Naldini 1999.

10 Depending on the taxation system, these may take the form of family quotient as in France, where the family and not the individual is the subject of taxation, or of tax deductions where the married couple (as in Germany) or the individual is the subject of taxation.

11 Moreover, researchers point out that joint custody might have adverse effects when one of the parents is abusive, or violent, restricting the ability of the other parent to reconstruct a more viable life for her/himself and her/his children – which is probably the main reason why the couple broke up to begin with.

12 This differentiation between the two countries is recent. They looked much closer on this subject ten years ago, before the UK government passed the recent law on child

support. This different development might be taken as an indicator of the different definition of the family in the two countries, which dates back at least to the beginning of the century: with the British focusing more on marriage and on 'proper' gender relationships, while the French focus more on children. See Pedersen 1993, Saraceno forthcoming

13 In the case of Norway this concerns only childcare for the under 3s. Coverage for children between 3 and 6 is similar to that of other Scandinavian countries.

14 We refer here to caring obligations and services. In these countries, in fact, there is a minimum income guarantee for the elderly, in the form of a means-tested social pension for those who are not entitled even to a minimum, contributory, work pension. The disabled elderly, analogously to all the severely disabled, are also entitled to a non means-tested accompanying indemnity.

15 In the Netherlands home care, granted universally on the basis of severity of need, is financed not out of the public budget but through a compulsory insurance, similar to that first introduced in Germany. See Knijn 1998.

16 Another area is that of accompanying and social integration measures for the poor or the long-term unemployed.

17 Third sector enterprises and provisions include both voluntary agencies and non profit ones. Therefore services providers within the third sector may be either unpaid for volunteers or paid for workers. Recent developments in this field witness both shifting boundaries within this sector between volunteer and non profit organizations, with an increasing role of the latter (or transformation of the former into the latter), as well as the presence of a mix between volunteer and unpaid work in both. Women are highly present among volunteers, particularly those performing social work. For the Italian case see Barbetta 1996.

18 It should be noticed that this distinction between intensity and width is not always clear in debates over 'familism' (and amoral familism) since Banfield's (1958) influential work. As a matter of fact, families studied by Banfield in Montegrano were far from adhering to the stereotype of the large southern Italian family. They were nuclear families where each household maximized the resources to its own members, with little solidarity across kin networks.

19 At the same time, they – as traditionally Italian emigrants did – may use their kin networks to help them emigrate.

References

Anttonen, A. and Sipilä, J. (1996) 'European Social Care Services: Is it Possible to Identify Models?', *Journal of European Social Policy*, Vol. 2: pp. 87–100.

Arendell, T. (1995) *Fathers and Divorce*, Thousand Oaks, Cal.: Sage.

Banfield, E. (1958) *The Moral Basis of a Backward Society*, New York: The Free Press.

Barbagli, M. and Saraceno, C. (1998) *Separarsi in Italia*, Bologna: il Mulino.

Barbetta, G.P. (ed.) (1996) *Senza scopo di lucro*, Bologna: il Mulino.

Bradshaw, J., Ditch J., Holmes H. and Whiteford P. (1993) *Support for Children: a Comparison of Arrangements in Fifteen Countries*, London: HMSO.

Bradshaw, J. *et al.* (1996) *The Employment of Lone Parents: a Comparison of Policy in 20 Countries*, London: Family Policy Studies Centre.

Daly, M. and Lewis, J. (1998) 'Introduction: Conceptualising Social Care in the Context of Welfare Restructuring', in Lewis (ed.), pp. 1–24, Aldershot: Ashgate.

Ditch, J., Barnes, H., Bradshaw, J. (eds) (1996) *A synthesis of national family policies, 1995*, Brussels: European Observatory of National Family Policies.

Esping-Andersen, G. (1999) *Social Foundations of Post-Industrial Economies*, Oxford: Oxford University Press.

Esping-Andersen, G. (1990) *The Three Worlds of Welfare Capitalism*, Cambridge: Polity Press.

Evers, A., Pijl M., Ungerson C. (eds) (1993) *Payments for Care. a Comparative Overview*, Aldershot: Avebury.

Evers, A. and Svetlik, I. (eds) (1993) *Balancing Pluralism, New Welfare Mixes in Care for the Elderly*, Aldershot: Avebury.

Facchini, C. and Scortegagna, R. (1993) 'Italy: Alternatives to Institutionalization and Women's Central Role', in Leseman and Martin, pp. 33–69.

Fagnani, J. (1994) 'A Comparison of Family Policies for Working Mothers in France and West Germany', in Hantrais and Mangen (eds).

Fagnani, J., Rassat, E. (1997) 'Garde d'enfant et/ou femme à tout faire?', *Les employées des familles bénéficiaires de l'aged*, no. 49, September.

Gambardella, D. (1998) *Chi guadagna e chi spende*, Napoli: Descartes.

Gauthier, A.H. (1996) *The State and the Family: a Comparative Analysis of Family Policies in Industrial Countries*, Oxford: Clarendon Press.

Gidron, B., Kramer, R.M., Salamon, L.S. (eds) (1992) *Government and Third Sector. Emerging Relationships in Welfare States*, San Francisco: Jossey-Bass.

Gornick, J. *et. al.* (1997) 'Supporting the Employment of Mothers: Policy Variation Across Fourteen Welfare States', *Journal of European Social Policy*, VII, 1, 45–70.

Hantrais, L. and Letablier, M.-T. (1996) *Familles, travail et politiques familiales en Europe*, Cahiers du Centre d'Etudes de l'Emploi, Noissy-le-Grand: Presses Universitaires de France.

Hantrais, L. and Mangen, S. (eds) (1994) *Family Policy and the Welfare of Women*, Loughborough: Cross-national research papers.

Hobson, B. (1990) 'No Exit No Voice: Women's Economic Dependency and the Welfare State', *Acta Sociologica*, 33: 235–50.

Hobson, B. (1994) 'Lone Mothers, Social Policy Regimes and the Logic of Gender', in Sainsbury (ed.), pp. 170–87.

Holland, S. (1993) *The European Imperative. Economic and Social Cohesion in the 1990s*, (Nottingham, England, Spokesman Bertrand Russell House.)

Höllinger, F. and Haller, M. (1990) 'Kinship and Social Networks', *European Sociological Review*, 6, 2: 103–24.

James, E. (ed.) (1989) *The Non-Profit Sector in International Perspective*, Oxford: Oxford University Press.

Jensen, A.M. (1999) 'Partners and Parents in Europe: a Gender Divide', in Leira (ed.), pp. 1–30.

Knijn, T. (1994) 'Fish Without Bikes: Revision of the Dutch Welfare State and its Consequences for the (In)dependence of Single Mothers', *Social Politics*, I, 1 (Spring): 83–105.

Knijn, T. (1998) 'Social Care in the Netherlands', in Lewis (ed.), pp. 85–110.

Knijn, T. and Kremer M. (1997) 'Gender and the Caring Dimension of Welfare States: Toward Inclusive Citizenship', *Social Politics*, IV, 3: 328–61.

Kramer, R.M. (1992) 'The Roles of Voluntary Social Service Organizations in Four European States: Policies Trends in England, the Netherlands, Italy and Norway', in S. Kuhnle and P. Selle (eds) *Government and Voluntary Organizations*, Brookfield: Edward Elgar.

Kurz, D. (1995) *For Richer, For Poorer: Mothers Confront Divorce*, New York: Routledge.

Langan, M. and Ostner, I. (1991) 'Gender and Welfare: Towards a Comparative Framework', in Room G. (ed.) *Towards a European Welfare State?*, pp. 127–50, Bristol: SAUS.

Le Grand, J. and Bartlett, W. (1993) *Quasi-Markets and Social Policy*, London: Macmillan.

Leira, A. (1998) 'Caring as a Social Right: Cash for Childcare and Daddy Leave', *Social Politics*, autumn, pp. 362–78.

Leira, A. (1993) 'The 'Woman-Friendly' Welfare State? The Case of Norway and Sweden', in Lewis (ed.), pp. 49–71.

Leira, A. (1992) *Welfare States and Working Mothers. The Scandinavian Experience*, Cambridge: Cambridge University Press.

Leira, A. (1999) 'Introduction', to Leira (ed.), *Family change, practices, policies and values*, pp. ix-xxii, Stamford, Conn.: JAI Press.

Leseman, F. and Martin, C. (eds) (1998) *Les personnes âgées. Dépendence, soins et solidaritées familiales. Comparisons internationales. Les Etudes de La Documentation Française*, Paris.

Lewis, J. (1992) 'Gender and the Development of Welfare Regimes', *Journal of European Social Policy*, II, 3: 159–73.

Lewis, J. (1997) 'Gender and Welfare Regimes: Further Thoughts', *Social Politics*, IV, 2: 160–77.

Lewis, J. (ed.) (1998) *Gender, Social Care and Welfare State Restructuring in Europe*, London: Ashgate.

Lewis, J. and Åström G. (1992) 'Equality, Difference and State Welfare: Labour Market and Family Policies in Sweden', *Feminist Studies*, XVIII, 1: 59–87.

Lewis, Jane (ed.) (1993) *Women and Social Policies in Europe: Work, Family and the State*, Cheltenham: Edward Elgar.

Martin, C. (1995) 'Father, Mother and the Welfare State. Family and Social Transfers after Marital Breakdown', *Journal of Social Policy*, 5, 1: 43–63.

Martin, C. (1997) *L'après divorce. Lien familial et vulnérabilité*, Rennes: PUR.

McLaughlin, E. and Glendinning, C. (1994) 'Paying for Care in Europe: Is There a Feminist Approach?', in Hantrais and Mangen (eds).

Millar, J. and Warman, A. (1996) *Defining Family Obligations in Europe. The family, the State and Social Policy*, report to the Joseph Rowntree Foundation.

Naldini, M. (1999) *Evolution of Social Policy and the Institutional Definition of Family Models. The Italian and Spanish Cases in Historical and Comparative Perspective*, PhD thesis, EUI, Florence, October.

O'Connor, J.S., Orloff, A.S. and Shaver, S. (1999) *States, Markets and Families*, Cambridge: Cambridge University Press.

OECD (1994) *Caring for Frail Elderly People*, Social Policy Studies, no. 14. Paris: OECD.

OECD (1996) *Caring for Frail Elderly People. Policies in Evolution*, Social Policy Studies, no. 19. Paris: OECD.

OECD (1990) *Lone Parents: the Economic Challenge*, Paris: OECD.

Orloff, A. (1993) 'Gender and the Social Rights of Citizenship: State Policies and Gender Relations in Comparative Research', *American Sociological Review*, 58, 3: 303–28.

Ostner, I. (1994) 'Back to the Fifties: Gender and Welfare in Unified Germany', *Social Politics*, I, 1 (Spring): 32–60.

Phillips, A. and Moss, P. (1998) *Who Cares for Europe's Children?*, report of the European Childcare Network, Brussels: Commission of the European Communities.

Sainsbury, D. (1996) *Gender, Equality and Welfare States*, Cambridge: Cambridge University Press.

Sainsbury, D. (ed.) (1994) *Gendering Welfare State*, London: Sage.

Saraceno, C. (1994) 'The Ambivalent Familism of the Italian Welfare State', *Social Politics*, I, 1 (Spring): 32–59.

Saraceno, C. (1997) 'Family Change, Family Policies and the Restructuring of Welfare', *Family, Market and Community*, Social Policy Studies, no. 21: 81–100. Paris: OECD.

Saraceno, C. (1998) *Mutamenti della famiglia e politiche sociali in Italia*, Bologna: il Mulino.

Scheiwe, K., 'Labour Market, Welfare State and Family Institutions: the Links to Mothers' Poverty Risks', *Journal of European Social Policy*, vol. 4, no. 3: 201–34.

Seltzer, J.A. (1991) 'Legal Custody Arrangements and Children's Economic Welfare', *American Journal of Sociology*, vol. 96, 4: 895–929.

Sørensen, A. (1999) 'Family Decline, Poverty and Social Exclusion: the Mediating Effects of Family Policy', in Leira (ed.), pp. 57–78.

Therborn, G. (1993) 'The Politics of Childhood: the Rights of Childhood in Modern Times', in F.G. Castles (ed.) *Families of Nations: Patterns of Public Policy in Western Democracies*, Aldershot: Dartmouth.

Twigg, J. (ed.) (1993) *Informal Care in Europe*, York: University of York Social Policy Research Unit.

Ungerson, C. (1997) 'Social Politics and the Commodification of Care', *Social Politics*, IV, 3: 362–82.

Waerness, K. (1998) 'The Changing "Welfare Mix" in Childcare and in Care for the Elderly', in Lewis (ed.), pp. 207–28.

7 Combining work and family

Nordic policy reforms in the 1990s

Arnlaug Leira

Introduction

Ever since the mid-1950s when Alva Myrdal and Viola Klein (1956) advocated married women's right to enter employment, questions concerning the combination of work and family responsibilities have become increasingly important in social research in the Scandinavian countries, and central issues in policy reform.[1] For decades the model family of industrialism centred around the male breadwinner and the female homemaker/carer has been declining, and replaced by the dual-earner family as numerically the dominant family form. Women's labour market participation has increased dramatically, as evidenced in particular in the mass entry of mothers into the labour market. However, these processes are not unique to the Nordic countries; in the 1990s the increase in mothers' participation rates is registered across the welfare states of the West. The emergence of the dual-earner family shows empirically how the relationship between production and social reproduction is being changed, transforming the everyday time structures as well as the gender balance of employment.

This shift in family form is often regarded as necessitating the intervention of the welfare state in order to 'harmonize' work and family obligations. Yet, in several countries motherhood change has preceded welfare state reform (Leira 1992; see also EC Childcare Network 1996), and the problems of reconciling waged work and childcare have not all been resolved. Increasingly, however, the questions are being politicized and entered on the political agenda, not only of individual welfare states, but also of the European Union. Moreover, the combination of work and family is gradually being redefined from being a women's issue only, to represent a concern of working parents, both fathers and mothers (EC Childcare Network 1994; OECD 1995).

This chapter discusses recent policy approaches of the Nordic welfare states towards the combination of job and family commitments of both mothers and fathers. Generally speaking, the reconciliation of employment and childcare has been addressed by three sets of policies that may roughly be interpreted as interlinked with different family models:

- the cash for childcare schemes (or home care allowance) that promote or sustain the traditional gender-differentiated family;

- state-sponsoring of childcare which facilitates the employment of mothers and the dual-earner family;
- legislation concerning paid maternity, paternity and parental leave, which supports dual-earner and care-sharing parenthood (Leira 1998).

While policy analysis has dealt more with the employment rates of mothers, the main focus of my discussion is on policies that affect the gendered division of paid and unpaid work and care at home, and care for children in particular. The chapter examines the two seemingly contradictory developments in policies related to the combination of work and family, the cash benefits for childcare and the 'daddy leave'. Special attention is paid to the parental leave and the father's quota, potentially very radical reforms, projecting as they do an image of fathers as both economic providers and carers for children. Drawing upon data from Finland, Denmark and Sweden, the core material for the presentation is based on the Norwegian experience.[2]

The state and working parents

During the 1970s and early 1980s, the first and foremost gender equality project of the Nordic welfare states was to encourage women's integration in the labour market. By the early 1990s in Denmark, Finland, Norway and Sweden, women's labour market participation was approaching that of men, and the participation rates of mothers of pre-schoolers ranged from 84 per cent in Denmark to about 75 per cent in Norway (EC Childcare Network 1996; NORD 1998). Obviously, family patterns and practices were changing, and actualizing the political debates concerning the combination of wage-work and childcare. Taking up employment, Nordic mothers challenged the traditional division of labour by gender; a beginning of motherhood change that preceded the institution of expansive state-supported child-care and generous parental leave schemes. At first, the transformation of motherhood apparently made little impact on the practices of fathers. However, small-scale studies from all the four countries indicate that from the late 1980s/early 1990s new models of motherhood are being accompanied by shifts in the making of fatherhood (e.g. Näsman 1990; Brandth and Kvande 1993; Carlsen 1993; Sundberg 1993; see also Forsberg 1993). In Norway, time budget studies from three decades demonstrate that fathers in the 1990s on average spend more time with their children than fathers in the past, but the participation of fathers at home and with children does not equal the time spent by mothers in employment or the time mothers spend with children (Kitterød and Lømo 1996). Moreover, Norwegian fathers of young children belong to those categories of employees who work the longest weekly hours (Ellingsæter 1990).

In Denmark, Finland, Sweden and Norway state-sponsored day-care for children and parental leave policies facilitate the combination of employment and childcare. However, this is not to say that reproduction policies have developed according to one Nordic master plan (Leira 1992). Discussing the parental leaves schemes of eight European countries, Bruning and Plantenga (1999) argue that Denmark, Finland and Sweden represent three different models when it comes to childcare arrangements. The obvious similarities may sometimes mask notable differences when it comes to how the policy package is made up, and the eligibility requirements, coverage and rationales of different schemes. Sweden has introduced the more generous parental leave scheme, which is still, after some cutbacks, extensive by Nordic comparison. In the mid-1990s entitlements were to 450 days of leave altogether, including maternity, paternity and parental leave, of which 360 days are given with wage compensation of 75–80 per cent, the remaining days at a flat, lower rate (for details, see Bekkengen 1996). For older pre-school children Sweden aims to accommodate all children whose parents wish it in publicly sponsored day-care. Compared with the other Nordic countries, Denmark offers a relatively short period of paid maternity and parental leave following the birth of a child, twenty-four weeks, but is the top provider when it comes to publicly sponsored childcare for the under threes. A childcare leave (*børnepasningsorlov*) facilitates a prolongation of the parental leave (see Rostgaard 2000 for details about the Danish provisions). Finland's paid parental leave is more extensive than Denmark's, and a cash benefit (home care allowance) offers the opportunity to prolong the leave of absence by giving parents a choice between a place in state-sponsored day-care or receiving the cash transfer. The proportion of children under 3 accommodated in publicly sponsored day-care has since decreased (Salmi 2000). The Norwegian leave scheme in connection with pregnancy and the birth of a child covers fifty-two weeks with wage compensation at 80 per cent. The Norwegian policy package at present is the only one in the Scandinavian region which both includes a cash benefit for childcare and reserves a special period of the parental leave for fathers.

From the early 1970s, relatively early on in the process of mothers turning towards paid employment, Denmark, Finland and Sweden introduced comprehensive state-sponsoring of childcare services. In Norway provision developed more slowly, but has been gaining ground. In 1996 almost half of all Danish children under 3 years of age attended publicly funded day-care. For Sweden it is about 40 per cent, and in Finland and Norway about 25 per cent. For children aged from 3 to school age, provision is higher in all the countries. Sweden and Denmark were the top providers, offering places to more than 80 per cent of all children in the age group, while Norway accommodated 75 per cent and Finland 63 per cent (NORD 1998: 62).

In the Nordic countries, as in the EU member states, legislation has been instituted to promote the carer aspects of fatherhood. The concept of 'maternity leave' has been expanded and transformed to include the right of fathers to care for an infant. The right of fathers to share the leave period was introduced first in Sweden in 1974 to be followed later by the other countries. In the 1990s Norway and Sweden have further promoted fatherhood reform via the introduction of a special quota for fathers in the parental leave scheme.

In addition, policy reforms have also facilitated more traditional family forms, as seen in the cash benefits for childcare legislated in Finland, Sweden and

Norway, although in Sweden this scheme was in existence for only a short period of time (see Leira 1998 for details).

Thus, during the 1990s in Norway, welfare state intervention in relation to the combination of work and family has taken different forms. The former Labour government aimed at providing state-sponsored places in childcare for all children whose parents wished for it by the year 2000, and provision of new places has been stimulated; the period of paid leave in connection with the birth of a child has been expanded and fathers' rights to care for a young child strengthened by the 'daddy quota' mentioned above. The most recent addition to the 'family policy package' is the cash transfer for childcare, introduced by a centre minority coalition government with support by political parties to the right.

The different reception of the two later reforms deserves to be mentioned: The daddy quota, a reform aiming to change the gender division of labour at home and projecting the image of fathers as capable carers, met with little political opposition in Norway, although when first debated in Sweden in the 1970s it was opposed (Karlsson 1996). The proposal for reform was shelved, and not revived until the 1990s. In the 1990s, in Norway, changing fatherhood apparently was not really a hot political issue, perhaps because the fathers' quota was regarded more as 'token politics' than as an important challenge to the gender balance in paid and unpaid work. Or, perhaps new norms concerning masculinity in the family setting and in the field of employment had been spreading and preparing the ground for new ways of perceiving fatherhood.

The proposal for a cash benefit scheme, on the other hand, caused heated political debate when introduced in Norway, as similar schemes had done earlier in Finland, and Sweden. This is hardly surprising, considering that the cash benefit was regarded by critics as a break with the gender equality policies in which women's access to the labour market was an important aim and the provision of state-sponsored, high-quality childcare a means to that end, in addition to being regarded as advantageous for children.

The discussion surrounding the introduction of cash for childcare schemes in Finland, Sweden and Norway highlights political conflicts when it comes to family values and which family models to support; the ones in which mothers stay at home, or the ones in which they are employed. In the 1980s and 1990s, parties to the Centre and Right in Finland, Norway and Sweden have advocated more direct economic subsidies to families with young children, while the Social Democrats and parties to the left argue more strongly for women's rights to economic independence and for state-sponsored high-quality childcare and parental leave.

Cash benefits for childcare

From 1998 the Norwegian cash benefit scheme includes families with children aged 12–36 months (for the first year after birth childcare arrangements presumably being provided via the parental leave legislation and the lump sum paid to the mothers who do not qualify for paid leave of absence from work).

The cash benefit is not means- or needs-tested and does not have to be reported for taxation. Cash transfers for childcare are instituted with different rationales in different countries. In Norway the intentions of the scheme recently legislated are three-fold:

- to ensure families have more time to care for their own children;
- to give families a real choice with respect to which form of care they select;
- to provide greater equity between families with respect to the state subsidies received for childcare regardless of the form of care used (Ot. prp. no. 56, 1997–98: 1).

As has been pointed out in the discussion preceding legislation, these aims may conflict. One intention of the scheme is to give families more time for children, but the cash benefit scheme does not state that the parents have to care for the child on a full-time basis, the only condition being that the child does not attend state-sponsored day-care. Since parents are free to use the cash transfer as they please, it is not really framed as a measure specifically related to caring; for the families eligible it rather adds to the universal child benefit. Some of the families receiving the benefit may opt for private and/or informal childcare arrangements while keeping up their employment or other activities, e.g. education, and not spend more time with their children. However, for some parents the cash benefit may work as intended, and offer more choice with respect to staying at home, for example, by reducing the costs of a prolonged leave of absence or making reduced working hours economically more feasible. In such cases and for those parents who had intended to stay at home anyway, the cash benefit may be interpreted as a compensation for income not earned, or as a 'caring wage'.

In the Norwegian debate it has been argued that the cash for childcare scheme may reduce some inequalities between families with one and two incomes, and between those families who use state-sponsored day-care for their children and those who do not. The proposal for the Act concerning cash benefits for parents with children aged 12–36 months, as noted above, states that the scheme is to equalize the subsidies families receive for childcare. Paying in cash a sum that equals state-sponsoring of a place in day-care to families who do not make use of such a place is said to offer all families with young children better opportunities to choose between forms of childcare. Critical voices have pointed out that it is fairly unusual to promote equity by subsidizing the non-use of a public good, and, needless to say, to make the parental choice a real one a sufficient supply of extra-familial childcare is needed. Unlike the reform in Finland that gave parents a real choice between a place in publicly funded childcare or a home care allowance, the Norwegian scheme does not make it mandatory for local authorities to provide a place in publicly funded childcare if that is the preference of the parents. Since state-sponsored, high-quality childcare is not universally available, and demand in several places exceeds supply, real choice is limited.

Often advocated in gender-neutral terms, choice does not appear as an option for the majority of fathers, since for most families income would generally be more reduced if fathers were to stay at home with the children. Thus, it is unlikely that the reform will contribute to fathers spending more time with children. In effect, parental choice may also encourage or sustain a traditional gendered division of labour. Since payment is far below income from even a low-paid job (as is the case for the present scheme in Norway) the arrangement presupposes additional income, that is, a breadwinner who takes on the main responsibility for economic provision. The cash benefit has been interpreted as the state's gift to the men (Andenæs 1997). The experience from Finland shows that the home care allowance is predominantly taken up by women (Sipilä 1995). In an assessment of the Finnish scheme, Sipilä and Korpinen (1998: 276) observe 'that it has been interesting to see just how extensively generous cash benefits could seem to change the traditional Scandinavian model of wage-earner motherhood'. This may be overstating the case (Salmi, personal communication 1998) and, in any case, the impact of the Norwegian reform may be different from the Finnish, i.e. because the reforms are differently structured, and, unlike in Finland, unemployment rates in Norway have been low in the period following the reform. However, the cash benefit scheme as such entails very little change in traditional family arrangements as regards the combination of economic provision and childcare. To modify the male breadwinner/female carer family model is not a stated aim of this reform, but may rather support its continuation.

Some studies conducted prior to legislation indicate that the cash transfer for childcare may influence the time use of parents, especially mothers, at home and at work. According to one study commissioned by the Ministry of Children and Family Affairs in which parents have been asked about their plans, three out of four of the parents with children in the age group eligible, that is the 1- and 2-year-olds, stated that they intended to use the cash benefit. Of this group, 63 per cent reported that the parents would look after the children, 23 per cent planned to make use of a child-minder, 5 per cent opted for playgrounds or private arrangements and some were not yet decided. According to the reports, the mother is typically the 'cash transfer parent'. Among the families who plan to take up the cash benefit, 86 per cent reported that the mother was to be the main or only carer, 11 per cent planned for the parents to share childcare, and only in 3 per cent of the families did the fathers plan to stay at home with the children (St. prp. 53, 1997–98: 28–29).

Another survey conducted by Statistics Norway among mothers with children in the cash benefit age group gives more detailed information about the plans for take-up. Approximately 60 per cent of the mothers intended to make use of the cash benefit. Of these, one in three will reduce working hours, 28 per cent will stay at home, and the others have no plans for changing their hours in employment (Rønning 1998). Among employed mothers, 56 per cent expected to reduce their working hours or stay at home full-time. A smaller share of the mothers with higher education than those with fewer qualifications planned to use the cash benefits, as did a smaller share among those with high income than those with low (Hellevik 1999). If the parents are to practice as they plan, 'the result will be a decline in the share of children below school age with a place in a day-care centre for the first time since the start of the 1970s, and an increase in the share of children who are minded by a child-minder for the first time in the 1990s.' (Hellevik 1999: 71.)

So far, however, little is known in detail about the ways in which the cash transfer has actually influenced parents' management of work and family obligations, which families do make use of it or how it is used. Since one of the aims stated was to increase parents' time with their children it is, of course, of interest to know more about take-up, for example whether the cash benefit is used for a prolonged job break, or to reduce parents' working hours, and also about which forms of childcare are in fact being subsidized, for example, the care by parents, by child-minders, nannies, relatives and friends or others. According to the National Insurance Office approximately 70–80 per cent of families with children in the age group eligible receive the cash. However, local take-up varies, which may have to do with variations in women's access to the labour market, and the local provision and cost of publicly sponsored childcare as well as differences with respect to motherhood and family values. The take-up rate indicates that parental (most likely maternal) time with children may have increased. It may also indicate that the demand for childcare is channelled from the use of state-sponsored services (the full-time use of which excludes access to the cash benefit) to informal, unregistered services for which the costs may be covered by the non-taxable cash transfer. (When a 1999 survey conducted by Statistics Norway, a follow-up of the one done in 1998, is analysed, more information on this and a number of other issues will be available.)

Some recent developments are registered in childcare statistics. For the first time in years the annual production of new places in publicly sponsored childcare is reduced from 16,400 in 1997 to 3,350 in 1998. Altogether there is a slight increase in the proportion of children aged 0–5 years who attend state-sponsored day-care, from 51 per cent in 1997 to 52 per cent in 1998 (Ukens statistikk 25/99: 3). A number of childcare services in private ownership have closed down, or may have to, due to economic problems (*Aftenposten*, 24 June 1999). Moreover, newspapers report that the informal labour market in childminding is flourishing (*Aftenposten*, 27 February 1999), but systematic data are not yet available. Government plans for 1999 indicate only 2,500 places as the aim of production for 1999 (Ministry of Children and Family Affairs, St. prp. 1, 1998–99: 136). The reduction in the provision of new places may signal that the aim formerly stated, of providing places in state-sponsored childcare for all children whose parents wish for it, may not be met in the year 2000. However, the government is probably right when stating that the cash transfer will reduce the demand for places in state-sponsored day-care. Still, the problem of a real choice for parents with respect to which form of childcare they prefer is not solved, as long as the supply of such childcare does not meet the demand.

Access to day-care for children is not only about available places but also about affordable prices. An OECD (1999) expert group examining the development in early childhood education and care, and reporting on a number of issues, comments on the high parental fees in state-sponsored childcare in Norway, adding that the pricing policies may disadvantage children from families with low income when it comes to access. The report also points to the possibility that the cash transfer may increase existing inequalities between children in this respect.

Parental leave

From the mid-1970s, the Nordic welfare states introduced an important reconceptualization of the state/market/family relationship, in the form of expanded entitlements to paid leave of absence in connection with the birth of a child.[3] Generally, these leaves give priority to the demands of social reproduction over those of production, they establish the primacy of parental obligation to children's care over the demands of the workplace, and they facilitate the combination of work and family obligations for both parents. Fathers as well as mothers are included in legislation that connects the concepts of 'worker' and 'carer' (Leira 1992). The legislation provides an interesting example of welfare state intervention in the general framework for employment to include the childcare responsibilities of wage-workers, and not leaving the care commitments solely to individual arrangements or negotiations between the labour market parties (see also Ellingsæter and Rønsen 1996; Bekkengen 1996).

In Norway, since 1993, employed parents have been entitled to leave of absence for forty-two weeks with 100 per cent wage compensation or fifty-two weeks at 80 per cent, while retaining job security and social security rights. (In accordance with the general rules of the National Insurance scheme there is a maximum limit to wage compensation.) Following the paid parental leave each of the parents is entitled to one year of unpaid leave, with job security. (For an overview of different forms of leave related to the combination of employment and childcare, see NOU 1995: 27; Ellingsæter and Hedlund 1998.) The rights of employed parents to leave of absence in connection with the birth of a child (or parental leave for short), comprise maternity, paternity and parental elements. Three weeks before the birth are reserved for the mother, and are lost if she does not make use of them. The six weeks following delivery are reserved for the mother, as obligatory leave. Four weeks of the total leave period, that is, the 'daddy quota', are reserved for the father. In addition to the general leave, all employed fathers are entitled to two weeks of unpaid paternity leave in connection with the birth of their child. What remains of the leave, parents have the right to share.

Apparently, Norwegian fathers were not much attracted by the right to share parental leave. When introduced in the late 1970s take-up was negligible, (perhaps because the total leave period was relatively short, eighteen weeks) and remained low later on, too, when the period of leave was gradually extended. However, the right of fathers to two weeks of leave from work when their child was born (paternity leave or 'daddy days'), rapidly became popular, even if it did not come with wage compensation in Norway. (Following collective agreements public sector employees have the right to wage compensation when taking the 'daddy days' at the birth of a child, as have some of those in private sector employment.)

According to more comprehensive overviews (EC Childcare Network 1994; OECD 1995), the right to share parental leave in countries with gender-neutral leave policies has not been much in demand by fathers; less than 5 per cent of the fathers have made use of this entitlement. Similar experiences are reported from the Nordic countries: in the early 1990s almost half of all Finnish fathers took paternity leave, but very few used the right to parental leave or the home-care allowance (EC Childcare Network 1994). In 1993 slightly more than half of Danish fathers took up the two weeks of paternity leave, but only 3 per cent used four weeks or more out of the ten weeks of parental leave that might be shared (NOU 1995: 27: 33). (However, as pointed out by Søren Carlsen (1993), parental leave statistics do not tell the whole story about the time fathers spend with their children, since arrangements for time with children are made outside the framework of the leave.) According to the OECD report, Swedish fathers provided the only exception; in 1987 one in four of the eligible fathers took up some of the leave (OECD 1995: 187). At the end of 1992, 45 per cent of the fathers of children born in 1991 had taken up the right to parental leave, spending on average 63 days of it. The proportion of leave-takers increased over time, and after the child's first year (NOU 1995: 27).

Generally speaking, parental leave is almost exclusively used by mothers, a fact that has been much debated in the Nordic countries. Some authors point to an unwillingness among mothers to allow fathers in on their traditional domain, others to the reluctance of fathers to take up female stereotyped tasks such as infant care (for a review of the Nordic discussion, see Bekkengen 1996; Einarsdottir 1998). The OECD report summarizes the socioeconomic characteristics of the Nordic fathers who made use of the right to share parental leave on a voluntary basis: they are well-educated, with permanent jobs and high income. The father's use of the leave is highly correlated with the mother's labour market attachment. A Norwegian study, examining couples' behaviour with respect to parental leave, finds 'that the user group is alike in that both the mother and the father have a high level of education and income. . . . the labour market position and the earning power of the mothers are strong . . . [and] strengthens their bargaining position in the family' (Brandth and Kvande 1993: 231).

Moreover, evidence from several countries indicates that the organization of work and workplace culture may influence fathers' use of the leave (EC Childcare Network 1994). In Norway, family economy may represent a barrier to the fathers' take-up of the leave since there is a maximum limit to wage replacement and the father's compensation is dependent on the mother's hours of employment.

Daddy quota: fatherhood by 'gentle force'

The introduction of a daddy quota in the parental leave scheme shows a very interesting development in political thinking concerning the relationship between families, labour markets and the state. Instituting a right of employed fathers to care for their children signals a new policy approach to fatherhood and gender equality; a state intervention in employment via the general work environment legislation to promote the carer aspects of fatherhood. Reserving one part of the leave for the father also represents an effort to influence the division of labour at home and to change the gender balance of caring rights and responsibilities (Leira 1998).

In both Norway and Sweden the proposal for a 'daddy leave' was argued from different perspectives, as in the best interests of father and child and as a means to promote gender equality further (see Bekkengen for a discussion of the Swedish discourse about *pappamånaden* (the daddy month) and Leira (1998) for an overview of some of the arguments used in Norway).

According to the Norwegian scheme, four weeks of the parental leave are reserved for the father, a period which may be lost to the family if he does not use it. However, fathers do not have an individual, independent right to use the parental leave or fathers' quota, the right is derived from the mother's right to paid maternity leave: that is, the father's entitlement is conditioned upon the mother's fulfillling the requirement of having been employed during the six months prior to giving birth and at a minimum of working half-time, and the father has to meet similar employment requirements. Moreover, the father's degree of wage compensation depends upon the mother's working hours. If the mother is employed less than full-time, the father's wage compensation is reduced accordingly. This construction has been repeatedly criticized and policy reform demanded to establish the independent right of fathers in relation to the parental leave scheme (e.g. NOU 1995: 27).

The 'daddy leave' is generally not transferable to the mother. If the father does not make use of the four weeks, they are lost for the family. Exceptions are made in cases in which the father is not eligible for the leave, or the mother is a single parent, or when the father has been granted a special dispensation (NOU 1995: 27: 12). Thus there are strong incentives for fathers to make use of their quota, and approximately 70 per cent of the eligible fathers do. Any fears that fathers might resent being 'pushed' to fatherhood have, so far, been proved wrong. The overall very positive response among fathers is in marked contrast to the modest take-up of the right to share parental leave on a voluntary basis which was not sufficiently tempting to bring fathers home. 'Earmarking' of part of the leave period, and not allowing for easy transfer to the mother have proved very effective when it comes to increasing the take-up rates. This is all the more remarkable, considering that the reform was not introduced as a response to demand from large groups of men or strong male-dominated organizations. The Norwegian experience with the father's quota differs from the one registered in Sweden by Sundström and Duvander (1997). In 1994, according to their study, that is before the 'daddy month' was instituted, fathers made up slightly more than 28 per cent of the parents using the leave. The fathers' share of parental leave made up only 11.4 per cent of all the days of parental leave taken. In 1996, the year following the institution of the father's month, fathers made up 31 per cent of the parental leave consumers, spending 10.1 per cent of all parental leave days taken (Sundström and Duvander 1997: Table 7.1: 7). However, as noted above, before the quota was established, the right to care for an infant was more popular among fathers in Sweden than among fathers elsewhere.

Small-scale studies of Norwegian fathers' use of the daddy quota show that fathers have accepted being gently pressured to take leave of absence. In 1996 Borghild Godal interviewed twenty fathers of new-born babies, asking about their use of the entitlement, whether they had taken it up or not, and why they had chosen as they did. The great majority of these fathers, whether quota users or not, were positive towards the reform, and found the push towards childcare a good idea. Generally, they saw it as important for fathers to spend more time with their very young children (see also Øverli 1995). The quota also made it easier for those who wanted the leave to approach employers.

In Godal's study none of the fathers who had asked for daddy leave was refused, but aspects of the work situation did influence take-up. Some of the men felt that employers were not keen on the reform. For various reasons, some of the fathers did not feel at ease about asking for leave, and had not done so. Some families experienced an income reduction, i.e. because of the ways in which fathers' wage compensation is linked with mothers' hours of employment, but gave priority to father's time with the children over income. However, some fathers did not have to make a choice in this respect, but received full wage compensation during the leave period.

Godal also reports some very interesting differences in the arrangements made by fathers and mothers for the father's leave. In some families mothers returned to work while the father was charged with the main responsibility for taking care of the infant, while other parents added the leave to their holidays and spent the leave period together. The author warns against simple conclusions such as taking the use of the quota as an indicator of fathers' involvement with their children. In her material, some of the fathers who made use of the leave were the main carers, in other cases they were rather mothers' helpers. On the other hand, some of the fathers who did not make use of the leave did 'parent-shifts' at home, taking the main responsibility for the child(ren) (Godal 1997).

The general reception of the quota is examined in a nationwide representative survey among 3,000 Norwegian men who became fathers in 1995, with 63 per cent responding (Brandth and Øverli 1998). According to this study 70 per cent of the respondents were entitled to the father's quota/parental leave; of those entitled, 78 per cent made use of their right, 22 per cent did not. Seven per cent of the respondents had been granted a dispensation, so that the right to the quota weeks was transferred to the mother. Generally, the fathers were positive about the quota, and did not much mind the gentle 'pressure' to take up caring for children. On average, the fathers responding had spent 3.9 weeks on leave, and their partners 44.1 weeks. The most common practice among the fathers was to spend four weeks on leave; among the mothers it was fifty-two weeks.

According to the reported take-up, fathers may be classified as non-users, quota users and long-leave users. Demographic characteristics such as age and number of children are of little importance when it comes to fathers' take-up of the leave, while use is correlated with socio-economic background and work-related conditions. The choice not to use the quota is often linked with work-related conditions, and with economic concerns. The non-users are more likely to be employed in the private sector, often in managerial jobs, and working long hours. An annual income above or below the average reduces the likelihood of fathers' take-up, as does temporary employment. Non-users are more likely to have partners who work part-time and have low income. What most of all reduces the likelihood of quota use is an annual income above NKr300,000 (Brandth and Øverli 1998: 36–7).

The majority of quota users were the main carers for children in the sense that the mothers had returned to full-time or part-time employment, while approximately one in three of the fathers (35 per cent) has used the quota while the mother was still at home. The main reasons for taking leave are that fathers want to spend more time with their child, and get to know their children better. Moreover, they do not want to lose any of the leave time available for the family. Fathers who have an annual income at medium/high level, who are permanently employed, in the public sector, and work normal hours are more likely to use the quota. However, the likelihood of fathers using the quota is most influenced by their partner's income and working hours. When the mother has an income above NKr200,000 and works more than thirty hours per week, the father is more likely to use the quota (Brandth and Øverli 1998: 36–7). When asked why they did not go for a longer leave period, more than 40 per cent of the fathers replied that the mothers wanted to use what remained, and about one in four reported that job concerns prevented a longer leave period.

When it comes to the long-leave users, that is, the 10 per cent of quota users who took up more than six weeks of leave and added part of the parental leave to the quota and the daddy days, they have higher education and income, relatively high-level jobs, and are predominantly employed in the public sector. In addition, their partners are relatively high-level, white collar workers, or self-employed, they work full-time and they have relatively high income (see also Gjerstad and Kvande 1998). A larger proportion of the long-leave users than of those taking shorter leave agreed that taking leave represents a threat to career advance (Brandth and Øverli 1998: 58). The report also shows that the fathers who spend the quota period or more at home are more likely to share housework and childcare with the mother.

In Norway the daddy quota appears as an important contribution to turning the trend in fathers' use of the right to care, but does not, of course, explain it all. During the 1980s and 1990s new images of fatherhood may have influenced fathers' and mothers' attitudes to fathers' caring. As indicated in research from several countries, a change in the norms constituting 'good fatherhood' and masculinity was under way in the period when the introduction of the quota was advocated (see, e.g. EC Childcare Network 1993; Leira 1998). In Norway, this is captured in popular expressions such as 'diaper-shift workers' and 'caring fathers', that is concepts of fatherhood that supplement the concept of the 'employed mother'. As mentioned above, Norwegian fathers were changing their everyday practices; time budgets show that fathers in the 1990s spent more time with their children than the fathers of the 1970s. As the quota for fathers was introduced together with a general expansion of the parental leave period, establishing a right for the fathers did not imply taking time from the mother. On the contrary, the quota added to the total leave.

When compared with the right to share the greater part of the leave period on a voluntary basis, the quota apparently did make a difference with respect to take-up. Obviously, reserving a period for the father made it easier to argue for a job break for those men who wanted to be more involved with childcare. The support of legislation which clearly states that the family loses four weeks of the parental leave if the father does not use it greatly improves the father's position when negotiating with reluctant employers, and reduces parental bargaining concerning the use of these weeks (Leira 1998). More generally, the future success of the quota, in the sense of its being used, most probably depends on labour market development and on the economic activity rates of both mothers and fathers. As long as the labour market is secure, as it is at present in Norway, and as long as taking up father's leave does not appear to interfere with the image of the 'good worker', chances are that fathers will use the right to leave of absence.

Cash for childcare and daddy leave – similar or different

At first glance, the cash for childcare and the paid parental leave may appear as rather similar, for example, both entail cash transfers to parents and a stated aim of both reforms is to increase parents' time with their children. However, as instituted in Norway, the eligibility criteria and the institutional framework of the two reforms are rather different. Despite the similarities the two sets of cash transfers also have different rationales and I have argued that the reforms represent distinctly different approaches to the combination of paid work and childcare; one implies a strengthening of the traditional gender arrangement, the other aims at challenging it by expanding on the concept of 'gender equality' to include changing not only the traditional gender balance in parental employment but also in infant care (Leira 1998). In no way underestimating the importance of these reforms for the care of children and the relationship between the child and both parents, in the following I will just touch upon some aspects having to do with gender equality, that is, the opportunities of both mothers and fathers to combine job and childcare commitments.

It is, of course, too early to assess what the combined effects of the cash for childcare and the parental leave/daddy quota will be on fatherhood, motherhood and childhood. The take-up of the father's quota and of the cash benefit as well indicates that a diversification of the ways in which work and childcare is combined is likely, and perhaps a polarization between family arrangements, with the dual-earner, care-sharing parents at one end, and gender-differentiated family arrangements of waged work and unpaid work and care on the other. However, more detailed information is needed about parents' use of the total 'policy package' aimed at work and family commitments. In a gender-equality perspective, one important question has to do with the influence of the cash benefit and parental leave on labour market attachment; for example, whether – and to what extent – the cash benefit will contribute to prolonged leaves or longer periods of reduced working hours, and whether the differences between mothers and fathers in this respect will increase. The studies referred to above indicate that the mother is the 'cash-benefit parent', and more than half of the employed mothers surveyed planned to reduce working hours or remain at home, whereas very few fathers intended to stay at home during the cash benefit period (Rønning 1998; Hellevik 1999).

Unlike the parental leave scheme, the cash benefit is not instituted with the aim of keeping up parents' (or mothers') labour market attachment and facilitating return. The gender-equality motivation of the parental leave which considers both mothers and fathers as economic providers and carers for children is absent from the cash transfer scheme. Access to parental leave and the daddy quota, on the other hand, presupposes that both mother and father have been employed prior to the birth of a child, they are both breadwinners. Eligibility for the leave presupposes previous labour market participation of some duration and the scheme offers both mothers and fathers a job break in order to care for their child. For Norwegian mothers, the right and obligation to paid leave following delivery is no news, but instituting a right for employed fathers to care in the work environment legislation represents a new approach to men's combination of job and family commitments. Moreover, a policy reform reserving part of the leave for the father represents an intervention by the state both in the general standards for employment and in family negotiations around paid and unpaid work and care. The parental leave and daddy quota signal the potentiality for comprehensive change in fathers' and mothers' approaches to employment and childcare.

In Sweden and Denmark, perhaps more than in Norway, it has been pointed out that if mothers only are to take long parental leave, they will be disadvantaged in the labour market, for example with respect to career advancement and income (Gupta and Smith 1999; Bekkengen 1996). On the other hand, Ellingsæter and Rønsen (1996) have argued that the long parental leave has encouraged and facilitated Norwegian mothers' attachment to the labour market. At first glance the positions may appear contradictory. However, in the first case, the comparison is between women and men, and in the second, the labour market prospects of women only are considered. Compared with the average use of leave among fathers, approximately four weeks, mothers on average spend forty-four weeks on leave, and may well be considered as less attractive for employers, and therefore relatively disadvantaged when it comes to career advance and income. On the other hand, the construction of the right to paid maternity and parental leave, stipulating as it does a period of labour market participation as precondition for the right to paid leave, may contribute to mothers' attachment and return to the labour market as Ellingsæter and Rønsen argue. A parental leave period of forty-four weeks or up to fifty-two weeks may in fact make return easier in a situation where high-quality state-sponsored day-care is scarce as it is for children under 3 in Norway, with provisions for the under ones being particularly meagre. Since men in general receive higher wages than women, the family is likely to have the income more reduced if men take a longer leave, thus it may be in the best interests of the household for women to be the main leave-taking parent. It does not, however, follow that it is in the long-term best interest of the mother to go for this division of labour.

For mothers working in female-dominated segments of the labour market, however, longer breaks may not represent severe barriers to later return. Several jobs considered as typically female do not offer elaborate career tracks, and taking longer leaves may not be regarded as a serious impediment to later return or career advancement as long as the labour market is secure. This applies to a number of jobs in the public sector labour market, for example, in health, education and welfare provision, such as pre-school teachers, teachers, nurses and nurses' helpers – who are much in demand.

Yet, it is worth noting, that the parental leave and daddy quota entail a right for fathers to care for a child, but not a responsibility to do so. The interrupted employment pattern, part-time work and absence for family reasons are still more associated with women's employment, and the combination of work and family still poses a dilemma more usual for women than for men. Gender equality in the labour market evidently is not what all mothers opt for; women plan for different motherhood models. However, as long as motherhood tends to outlast marriage and cohabitation and an increasing proportion of mothers experience periods as single providers, leaving the labour market for prolonged periods might, in the long run, turn out as an economic and social trap for mothers (Leira 1998). More generally, it is worth considering what Harriet Holter and Hildur Ve Henriksen wrote twenty years ago (1979: 209) 'whether the strengthening of women's position as mothers in the long run strengthen their position as women. A policy stimulating fathers to take care of their children over time may be more liberating to women.'

Notes

This chapter draws upon A. Leira (1988), 'Caring as Social Right: Cash for Childcare and Daddy Leave'. *Social Politics*, vol. 5, no 3: 362–378; and A. Leira (1999), 'Family Policy Reforms in the Scandinavian Countries: Cash for Childcare and Daddy Leave'. Paper presented at the European Seminar on Parental Leave, Brussels, January 1999.

1 In this chapter the term 'Nordic countries' is used to refer to Denmark, Finland, Norway and Sweden
2 In Norway, the right to leave of absence with wage compensation is established in the work environment legislation and the National Insurance Act (for details about the Norwegian scheme, see, e.g. NOU 1995: 27). The term 'parental leave' is sometimes used more comprehensively, to refer to all the different rights to paid and unpaid leave of absence in connection with the last weeks of pregnancy, childbirth and the early years of an infant's life, including maternity rights, paternity rights and the rights that parents may share to stay at home during the child's first year. The right to leave also includes the option for more flexible use, that is, a time account scheme, in which part-time leave and part-time work is combined. Moreover, following on the period of paid

leave, each of the parents has the right to one year of unpaid leave with job security. The term also includes the right for each parent to leave of absence when a child aged 0–12 years or the regular child-minder is ill.

3 Parental leave is sometimes used in a more restricted sense, for the special period of leave that parents may share, during the child's first year of life. In this chapter 'parental leave' is sometimes used for the scheme as a whole, some times for the part of the leave that the parents may share.

References

Aftenposten, 27 February 1999.

Aftenposten, 24 June 1999.

Andenæs, A. (1997), 'Kontantstøtte en gavepakke til mannen', in *Dagbladet*, 15 Sept 1997, Oslo.

Bekkengen, L. (1996), *Mäns föräldraledighet. En kunskapsöversikt*, Karlstad: Högskolan i Karlstad. Arbetsrapport, 96: 12.

Brandth, B. and Kvande, E. (1993), 'Changing Masculinities: The Reconstruction of Fathering', in Leira, A. (ed.) *Family Sociology – Developing the Field*, report 1993: 5, Oslo: Institute for Social Research.

Brandth, B. and Øverli, B. (1998) *Omsorgspermisjon med 'kjærlig' tvang. En kartlegging av fedrekvoten*, Trondheim: Allforsk rapport.

Bruning, G. and Plantenga, J. (1999) 'Parental Leave and Equal Opportunities: Experiences in Eight European Countries', *Journal of European Social Policy*, vol. 9 (3).

Carlsen, S. (1993) 'Men's Utilization of Paternity Leave and Parental Leave Schemes', in S. Carlsen and J. Larsen (eds) *The Equality Dilemma: Reconciling Working Life and Family Life, Viewed in an Equality Perspective*, Copenhagen: Danish Equal Status Council.

Deven, F. *et al.* (1998) *State of the Art Review on the Reconciliation of Work and Family Life for Women and Men and the Quality of Care Services*, London: Department for Education and Employment, Research Report 44.

Einarsdottir, T. (1998) *Through Thick and Thin. Icelandic Men on Paternity Leave*, Reykjavik: Committee on Gender Equality.

Ellingsæter, A.L. (1990) *Fathers Working Long Hours. Trends, Causes and Consequences*, working paper no. 2, Oslo: Institute for Social Research.

Ellingsæter, A.L. and Hedlund A.-M. (1998) *Care Resources, Employment and Gender Equality in Norway*, Oslo: Institute for Social research. Report 5.

Ellingsæter, A.L. and Rønsen, M. (1996) 'The Dual Strategy: Motherhood and the Work Contract in Scandinavia', *European Journal of Population*, 12: 239–60.

European Commission Childcare Network (1996) *A Review of Services for Young Children in the European Union 1990–1995*, Brussels: European Commission, Equal Opportunities Unit.

European Commission Childcare Network (1994) *Leave Arrangements for Workers with Children*, Brussels: European Commission, Equal Opportunities Unit.

European Commission Childcare Network (1993) *Men as Carers: Towards a Culture of Responsibilities, Sharing and Reciprocity between the Genders in the Care and Upbringing of Children*, report of a seminar held in Ravenna, 21–22 May 1993, Brussels: European Commission, Equal Opportunities Unit.

Forsberg, H. (1993) *Doing Fatherhood*, paper presented at the XXX seminar of the CFR, ISA, Annapolis MD, 6–9 November.

Godal, B. (1997) *Fedre i forandring*. Cand. polit. dissertation: Department of Sociology, University of Oslo.

Gjerstad, B. and Kvande, E. (1998) *Fedre mellom arbeid og permisjon*, Trondheim: Allforsk notat 1998: 5.

Gupta, N.D. and N. Smith (1999) *Children and Career Interruptions: Effects on the Earnings Capacity of the Parents*, paper presented at the Gender and Employment Seminar, Stockholm, June.

Hellevik, T. (1999) *Kontantstøtteordningens effekter for barnetilsyn og yrkesdeltakelse*, Oslo: NOVA- rapport 4/99.

Holter, H. and Ve Henriksen, H. (1979) 'Social Policy and the Family in Norway', in J. Lipman-Blumen and J. Barnard (eds) *Sex Roles and Social Policy*, London: Sage.

Karlsson, G. (1996) *Från broderskap till systerskap. Det socialdemokratiska kvinnoförbundets kamp för inflytande*, Lund: Arkiv förlag.

Kitterød, R.H. and Lømo, A. (1996) 'Småbarnsforeldres tidsbruk 1970–90', in B. Brandth and K. Moxnes (eds) *Familie for tiden. Stabilitet og endring*, Aurskog: Tano Aschehoug.

Leira, A. (1992) *Welfare States and Working Mothers. The Scandinavian Experience*, Cambridge: Cambridge University Press.

Leira, A. (1998) 'Caring as Social Right: Cash for Child Care and Daddy Leave', *Social Politics*, vol. 5, no 3: 362–78.

Leira, A. (1999) *Family Policy Reforms in the Scandinavian Countries – Cash for Childcare and Daddy Leave*, paper prepared for the European Parental Leave Seminar, Brussels, January.

Myrdal, A. and Klein, V. (1956) *Women's Two Roles*, London: Routledge and Kegan Paul.

Näsman, E. (1990) 'The Importance of Family Policy for Fathers' Care of their Children', in EC Childcare Network (ed.) *Men as Carers for Children*, report of a seminar held in Glasgow, 18–19 May), Brussels: European Commission Equal Opportunities Unit.

NORD 1994: 3, *Women and Men in the Scandinavian Countries: Facts and Figures 1994*.

NORD 1998: 1, Yearbook of Scandinavian Statistics.

NOU 1995: 27, *Pappa kom hjem*, Oslo.

Nurmi, K. (1997) *Gender, Equality and Welfare State Models*, Department of Social Policy Series 14/1997, Turku: University of Turku.

OECD (1995) 'Long-term Leave for Parents in OECD Countries', Ch. 5, in *Employment Outlook*, pp. 171–96.

Ot. prp. 56 (1997–98) *Om lov om kontantstøtte*.

OECD (1999) *Early Childhood Education and Care Policy in Norway: Country Note*.

Øverli, B. (1995) *Fedrekvote og nye faderskap. En kvalitativ studie av menn og omsorg*. Cand. polit. dissertation, Department of Sociology, University of Trondheim.

Rostgaard, T. (2000) 'Parental Leave in Denmark', in Moss P. and F. Deven (eds) *Parental Leave: Progress or Pitfall?*, Brussels: NIDI CBGS Publications 35.

Rønning, E. (1998) *Barnefamiliers tilsynsordninger, yrkesdeltakelse og økonomi før innføring av kontantstøtte*, Oslo: SSB notater 98/6.

Salmi, M. and Lammi-Taskúla, J. (2000) 'Parental Leave in Finland', in P. Moss and F. Deven (eds) *Parental Leave: Progress or Pitfall?*, Brussels: NIDI CBGS Publications 35.

Sipilä, J. (1995) 'The Right to Choose: Day Care for Children or Money for Parents', in R. Page and J. Baldock (eds) *Social Policy Review* 6: 159–69, Canterbury: Social Policy Association.

Sipilä, J. and Korpinen, J. (1998) 'Cash versus Child Services in Finland', *Social Policy and Administration*, vol. 32, no. 3: 263–77.

St. meld 4, (1988–9) *Langtidsprogrammet 1990–93*.

St. prp. 53 (1997–98), *Innføring av kontantstøtte til småbarnsforeldre*.

Sundberg, E. (1993) *From Vikings as Fathers to Fathers as Vikings*, paper presented at the conference 'Men as Carers: Towards a Culture of Responsibilities, Sharing and Reciprocity between the Genders in the Care and Upbringing of Children', 22 May: Ravenna.

Sundström, M, and Duvander, A.-Z. (1997) 'Föreldraförsäkringen och jämställdheten mellan kvinnor och män', in I. Persson and E. Wadensjö (eds) *Offentlig och kollektiv välfärd och ekonomisk jämställldhet mellom kvinnor och män*, Stockholm: Commission on Women's Power.

Ukens statistikk 21–25 June, 1999, Oslo: Statistics Norway.

8 Childcare policies in Japan

Postwar developments and recent reforms[1]

Ito Peng

Introduction

Since the introduction of the child welfare reform legislation in 1996, childcare has become one of the most widely debated policy issues in Japan. The debates have ranged from the topic of how should childcare be arranged, who should care for children under what circumstances, what should be the role of the state with respect to childcare, and how the cost of childcare should be arranged. For many outside observers the childcare system in Japan may appear quite generous (Boling 1998), and the current reform may seem to signify a further progressive step towards greater socialization of childcare. After all, about one-fifth of all pre-school-age children in Japan are in public childcare, and the national figure shows that there are still more spaces available, as the total childcare enrolment rate is only about 87 per cent of the available spaces (Japan – Ministry of Health and Welfare 1998). However, a closer examination of the current childcare system and the nature of the recent reform reveals a rather different story

First, it is difficult to assess adequately the generosity of childcare provision simply by looking at figures. Having one-fifth of pre-school-age children attending public childcare may seem considerable if compared with the countries like the US, Canada or the Netherlands where the figures are below 10 per cent, but it is very low when compared with countries like Sweden, Denmark, and France, where over 25 per cent of pre-school-age children are in public day-care. Rather, the important issues related to the current childcare system and the recent reform in Japan have to do with the fact that the existing system is functionally and procedurally obsolete and has been in need of a reform for some time; but that the recent reform does not really address these issues. Instead of extending social care to families with small children, the reform has been used as a tool to achieve the state's pronatalist and welfare state restructuring objectives. Procedurally, a large number of families with small children are unable to access public childcare because they do not meet the needs test, and functionally most of the public childcare centres are operating in a way that is no longer in keeping with the actual needs of the family. Although the childcare reform has been promoted as a policy to enable families to harmonize work and family responsibilities, the real goal is not about increasing employment options for mothers nor ensuring a greater gender equality at home or in the labour market. Rather, the reform is more aimed at preventing possible social and economic problems that may arise from a continuing decline in the total national fertility rate and to introduce the concept of free market competition to an otherwise highly regulated system.

The residual nature of the existing childcare system in Japan stems from its original policy premise of serving a protective custodial function for children 'lacking in care' at home rather than a supportive function for the family. That is, public childcare in postwar Japan was established to serve children who came from full-time working single-parent families or from full-time working two-parent families, and who had no other relatives or adults to take care of them while their parents were working.[2] As such, public childcare was never intended to be a social support for maternal employment; rather it was meant to be a safety net to protect children whose mothers had no choice but to work. The childcare reform of 1996 claims to correct this historical legacy by making childcare available to families with small children, but its motivations and the nature of the reform are complex and multidirectional, and because of this it must be assessed carefully. First of all, the childcare reform has been motivated by a number of conflicting objectives: on the one hand, there is a desire to address the growing public demand for more childcare and for a reform of the existing childcare system; on the other, the reform would not have been possible if it was not actively promoted by the policy bureaucrats as a strategy to raise the country's total fertility rate, which, in turn, has been fuelled by the state's anxieties about the immediate and the longer-term problems associated with the ageing of the society. The extension of childcare and the promotion of women's labour market participation proposed in this reform therefore have less to do with achieving gender equality; instead, more to do with helping women to take on a greater share of work and care responsibilities in the future. What this reveals is the tension between the state's fiscal and economic impulses towards welfare management and economic stimulus, counteracted by social and demographic pressures for welfare extension brought about by the changes in gender relationships within the family and the labour market. The result is a selective extension of social welfare along with an attempt to integrate the market economy within the provision of social care services. It also highlights the shift in the interdependencies of the state, the market and the family.

This chapter seeks to understand the recent reform in the childcare system in Japan by examining the current childcare system and what the reform is trying to accomplish. This will allow insight into how Japan deals with a common issue, which is shared by many of the western welfare states, that of childcare and the socialization of childcare. It will also permit discussion on how childcare interlocks with the other social and economic issues such as the changing gender relationship, ageing of the society, economic development, and welfare state restructuring. Studying Japan is also important because it helps us understand how a non-western welfare state deals with the problems of rapid ageing, shifts in the family structures and gender relations, women's labour market participation, and welfare state restructuring. The first section will outline the postwar childcare system in Japan and identify some of its features and problems. This will be followed by a discussion on some of the key areas of reform introduced in the 1996 childcare reform legislation. Next, I will discuss why childcare has become such an urgent policy issue today. Finally, the last section will assess the childcare reform in terms of what it is trying to accomplish.

Childcare system in Japan: its structure and features

Overview of the postwar Japanese childcare system

The current childcare system in Japan is based on the Child Welfare Law established in 1947.[3] According to Article 24 of this legislation, the state has the legal obligation to provide childcare to pre-school-age children (that is, children under the age of six) who are found 'lacking in care' at home. When it is proved that a child is 'lacking in care' at home, the local governments then must place the child in certified childcare. The childcare in Japan is broadly divided into two categories: the certified (*ninka hoiku*) or the uncertified (*ninka-gai hoiku*). Certified childcare may be run by the state (in which case, most often by local governments), or it may be operated by the registered private organizations (*fukushi hojin*) which are, in most cases, non-profit organizations. In either case, certified childcare must meet the basic standards and regulations set by the state (that is, the Ministry of Health and Welfare) and are regularly inspected by government officials.[4] Uncertified childcare, on the other hand, does not have to comply with the state regulations. However, what really distinguishes the Japanese childcare system from that of other countries is that in Japan, included in the regulations for certified childcare are the conditions that it must accept the price set by the state; and that it can only accept children who are referred by the local governments. In other words, all certified childcare, whether public or private, is almost completely regulated by the state as to its price and clientele. Since it cannot accept children other than those who are placed there by the local governments, it basically operates as the childcare agency of the state. Under the current system, parents cannot make direct arrangements with a certified childcare centre to have their children looked after. Parents must first register with the local government and pass the needs assessment test before they are allowed to put their children in a certified childcare centre. The only way in which parents can put their children in childcare without going through the local government is to use uncertified childcare, which may be expensive and is a highly insecure system as it is not regulated. In summary, in Japan the entire certified childcare sector, public and private, is a state monopoly. Even though it is the most desired option for parents who wish to put their children into childcare, its access is limited as only those children who are deemed 'lacking in care' at home are given access.

The cost of certified childcare is, as mentioned above, set by the Ministry of Health and Welfare of the central government, and is based on the age of the child. The parental contribution for the certified childcare is calculated on a sliding scale based on the family's income, with the remainder shared equally by the central and the local governments through general taxation. Currently the parental contributions are divided into ten levels, ranging from no cost for those with income equivalent to the public assistance level to full cost (i.e. no subsidy) for those in the two highest income brackets. For these families the cost may come close to ¥100,000 a month (about $900 a month – $1 = ¥110) per child, depending on the age of the child. Not surprisingly, this system is of tremendous benefit to families with low incomes, particularly single-mother families as their average income is only about 34 per cent of the average income of two-parent families with children (Japan – Ministry of Health and Welfare 1996). As the total household income approaches the average household income, the cost effectiveness of certified childcare becomes more dependent on the income level of the second wage earner which in most cases is that of the mother. The cost of the uncertified childcare, on the other hand, is not regulated and therefore depends on the market force. Many uncertified childcare centres also allow parents to put their children on a part-time basis and/or offer more flexible arrangements and therefore may be more cost-effective for families with part-time working mothers.

In 1997 there were a total of 22,401 certified regular (that is, for children between the ages of 2 and 6) childcare centres in Japan, of which 13,074 or 58.4 per cent were publicly run and 9,327 (41.6 per cent) were privately operated, with a total of about 1,643,000 children registered in them. In addition to these there were 7,850 certified childcare centres for children under 2 years of age (2,790 public and 5,141 private), but of these only 20.6 per cent of the public and 55.2 per cent of the private childcare centres were actually operating (Japan – Ministry of Health and Welfare 1998). One reason is that childcare centres for under-twos, and particularly those for under-ones, are much more expensive to operate compared with regular childcare centres as they require a much higher staff to child ratio, and additional requirements such as special baby and infant food and supplementary provisions (Zenkoku Hoikudantai Rengokai and Hoikukenkyusho, 1997). In addition, the cost of relief childcare workers and cooks are not included in the per unit cost set by the state in the case of childcare centres for under-twos (Maruyama, 1998).[5] Many of the regular childcare centres, therefore, may meet the conditions and receive certification to provide care for infants under 2 years of age, but choose not to undertake the operation because of the high running cost involved.

In addition to the certified childcare centres, there were also 9,387 registered uncertified childcare services in 1997, of which 4,339 were regular childcare centres with 78,404 children registered, 573 were baby hotels (night-care centres for babies and small infants) with 15,693 children, and another 3,881 'other types' of childcare (which include workplace childcare and small-scale childcare centres which accommodate thirty or fewer children) with 125,359 children registered in them (Zenkoku Hoikudantai Rengokai and Hoikukenkyusho 1997).[6] Finally, there are also unregistered and uncertified childcare services, most of which are thought to be in the form of informal childcare arrangements, including baby-sitters and child-minders. However, since these arrangements are often made privately it is unclear how widespread they are. A recent survey shows that the great majority of children below the age of 2 are being looked after by their families or through some sort of private care arrangements; among 3-year-olds about one-third are being looked after by their families or through private care arrangements, while the same number, respectively, are in kindergarten and childcare centres. Among children aged 4–6, about half are in kindergarten while about a quarter are being looked after by their families/private arrangements and another quarter are in childcare (see Figure 8.1).[7]

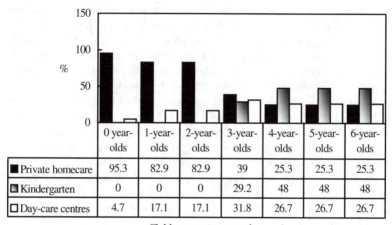

	0 year-olds	1-year-olds	2-year-olds	3-year-olds	4-year-olds	5-year-olds	6-year-olds
■ Private homecare	95.3	82.9	82.9	39	25.3	25.3	25.3
▣ Kindergarten	0	0	0	29.2	48	48	48
☐ Day-care centres	4.7	17.1	17.1	31.8	26.7	26.7	26.7

Child-care arrangments by age (percentages)

Figure 8.1 Childcare arrangements for pre-school-age children, 1997

Source: Japan – Ministry of Health and Welfare (1998).

One of the problems associated with the Japanese childcare system is that, because of the strong state monopoly and control over both the public and private certified childcare, these places have developed into very rigid and bureaucratic institutions. For example, most of these childcare centres operate only during regular office hours, that is from 8:00 a.m. to 6:00 p.m., Monday to Friday, and in some cases Monday to Saturday. They also only take children on a full-time basis.[8] Compared with these, uncertified childcare centres offer more flexible hours, including evening and overnight childcare services for parents who work at night or irregular hours, as well as offering options for full- or part-time childcare. It has become increasingly obvious that the placement conditions and the rigidity of the hours of the certified childcare centres are not in keeping with the actual working conditions and the needs of many families with working mothers. For example, while office hours are normally 8:00 a.m. to 6:00 p.m., Monday to Friday, most workers cannot leave their work by 6:00 p.m. and are often expected to work on Saturdays as well. Moreover, in large cities like Tokyo, where the average commuting time is one-and-a-half hours each way, most working parents cannot reasonably reach a childcare centre in time to collect their children. Yet, on the other hand, the uncertified childcare centres are not regulated and therefore they could be unsafe and, depending on the services offered, could also be very expensive (Nihon Jido Mondai Chosakai 1992). Moreover, there is a widespread assumption that while it may be acceptable to put a child into certified childcare, it is not quite proper to use uncertified childcare, as the eligibility criterion (the test of a child's need for childcare) for certified childcare has itself become a form of social and economic test of legitimacy for mothers.

In total about 21 per cent of all pre-school-age children in Japan are in certified childcare. The enrolment rate is, however, highest among 3-year-olds, about 32 per cent of whom are in childcare, and lowest among those less than one year old (see Figure 8.1). For children between the ages of 4 and 6 kindergarten is a more commonly used form of childcare. Many middle-class parents prefer to send their children to kindergarten, some of which are now accepting children from the age of 3, because they provide more educationally focused programmes than those offered by childcare centres. Unlike the certified childcare, which is a child welfare service provided by the Ministry of Health and Welfare, kindergartens in Japan are regulated by legislation concerning private education. Hence, like other private schools in Japan, kindergartens are generally run by private enterprise or the non-profit educational organizations and are regulated by Ministry of Education guidelines. Since most kindergartens only provide half-day programmes they provide access to two-parent families where mothers work part-time. They can also be a cheaper option for middle- to higher-income families, as the fees for kindergartens are normally not based on income.

Some of the specific features of the Japanese childcare system

There are three specific and important features to the current childcare system in Japan. First, as mentioned earlier, the current childcare system is located within the framework of the child welfare system and is regulated by the child welfare law. At first, this may not seem a very significant point; however, as will be discussed below, the child welfare system's specific orientation to child protection has seriously narrowed the scope of childcare. Second, as part of the child welfare system, childcare, like most other postwar social welfare services in Japan, also operates within the framework of a mandatory placement system (*sochi seido*), that is, its implementation is strictly based on the idea that the state has the legal obligation to place a child in a childcare institution once the child's need for care is established. Finally, in Japan local governments can use both the public and private childcare centres to meet their childcare needs. As mentioned above, while both public and private certified childcare centres in Japan operate largely as if they were state institutions, there are also some subtle differences between them, the most crucial being the way these institutions are managed, and this has an implication for the overall cost. This has led to an increasing preference for using private certified childcare centres in recent years.

Childcare as a part of the child welfare system

The fact that childcare is found within the child welfare system has meant that its basic orientation is premised on child protection, not social support for mothers or parents. As a result, childcare has been treated in a manner much like that of other forms of child protection. While this is understandable given that the child welfare law was introduced in 1947, it is now clearly evident that such an approach to childcare is no longer in keeping with the social and economic reality of the majority of families in Japan. The original intention of the public childcare system was to protect pre-school-age children who were left uncared for during the day while parents were out working or were unable to provide proper care due to disability or illness. During the first decade after the end of the Second World War there were a large number of children lacking in childcare at home because of the economic depression and of a large number of single-mother families. For example, until 1955 there were over a million households, about 3 per cent of *all households* in Japan that were headed by single mothers, most of whom were widows who had to work to support their families. In addition to this there were many other families who had to depend on two or more incomes in order to survive the economic hardship. The childcare legislation was thus introduced as a part of the child welfare law with the specific purpose of protecting small children of working mothers. Not surprisingly, once established, it became the primary form of care for pre-school-age children of single-mother families and low-income two-parent families. Partly because of this there was also a strong social stigma attached to putting children into public childcare. However, with the rise in married women's labour market participation since the 1970s, public opinion about childcare has been shifting (see Table 8.1). As a large number of children from middle-class two-parent families began to enter the childcare system, it has created a new pressure for change.

Another problem associated with childcare as a part of child welfare system is that because child welfare is highly residual in Japan, this has seriously restricted the types and methods of provision for childcare as well. Regardless of public demand, local government will place a child in childcare only when it deems that the child is in need of care. Parents are therefore obliged to provide proof that their child is truly lacking in care at home, which usually involves proof of full-time employment for both parents or proof of illness or disability and, as well, some convincing evidence that there is no other means of childcare support available. Mothers who work part-time or families that can make other formal or informal childcare arrangement with family members, neighbours, or by arranging working hours, do not generally qualify for public childcare. This has resulted in a large number of two working parent families who need childcare being disqualified from accessing the certified childcare system.[9] Also, because most certified childcare is available only during regular office hours, parents who work in the evenings or who work in shifts are unable to use this system even if they qualify.

Table 8.1 The breakdown of the children in childcare by family background,
1960–94

	Children from families receiving welfare assistance	Children from families with income below taxable level	Children from families with income above taxable level
		(%)	
1960	5.6	74.7	19.7
1965	3.7	73.3	23.0
1970	2.5	66.5	31.0
1975	1.7	35.5	62.8
1980	1.7	34.8	63.5
1985	2.1	25.7	72.2
1990	1.6	26.6	71.8
1994	1.0	23.7	75.3

Source: Japan – Ministry of Health and Welfare (1994) *Riyoshiyasui Hoikusho wo Mezashite (Towards Accessible Childcare Centres)* (Tokyo: Ministry of Health and Welfare).

However, in addition to the problem of needs assessment, the state's notion of what constitute a child 'lacking in care' has also fluctuated with time along with the changes in the state's and the public's sentiments about women's primary roles and what constituted a good mother (Shimoebisu 1994). A quick historical survey of the postwar family and childcare policies in Japan reveals that the definition of a child lacking in care was relatively liberally interpreted until the 1950s. However, starting with the consolidation of the conservative Liberal Democratic Party into a single party in power and the introduction of the so-called '1955 Regime' (*55-nen taisei*) characterized by the formation of a corporate-centred economic and welfare model and the implementation of the ten-year economic plan, a noticeable change was seen in relation to the state's family and childcare policies. The formation of the state, business, and labour consensus to create a corporate-centred welfare system premised on the modern (western) middle-class family was reinforced by the new policy view that a family should constitute two parents and that pre-school-age children should be cared for by their own mothers. This policy assumption was also underlined by the introduction of the idea about the primacy of mother–child bonding in the 1950s, a notion which was largely borrowed from the West. As a result, the 1950s saw a strong policy aversion to maternal employment and it became much more difficult for families to put their children into certified childcare as the concept of a child 'lacking in care' became much more strictly interpreted.

However, as the social and economic conditions began to shift after the 1960s, so did policy interpretations about childcare. As the Japanese economy shifted into a high growth period in the 1960s, women were sought as a new source of labour. With a rise in married women's labour market participation and a greater acceptance of it, social policy also began to look favourably towards public childcare. As illustrated in Table 8.2, the number of childcare centres rose steadily throughout the 1960s and 1970s in keeping with the rise in the number

Table 8.2 Number of childcare places and children registered in public and private
certified childcare centres, 1949–95

	Childcare spaces			Number of children registered		
	Public	Private	Total	Public	Private	Total
1949			195,377			216,887
1952			380,989			502,345
1957			700,815			657,010
1960	424,092	309,553	733,645			689,242
1965	546,096	330,044	876,140	503,259 (92.2)	326,481 (98.9)	829,740
1970	752,710	442,222	1,194,932	690,344 (91.7)	441,017 (99.7)	1,131,361
1975	1,090,653	690,028	1,699,681	1,012,290 (92.8)	618,735 (89.7)	1,631,025
1980	1,321,677	815,051	2,136,728	1,188,340 (89.9)	807,742 (99.1)	1,996,082
1985	1,247,306	831,459	2,078,765	1,046,060 (83.9)	797,490 (95.9)	1,843,550
1990	1,171,637	807,822	1,979,459	957,249 (81.7)	766,526 (94.9)	1,723,775
1995	1,128,074	794,761	1,922,835	912,659 (80.9)	766,207 (96.4)	1,678,866

Note: The enrolment rate is given in parentheses.

Source: Zenkoku Hoikudantai Rengokai and Hoikukenkyusho (eds) (1997) *Hoiku Hakusho, 1997* (*White Paper on Childcare 1997*) (Tokyo: Sodo Bunka).

of working mothers. The notion of a child lacking in care also became much more liberally interpreted as the state's policies shifted in favour of maternal employment during this period. Unfortunately, with the fiscal and welfare crisis following the oil shock of 1974 and a shift to political conservatism in the 1980s, family policy in Japan entered a new period of policy ambivalence: this time women were encouraged to work to help the family maintain economic wellbeing but, at the same time, a much greater policy emphasis was put on women to provide care within the home.

The outcome of such bipolar policies towards the family was a gradual reduction in childcare spaces despite the steady rise in maternal employment throughout the 1980s. Overall, the cuts in welfare spending had resulted in the reduction of childcare places.

As shown in Table 8.2, from 1980 the number of childcare centres began to decline along with the actual enrolment rate. This is particularly noticeable among publicly run certified childcare centres which became a target for the welfare restraint exercise. Between 1980 and 1995 the number of children registered in publicly run certified childcare centres dropped by about 280,000 while the enrolment rate in these childcare centres declined from about 90 to 81 per cent. At the same time, there had been a gradual shift in the balance of childcare centres in favour of the private ones, as illustrated in a much more drastic decline in the number of public childcare places and enrolment rate compared with the private during this time.[10]

The mandatory placement system

The second important feature of the childcare system in Japan is that it is premised on the notion of the mandatory placement system (*sochi seido*). The mandatory placement system is considered a unique feature of Japanese social welfare and refers to the state's legal obligation to provide welfare upon the determination of needs.[11] In theory, it serves as an important legal basis to ensure that the state provides social welfare; however, in practice it has come to mean the power of the state to place an individual into a welfare institution. In the case of childcare, the local government has the power to, and generally does, decide which childcare centre to place children in, irrespective of the parents' wishes. It is therefore not uncommon for the local government to place siblings in different childcare centres to suit the needs of the local government.

This kind of issue has become increasingly contentious over recent years as the mandatory placement system has come under growing criticism as an undemocratic, anachronistic, and inefficient method of service provision. However, on the other hand, there is also concern that undermining this system will undermine the most important legal basis guaranteeing the state's provision of welfare services. What is interesting is that, in fact, much of the criticism of this system has come from central government. Since the 1980s central government has been leading the policy debate about the problems associated with the mandatory placement system. The system has been criticized for creating an unnecessary barrier to individual right to choose, and for creating inefficiencies in welfare services. With respect to welfare for the elderly, a significant reform was introduced during the 1980s to change this system. As a result, most of the institutional services for the elderly have been privatized and now operate outside the mandatory placement system. This has, in fact, brought about a greater choice for individuals but, at the same time, also resulted in a greater marketization and less regulation of the services. The 1996 childcare reform, like the reform of care services for the elderly in the 1980s, will replace the mandatory placement system with a contractual system whereby parents can make a direct service contract with the childcare centre. Within the context of the welfare restructuring which has been steadily proceeding since the 1980s in Japan, we can see that this will fit well into the scheme to abrogate the system of mandatory placement gradually and hence pave the way to a more private welfare arrangement.

Use of both public and private certified childcare

The third feature of the childcare system in Japan, the local government's ability to use both the public and private childcare centres to meet their childcare needs, has had two interesting results. First, it has made a nonsense of the public and private divide. Since both publicly and privately run certified childcare have to follow the same regulations set by the state and charge the same prices, and can only receive children who are placed there by the local government, they essentially function as state childcare centres. Also, since the privately run certified childcare centres receive all their money from the state in the form of the placement fees for children, there is very little difference between the private and public sectors as far as the funding base and the nature and contents of services are concerned. In fact, there is no market in the sense of access and competition here because the entire certified childcare sector is controlled by the state.

This begs the question as to why there should be private sector certified childcare in the first place. The reason is that private childcare centres run by non-profit or charity organizations had ante-dated the public childcare system, coming into existence well before the 1947 child welfare law was put in place. As illustrated in Table 8.3, in 1947 there were three times as many private childcare centres as public ones. In the early years, during the formation of the childcare system in Japan, private childcare centres fulfilled an important role in absorbing children who were in need of care as the state could not build childcare centres fast enough the keep up with their needs It was only in the 1960s, when the state had an adequate financial and organizational framework to build more public childcare centres, that the publicly run childcare centres began to outnumber the private ones. However, once the government had established the legacy of contracting out its childcare services to certified private childcare centres, it could not undo that relationship. In essence, the government had created a monopoly in which a limited number of private organizations were given exclusive access and public funding to provide childcare. In fact, in recent decades, the state has seen a great fiscal incentive to supporting certified private childcare centres over the public ones, as will be discussed below.

The second outcome of the state using both the public and private childcare centres to meet their childcare needs is that, in recent years, there has been an increasing government preference for using private over public childcare centres. As illustrated in Table 8.3, the ratio of public childcare centres has been gradually declining in relation to private childcare centres since 1975. For example, the rapid increase in the number of public childcare centre in relation to the private ones peaked in 1975 but has been declining ever since. The proportion of children enrolled in the public childcare centres compared with private ones has been dropping at a rapid rate also over the last couple of decades. The reason for this is that the employees of the public childcare centres are considered public servants while those working in private certified childcare centres are not, even though they are all certified and licensed childcare workers. The public sector childcare workers belong to the public services union and, as a result, their wages and working conditions are significantly better than those of the staff of the private childcare centres. For example, public sector childcare workers are not only generally paid higher wages compared with the private sector childcare workers, but as public sector employees they enjoy more generous welfare provisions and greater employment security. Indeed, it is quite common, for example, for private sector childcare workers (almost all of whom are women) to be laid off after about ten years of service because their salaries will then be too costly for the employers to make enough profit. In addition, whereas the salaries of the private childcare centre employees are paid out of the placement fee established by the state, the salaries of the public childcare centre employees are directly paid out of the local government's general payroll. This has meant that for local governments more saving could be made if they can cut the labour cost from their own general payroll and transfer the cost of childcare to placement fees which they share with the central government. Not surprisingly these labour management and financial reasons have led to local governments preferring to use certified private childcare centres over publicly run ones, particularly after 1980 when the central government began to impose welfare spending cuts by cutting back on its social welfare transfer payments and at the same time down-loading social welfare responsibilities to local government.

Table 8.3 Number of public and private certified childcare centres, 1947–95

	Public childcare	*Private childcare*	*Public/private*
1947	395	1,223	0.32
1952	1,855	3,268	0.57
1957	4,951	4,187	1.18
1960	5,571	4,221	1.32
1965	6,907	4,292	1.61
1970	8,817	5,284	1.67
1975	11,545	6,693	1.72
1980	13,311	8,725	1.53
1985	13,590	9,309	1.46
1990	13,371	9,332	1.43
1995	13,184	9,304	1.42

Source: Zenkoku Hoikudantai Rengokai and Hoikukenkyusho (eds) (1997) *Hoiku Hakusho 1997* (*White Paper on Childcare 1997*) (Tokyo: Sodo Bunka).

This section described the structure and features of the postwar Japanese childcare system. As a system created to meet the welfare needs of small children immediately after the Second World War, it is clear that the childcare system is now in need of a serious overhaul. I shall now describe the nature of the 1996 reform to show how the Japanese government has tried to reform the current childcare system.

The nature of the recent childcare reform

It is important to point out here that while we discuss childcare reform and its implementation we must also constantly keep in mind that there is a much larger and parallel development in welfare state restructuring in Japan. As part of a larger welfare state restructuring project which has been taking place since the

1980s, the 1996 childcare reform has more to do with policy concerns about the ageing of the Japanese society than with the care of children. During the 1980s much of the social policy was focused on the ageing society and reform of the social security system that affects elderly people. However, as the total fertility rate continued to decline in the 1990s, policy attention shifted to the social and economic implications of the low birth-rate and rapidly ageing society. Since the beginning of the 1990s the Japanese government has put much energy into reforming family policy, much of which focused on improving childcare as a way to promote childbirth. In 1994 a large reform package called the Angel Plan was introduced to provide and strengthen public support and social infrastructure for families with small children.[12] The plan proposed to expand childcare places, after-school programmes and other types of childcare services, as well as to increase the numbers of parks and playgrounds in cities, establish family counselling centres and telephone hotlines for parents with child-rearing concerns, and to provide various forms of housing support to families with children over the next ten years (Japan – Ministry of Health and Welfare 1994, 1997). To actualize this plan, the ministries of finance, health and welfare, and of municipal affairs introduced a joint five-year action programme in 1994, a good part of which involved reforming the childcare system. In particular, it called for an increase in the number of childcare places for 0–2-year-olds, the introduction of extended childcare services within the childcare system (that is childcare which will provide services from as early as 7:00 a.m. to as late as 10:00 p.m. to accommodate parents who have to work longer hours), a huge expansion in the number of temporary childcare centres by 1999, and the setting up of a large development fund to assist private sector business to develop the childcare market (Japan – Ministry of Health and Welfare 1997).

However, at the same time as the extension of childcare services is proposed, central government has also pressed forward on a decentralization policy by further down-loading social welfare responsibilities to local government. Almost immediately after the introduction of the five-year action programme, it became clear that local governments were unable to shoulder half of the expected costs as most of their social welfare expenditures were already heavily burdened by the expansion of care services for the elderly in the community. With local governments unable to come up with the necessary funds, the programme was soon revised with many of the proposed expansions significantly modified. To continue with its objective of childcare reform, however, central government then sought to restructure the framework of the childcare system in 1996 by way of legislative reform. The idea was that if the system of childcare provision could not be changed due to lack of funding, it should at least be reformed by changing the law. It is this reform which is now being pursued and which is at the centre of the policy debate.

The contents of the 1996 childcare reform can be summarized into three points:

- the replacement of the mandatory placement system with a system based on user (consumer) choice;

- the marketization of childcare services;
- cost containment through establishing a new family–state cost sharing arrangement.

The replacement of the mandatory placement system with a system based on user (consumer) choice

As mentioned earlier, the mandatory placement system has been under attack for some time now, not least from central government, which wants to reduce its constitutional obligation to provide social welfare. The 1996 childcare reform will gradually replace the mandatory placement system with an individual contract system. Arguing on the basis of freedom of choice and of efficiency, a new childcare placement system has been introduced whereby the local government will no longer, on its own authority, be able to place a child in a childcare centre. Instead, it is required to ask parents about their choice of childcare centre when considering the placement of children and, furthermore, parents can now theoretically sign contracts with childcare centres about care of their children.[13] In order to enable parents to make choices, the local governments are advised to publicize information on childcare centres in the local area, and childcare centres are also to provide information concerning their services. It is hoped that this will result in more choice and openness and a greater access to childcare services for the users. Also, it is argued that such a system will create more competition among certified childcare centres and thus lead to more efficient and better services.

A shift to a more user-centred system appears very positive; however, there are a number of issues which need to be considered. One is the question of choice. Since this applies only to certified childcare it is questionable whether there are real choices to be made. First, the number of certified childcare centres is limited and so most parents are not actually in the position to choose but rather have to accept whichever childcare centre can take their children. For example, as indicated in an earlier section, with children on waiting lists as high as 50 per cent in some cities, parents are more concerned about finding a place in a childcare centre than about choosing where to put their children. Also, since it makes most sense for parents to put their children in childcare either near their homes or near their work, the location is a much greater factor than the nature of services. In addition, as mentioned earlier, since these centres are still all controlled by the state not much can happen in the way of competition unless more changes are made. However, an even more basic issue is that a large number of families are not able to reach the stage where they can make a choice of childcare. Because of the 'lacking in care' criteria, most parents who want to put their children in childcare cannot access the certified childcare system in the first place. The increased parental choice would make sense if more certified childcare were made available and if more people were allowed to participate in the choice making, and this would require allowing more families to access childcare by reforming the childcare eligibility criteria, and by increasing the number of certified childcare places.

Another problem concerns the idea of doing away with the mandatory placement system. As with the case of welfare services for the elderly, the mandatory placement system has been systematically replaced by services based on individual contracts. While it is important to emphasize individual choice, it is also important to consider the fact that abrogating the mandatory placement system without installing the individual right to social welfare will only undermine the legal basis for the state's welfare provision. Critics argue that the current policy emphasis on increased individual choice and responsibility is a convenient rationale for breaking down this legal framework (Tamura 1997a, 1997b). Indeed, given the direction of welfare state restructuring, it seems to suggest that the state is gradually withdrawing from its welfare responsibility. Clearly, eliminating the mandatory placement system is a very effective way for the state to abdicate its legal responsibility to provide social welfare. Currently certified childcare centres make up about 40 per cent of all the welfare institutions under the mandatory placement system, and children in these places make up 73 per cent of all the clients served by mandatory placement institutions (Zenkoku Hoikudantai Rengokai and Hoikukenkyusho 1997). It is not difficult to discern from this that doing away with the mandatory placement system within the childcare system would imply a major restructuring of the postwar institutional welfare arrangement.

The marketization of the childcare services

One important aspect of the 1994 Angel Plan which was incorporated into the 1996 child welfare reform is the establishment of the Kodomo Mirai Zaidan (Children's Future Foundation) to promote the development of private-sector childcare services. The foundation received a set-up fund of ¥30 billion from the Ministry of Health and Welfare. The money was taken out of the reserve fund for the national child allowance programme to be used as grants and subsidies for the private sector to set up childcare services (that is, uncertified childcare centres and other new childcare services operated by private businesses). Since 1995 about ¥5 billion have been distributed annually in subsidies to the private sector to develop such services as 'station childcare' (*ekigata hoiku*), baby-sitting services, company day-care, and 24-hour telephone counselling services for parents with small children (Hoikukai 1994). Two areas of expansion since the development of the Kodomo Mirai Zaidan are the extended hours in childcare centres for children under the age of two (*encho nyuji hoiku*) – the segment of childcare that is facing the greatest shortage – and the station childcare – the childcare centres which are located in major train or subway stations for parents who commute to work. The fact that deregulating the childcare market and giving financial incentives for private sector involvement is given priority over expanding public childcare centres suggests a very specific way in which this reform is moving. It is clear that the extension of childcare is pursued in concert with the marketization of childcare services.

Containing the cost of childcare through a new cost-sharing arrangement

Another point of the childcare reform is to rearrange the cost-sharing burden of the existing childcare system. Currently the parental contribution rate is calculated on the household's total annual income. For the purpose of childcare, a standard chart is set whereby the total annual income is divided into ten levels, ranging from one for those who are welfare assistance recipients to 10 for those with total annual pretax income of over ¥9 million.[14] The parental contribution rate for regular childcare, for example, ranges from nothing (100 per cent subsidy) for those in the lowest income level (level 1) to nearly ¥100,000 a month (i.e. no subsidy) for those in level 10 (Japan – Ministry of Health and Welfare 1998).[15] Since the average income of a Japanese household in 1998 was approximately ¥7.5 million a year, one can assume that the regular childcare cost of such families was about ¥50,000 a month for each child, higher if the child is under the age of 2 and slightly lower if the child is aged 3 or older.

Under the reform a new calculation method will reduce the family income categories from the current level of ten to seven. Two contradictory reasons are given for this. One is that the new calculation method will apparently help equalize the parental contribution rates as the current method of calculation puts undue financial burden on the families in the middle and upper-middle end of the spectrum. This is underlined by the fact that a large number of children in childcare are from middle-class two-income families and that the parents of these children have been the most vocal in calling for a review of the childcare system. Another argument is that childcare costs should properly reflect the economic background of the users. This view, which represents the government position, differs slightly from the other one in that it calls for a general increase in the overall parental contribution rate. It has been argued that the current childcare system is serving a much higher income group than was originally intended in the 1940s. Hence, the overall childcare cost should be raised to reflect the middle-class background of the children who are currently in public childcare. The combined effect of these two rationales is the collapsing of the income level from ten to seven, and a higher childcare cost for more families, as the new method will upgrade three lower levels of income groups by combining them with income groups one level higher. In reality, the total parental contribution rate for childcare has already been rising steadily over the last couple of decades: from 1975 to 1995 the parental contribution for childcare rose from 35 per cent to 50 per cent of the total cost (Murayama 1997). It is expected that the new childcare reform may raise the total parental contribution to above the 50 per cent level.

This section discussed the nature of the 1996 childcare reform in Japan. It shows that the reform tries to do more than simply make the childcare system more flexible and keep in with the needs of the family today. Rather, the main body of the reform seems to point in a very different direction. By replacing the mandatory placement system with a user contract system, by putting so much emphasis on opening up the childcare market to the private businesses, and by rearranging the fee structures for certified childcare centre, the reform conforms to the welfare state restructuring plans set out by the Commission on Social Security System Review and the Ministry of Health and Welfare (Shakai Hoshoseido Shingikai 1995; Japan – Ministry of Health and Welfare 1996b).

The emergence of childcare as a policy issue

Now we need to go back and ask why did childcare become such an important policy issue in Japan in the first place. There are two main reasons to this: the first relates to the public demands for more childcare and for a reform of the existing childcare system; and the second to the state's pronatalist concerns about the declining birth rate underlined by the anxieties of the rapidly ageing society.

Public demands for more childcare and childcare reform

There has been a growing public demand for more public childcare and for a reform of the existing childcare system since the 1970s as a result of:

- the increase in mothers' labour market participation rate;
- the increase in the public awareness about childcare and childrearing issues;
- a shift in public attitudes towards public childcare.

The employment rate of mothers with young children in Japan has been rising steadily since the mid-1970s. For example, the employment of mothers with children under the age of 18 (in sectors other than agriculture and family business) rose from 30.1 per cent in 1979 to 43.3 per cent in 1996 (Japan – Rodosho 1997). This trend is particularly noticeable among those with pre-school-age children. As shown in Table 8.4, in 1996 the employment rate of mothers with a youngest child aged between zero and 3 was 28.2 per cent, while that of mothers with a youngest child between the ages of 4 and 6 was 50 per cent. This is a considerable increase compared with 1979 when more than 80 per cent of mothers with children under the age of 5 were staying at home. Of the working mothers, about half work full-time (that is, thirty-five hours or more per week): for example, 46.5 per cent of those whose youngest child is under 3 years old and 45.5 per cent for those whose youngest child is between the ages of 4 and 6 who were working worked full-time in 1996. Among mothers who were not working, 57.1 per cent of those whose youngest child was under 3 years old, and 63.7 per cent of those whose youngest child was between 4 and 6 years old reported that they were actively looking for work. These figures suggest not only that the employment rates of mothers with young children are reasonably high, but that a large proportion of those who are not working are seeking a job. They also indicate that most mothers today see childbearing not as a permanent condition but rather as a temporary period outside the workforce.

Evidence shows that the lack of childcare is a significant barrier to employment for many women in Japan. For example, surveys have found that mothers' employment rates rise steadily in relation to the age of the youngest child. As illustrated in Table 8.4, starting with 28.2 per cent for mothers whose youngest child in under 3, the employment rates of mothers increase steadily up to 70.9 per cent by the time their youngest child reached the ages of 15–17. The availability of childcare at home is an important factor contributing to maternal employment rate, as mothers living in three-generation households have a noticeably higher employment rate compared with those living in two-generation households (Table 8.5). The difference is most significant in relation to full-time employment. As shown in Table 8.5, the full-time employment rate of mothers whose youngest child is under the age of 3 is about twice as high in three-generation households compared with two-generation households (13.4 per cent and 27.6 per cent, respectively), suggesting that the possibility of having childcare at home makes a significant difference to mothers' employment rate and their types of employment.

The increase in mothers' employment since the 1970s had led to a number of public and policy debates which have further influenced public thinking about childcare issues. The first relates to concern about childcare as a necessary precondition for women's labour market participation. It argues that the lack of childcare was a serious barrier to women's entry into the labour market and therefore more childcare is needed to enable mothers to enter the labour market. This argument has been supported by government surveys which found that women (76.3 per cent) found the lack of childcare to be a more serious disabling factor to their work compared with caring for their elderly or sick family members (53.8 per cent) (Japan – EPA 1996), and that working mothers with pre-school-age children wanted most of all:

- more childcare;
- longer childcare hours;
- more financial support for their families (Japan – Rodosho 1997).

Other studies have also shown that despite the apparent changes in public attitudes towards a more equal relationship between men and women within the home, the majority of Japanese men continue to do very little in the way of housework and childcare. As a result, women continue to shoulder almost all of the childcare responsibilities despite the increase in their share of paid work. For example, comparative studies have found that the amount of time Japanese men spend on household chores has not changed over the last forty years: according to the 1955 national survey, men spent on average twenty-seven minutes a day doing household work compared with five hours and eighteen minutes for women; compared with this, men spent on average thirty-two minutes a day doing housework while women spent on average four hours and thirty-two minutes in 1995 (Kusatake *et al.* 1997). The amount of time husbands spend on household chores is also pathetically low whether their wives were full-time housewives or full-time workers: twenty-five minutes for husbands of full-time housewives and nineteen minutes for those married to full-time workers (Japan –

Table 8.4 Mothers' employment by the ages of the youngest child, 1996

Types of families	Total (x 1,000)	Ages of youngest child						
		0–3 years	4–6 years	7–9 years	10–12 years	13–14 years	15–17 years	18 and over
Total number of families with children	*18,010*	*3,120*	*1,660*	*1,520*	*1,570*	*1,230*	*1,990*	*6,940*
With mothers working	10,000	880	830	950	1,070	850	1,410	1,010
With mother working in sectors other than forestry or agriculture	7,800	710	660	770	890	670	1,120	1,980
Full-time	3,890	330	300	340	430	320	550	1,630
Part-time	3,920	380	370	440	460	350	570	1,350
With unemployed mothers	7,800	2,190	800	550	490	360	560	2,840
With mothers seeking employment	3,690	1,250	510	330	270	180	270	860
Total percentage of families with children	*100.0*	*100.0*	*100.0*	*100.0*	*100.0*	*100.0*	*100.0*	*100.0*
With mothers working	55.5	28.2	50.0	62.6	68.2	69.1	70.9	57.8
With mother working in sectors other than forestry or agriculture	43.3	22.8	39.8	50.7	56.7	54.5	56.3	42.9
Full-time	21.6	10.6	18.1	22.4	27.4	26.0	27.6	23.5
	(49.9)	(46.5)	(45.5)	(44.2)	(48.3)	(47.8)	(49.1)	(54.7)
Part-time	21.8	12.2	22.3	28.9	29.3	28.5	28.6	19.5
	(50.3)	(53.3)	(56.1)	(57.1)	(51.7)	(52.2)	(50.9)	(45.3)
With unemployed mothers	43.3	70.2	48.2	36.2	31.2	29.3	28.1	40.9
With mothers seeking employment	20.5	40.1	30.7	21.7	17.2	14.6	13.6	12.4

Note: Figures in parentheses are the percentage of mothers who were working full- or part -time among those working in sectors other than forestry or agriculture.

Source: Japan – Somucho (1996) Rodoryoku Chosa Tokubetsu Chosa (Special Survey of the Labour Power Survey).

Somucho 1992). These contradictions have underlined the childcare dilemma faced by women in Japan and contributed to the public debate about an obvious need for childcare, but childcare as a gender issue which needs to be addressed at a policy level.

Another debate which had greatly influenced the public demand for more childcare, quite unlike the first one, was about the safety issues concerning uncertified childcare. In 1981, a number of sensational cases involving the deaths of small infants in baby hotels outraged the public and attracted much political and media attention about the need for a more strict public enforcement of childcare regulation. The public investigation which followed from these incidences revealed that of the 587 such hotels which existed at the time, 94 per cent were operating in premises with no windows or emergency exits, and that most of them did not meet basic health and safety standards (Japan – Ministry of Health and Welfare 1981). The problem of baby hotels revealed a huge dilemma for mothers who worked in non-conventional jobs or for irregular hours. The widespread public image of baby hotels as rather unsavoury businesses catering mainly to the needs of lone mothers who had to work at night was also revised by the public investigation which showed that a

Table 8.5 Mothers' employment by type of employment, age of the youngest child and type of household, 1997

| | Household type and the age of the youngest child | | | |
| | Nuclear household | | Three-generation household | |
	0–3 years	*4–6 years*	*0–3 years*	*4–6 years*
Total (x 1,000)	2,540	1,230	580	430
(Per cent)	(100.0)	(100.0)	(100.0)	(100.0)
Total number of mothers employed (x 1,000)	640	560	240	270
(Per cent)	(25.5)	(45.5)	(41.4)	(62.8)
Self-employed (x 1,000)	40	40	0	10
(Per cent)	(1.6)	(3.3	(0)	(2.3)
Piecework at home (x 1,000)	30	20	10	10
(Per cent)	(1.2)	(1.6)	(1.7)	(2.3)
Family business (x 1,000)	40	70	40	20
(Per cent)	(1.6)	(5.7)	6.9)	(4.7)
Regular employment (x 1,000)	530	430	180	230
(Per cent)	(20.9)	(35.0)	(31.0)	(53.3)
Regular employment part-time (x 1,000)	300	260	80	110
(Per cent)	(11.8)	(21.1)	(13.8)	(25.5)
Unemployed mothers (x 1,000)	1,890	660	330	150
(Per cent)	(74.4)	(53.7)	(56.9)	(34.9)

Note: Part time refers to less than thirty-five hours of work per week.

Source: Japan – Somucho (1997) *Rodoryoku Chosa Tokubetsu Chosa* (*Special Survey of the Labour Power Survey*).

significant number of clients were professional women, such as nurses, who had no other place to leave their children while they were on night shift. The issue thus made clear the condition of a large number of working mothers who worked outside regular office hours and the diversity of their work. Public and media discussions on the safety issues of baby hotels thus brought the topic of childcare into the political limelight.

The hardship of working mothers notwithstanding, the 1980s also saw the discovery of the childrearing neurosis (*ikuji noirose*), a form of neurosis experienced by young, and often inexperienced, full-time mothers. With its symptoms ranging from depression and anxiety over childrearing to child abuse and neglect, the childrearing neurosis came to reflect not only the perceived personal inadequacies of the young full-time mothers, but also the disintegration of the traditional family system and supportive communities. In more recent years, however, the public discourse on childrearing neurosis has shifted noticeably from one of blaming mothers to a critique of the inordinate amount of childcare burden placed on women in Japanese society today (Anme 1996; Kato *et al.* 1997; Ohinata 1995). This new public discourse has opened the window for a policy debate about the need to provide social support to full-time mothers caring for pre-school-age children at home. Particularly following Ohinata's (1995) study showing widespread cases of childrearing neurosis among young, urban, middle-class mothers and Osaka City Childrearing Hotline's report on child abuse by mothers in 1996, there has been a heated policy debate about public childcare support for full-time mothers.

The pronatalist policy objective

As illustrated above, the public demands for more childcare and a reform of the existing childcare system emerged from a number of different directions. While they have all pointed to a need for childcare reform, and while all these factors have been noted by the policy-makers as contributing to the childcare reform of 1996, in reality the policy responses to them have been rather disappointing. For example, when the baby hotel crisis exposed the inadequacies of the childcare system, the government responses were simply to step up the public inspection of these premises, leaving aside the issue of the needs for childcare of mothers who worked outside regular office hours. The problem was that while these public and policy discourses called for a greater public support for mothers with small children, at a macro level the state's policy position with respect to welfare state restructuring was to established a new welfare mix by reasserting the traditional family structure based on the traditional gender roles. Hence despite calls for more public support for working mothers and the extension of childcare, the 1980s saw little government effort to take on the reform of the childcare system seriously. Indeed it is not an exaggeration to say that the Japanese government paid almost no attention to the issue of childcare until the mid- and long-term implications of the decline in the total national fertility rate became widely acknowledged by policy-makers. The Japanese government first began publicly to express its concern over the declining birth rate in 1990, when the Ministry of Health and Welfare reported a total fertility rate of 1.57 per population of 1,000 (the so-called 1.57 shock) for the year 1989. This figure has sparked a wave of anxiety among politicians and government bureaucrats because it marked the lowest fertility rate in Japan since the war. It broke the psychological barrier established in 1966 when the national fertility rate dropped from 2.14 per cent to 1.58 per cent within a year in reaction to the particularly bad luck associated with that year according to the Chinese astrological calendar (see Figure 8.2) (Kashiwame 1997).[16]

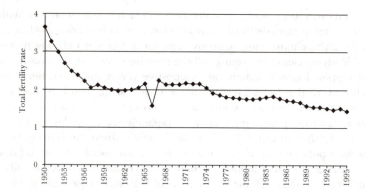

Figure 8.2 Total fertility rate, 1950–95

Underlying the anxieties of the low fertility rate was clearly a much more serious concern about the ageing of the society, which has been the main focus of policy debates in Japan since the latter half of the 1970s. The problem of imminent ageing of the Japanese society has been debated mainly in terms of its adverse effects on the economy and social welfare. In particular, the tenets of the state's ageing society policy discussion had been focused on the economic growth, the future welfare burden for the young people, and also in terms of the real income of the current generation of workers. The policy responses to the ageing society issue have been carried out in three ways: by restructuring the social welfare system, by encouraging women and the elderly to work, and by promoting a higher birth rate.

With the restructuring of the welfare system, for example, there has been a series of pension and healthcare reforms since 1980. Pension reforms have resulted in more individual contributions and a gradual increase in the pension age from 60 to 65. In healthcare, the insurance contribution rate has also been raised at the same time as a series of restrictions and service charges have been imposed to reduce the total healthcare cost. Social assistance programmes have been radically reformed and a greater emphasis has been put on individual self-support and family mutual assistance (Peng 1997a, b). The income tax system was also reformed in the 1980s providing special tax breaks for three-generation households and full-time housewives. By the end of the 1980s most of the mandatory placement institutions for the elderly were also replaced by private sector service providers, as the state sought greater fiscal rationalization by privatizing care services for the elderly.

Along with the restructuring of welfare, the Japanese government has also been encouraging women and the elderly to enter the labour market in order to sustain the country's economic productivity. Particularly, women have been targeted as an important source of (part-time) labour. Since the 1980s, a number of employment-related policies for women have been introduced to encourage women to enter and remain in the labour market. For example, an equal employment opportunity law was introduced in 1987 giving women the option to enter the career stream where they will be treated in the same manner as men. A new childcare leave legislation was introduced in 1992 allowing parents to take up to one year of leave after the birth of the child with 25 per cent of their previous salary, social insurance waiver, and employment guarantees. Also in 1995 a family-care leave bill was added to the childcare leave legislation enabling men and women to take up to four months of leave from their work in order to care for their elderly relatives.

Finally, many of the new support measures for working women have also been introduced to promote a higher birth rate. Most of these try to make it easier for women to care for their children while working. The Angel Plan introduced in 1994 also claimed to enable families (women) to take on work and childcare simultaneously by expanding the number of certified and uncertified childcare centres, and offering other forms of childcare beyond the regular childcare, such as extended childcare centres, night-care centres, after-school programmes for school-age children, temporary childcare centres for mothers who need childcare for a few hours a day or on an emergency basis, and family support centres which will provide consultations, guidance, and other support for families with children. The current childcare reform also aims to expand the types and numbers of childcare places for working mothers by enabling more private sector business to enter the childcare market.

What does the reform hope to achieve?

It is clear that given the problems and inadequacies of the childcare system established in 1947, it is now in need of a serious reform. However, as we begin to understand the nature of the 1996 childcare reform within the context of the welfare state restructuring, it becomes clear that, despite its claim of restructuring the childcare system to meet the needs of parents today, it is not really about addressing the needs of the families with small children. Rather, it is a new phase of an ongoing welfare restructuring project, an attempt to allay the state's anxieties about the possible social and economic problems associated with an ageing society. In this sense, childcare reform is a public investment, if not to reverse the trend of steady decline in the total fertility rate, at least to minimize some of the social and economic problems associated with society ageing. In order to understand what the reform is trying to accomplish, we will need to examine the social and economic imperatives associated with the low fertility rate and rapidly ageing population.

The economic imperatives

The economic imperatives relate to the concerns over the impact of global competition on the Japanese economy. Specifically there are two issues here. First, the Japanese are beginning to realize that the postwar Japanese corporate welfare system premised on the idea of life-time employment and automatic wage rises for men will gradually disappear in an increasingly competitive global economic environment. Indeed there has already been some shift in public and business views of what used to be regarded as the postwar middle-class household structure, that of a household made up of the male family wage-earner and full-time housewife. As discussed earlier, more than half of the so-called middle-class housewives now work outside the home, and the primary reason for their employment is to support the family income (Japan – Rodosho 1997). Under the current economic recession the corporate sector in Japan has begun to restructure by reducing the proportion of its core workers and replacing them with part-time and/or contract workers. Women are now sought both as a new source of labour by employers and as an important second wage-earner by the family. The decline of the postwar Japanese corporate welfare system therefore will effect changes not only in the labour market arrangements but also in gender relationships within and outside home. The childcare implication of this for the government is obvious.

The other economic concern is that as part of the economic restructuring policy, the government is also trying to create new markets for the private sector, and one way is by deregulating some of the public service sectors which had been more or less under state control. The impulse to deregulate childcare services is understandable: as more middle-class women find different kinds of work outside the home there will be not only more demand for childcare services but also a need for a greater variety of childcare. Given this condition, the traditional public childcare system, based on the idea of protecting children who are lacking in care, would clearly be too narrow. Yet, on the other hand, the cost of universalizing public childcare to allow all parents who need childcare a place would be too large, particularly at a time when the state policy towards the family is also trying to emphasize greater autonomy and self-reliance. One solution, as in this case, is to expand and deregulate the certified childcare services and to reassess the parental contributions for these services in a way that will ensure that middle-class families will take on a greater share of the childcare cost. The marketization of the childcare system is, therefore, a response to a mix of economic interests, which includes aims to enable women to work, to create new markets for the private sector, and to find ways to minimize the state's fiscal burden of childcare services. Breaking down the mandatory placement system which sets legal and institutional barriers to private businesses is the first step to deregulating childcare services. By getting rid of the mandatory placement system and allowing parents to make their own contracts with childcare centres the government hopes to circumvent the legal mandate for the state to provide childcare and to introduce the concept of free market competition in the existing public childcare system. To support the private sector's entry into the childcare market further, the government has introduced the Kodomo Mirai Zaidan providing grants and interest-free loans. These suggest that the current childcare reform may lead to an expansion of childcare, particularly to middle-class mothers, but it is not clear whether this will ultimately benefit them. The reason, as shown here, is that the reform will extend childcare services but, at the same time, it will bring about a greater marketization/privatization of these services and gradually a greater cost burden for the family.

The demographic imperatives

The second set of imperatives behind the childcare reform is demographic. The demographic objective of the childcare reform is to promote a higher birth rate by enabling families to harmonize work and childcare. However, underlying this objective as discussed earlier is a longer-term aim to address the future economic and social development concerns related to the low fertility rate and rapid ageing of the population. It is hoped that a reform of the child welfare system, including childcare and the provision of more family support will encourage families to have more children (Japan – Ministry of Health and Welfare 1994b). Future economic problems, such as the decline in labour power and the decline in economic growth, are dealt with by the childcare reform by way of extending childcare as an incentive for women to have children while working. This will no doubt solve some of the problems for women who are hoping to place their children in childcare. But here again, there are some contradictions. For example, while it hopes to remove some of the barriers for mothers working, the state has also been careful not to take on too strong a policy stance against employers. This can be seen in a lack of attention paid to the issue of childcare in the workplace, which was a popular topic until the 1980s. Protective legislation for working parents such as the 1992 parental leave law has also been left unenforced. According to the Ministry of Labour's own survey, for example, only 60 per cent of businesses have complied with the parental leave legislation in 1996. Moreover, even among employees who were working in companies which offered parental leave provisions, less than half (44.5 per cent) of women who gave birth and only a minuscule fraction of men (0.16 per cent) whose wives had given birth had actually taken the leave in 1996 (Japan – Rodosho 1997). Studies show that, despite the legal backing, very few women felt confident that they could securely take childcare leave from work beyond the legal minimum of sixteen weeks maternity leave (eight weeks before and eight weeks after the delivery). In the same studies it was found that the majority of women felt pressurized to return to work and feared significant personal antagonism against them in the workplace if they were to assert their legal right to take childcare leave (Japan – Rodosho 1997).

In the area of basic employment opportunities also, despite the existence of the equal employment opportunity law since 1987, the majority of women continue to face unequal treatment as evidenced by the large wage disparity between men and women, the lack of promotional opportunities for women, and the high incidence of sexual harassment against women (Japan – Ministry of Health and Welfare 1998). Since the equal employment opportunity law, like the parental leave law, also has no legal sanctions attached, employers are under no legal obligation to comply. These underline women's insecure position in the labour market and suggest an obvious lack of commitment to promoting gender equality in the labour market. In terms of childcare policies, this has resulted in much of the reform being focused on developing childcare services to accommodate the current work structure and the work demands placed on parents: by increasing the number and hours of childcare services, and by extending the private sector childcare provision while little attention is being paid to addressing the problems associated with the existing model of work itself.

The gender imperative

The third, and perhaps the least immediately apparent issue, is that of gender. Although the women's movement in Japan has not been strong compared with that of many western countries, Japanese women have been able to affect policy changes particularly in recent years by gradually shifting the gender relationships within the home and in a wider social context. Factors such as women delaying and/or opting out of marriage are now seen as the major underlying cause of the total decline in fertility in Japan. The government is particularly concerned about the rise in the average age of first marriage for women which increased from 24.2 in 1970 to 26.4 in 1996; and in the non-marriage rate among women (that is, the proportion of women who are still unmarried in their fifties) (from 2 per cent in 1960 to 5.1 per cent in 1995) (Japan – Rodosho 1997). Since both the rate of cohabitation (1.7 per cent in 1992) and birth outside marriage (1 per cent of all births in 1995) are extremely low in Japan, the above two factors – women delaying marriage and women's increasing non-marriage rate – are now considered as two crucial factors behind the low birth rate demographic outcome. In addition, the increase in the number of divorces among older couples has also alarmed policy-makers in terms of its social welfare implications. For example, the fact that the divorce rate among couples married for 15 years or more has risen from 12.7 per cent of all divorces in 1975 to 25.7 per cent in 1996 and that over 70 per cent of these divorce are initiated by women is now regarded not only as a sign that women are becoming increasingly disenchanted with their marriage, but also a possible social problem for men and women in their old age (Japan – Ministry of Health 1998). In either case, without making overt political demands, Japanese women are challenging the existing gender relationships by taking personal actions the outcomes of which prove to have serious demographic and political implications. From this perspective the current childcare reform, as part of a broader development in policies concerning the family in Japan, is an attempt to support and partially (although rather unsuccessfully) satisfy women, many of whom are choosing to disengage themselves from marriage and thus be diverted from their expected life-course which would have sustained the status quo.

Conclusion

In recent years the Japanese government has been making efforts to reform the childcare system. Unable to pursue its initial plan to expand and diversify public childcare services directly due to financial constraints, central government has opted to reform the childcare legislation which involves shifting the basis of childcare provision from that based on *sochi seido* (mandatory placement system) to the individual contract system, and the introduction of free market principles within the existing childcare system. It is generally considered that this reform will bring about a significant change in the nature of public childcare in Japan.

This chapter has examined the postwar childcare system and the recent childcare reform in Japan. On the surface the childcare reform of 1996 seems to suggest a progressive step towards greater socialization of childcare. However, a closer examination reveals a very different picture. While it claims to help women and families harmonize work and care, it has been very careful not to upset the current labour markets structure by pursuing to an excessive extent the issue of women's equal opportunities. Also, while the reform will bring about an extension of childcare, it will do so by way of expanding private childcare through the introduction of free market principles within the childcare system. As a result, the reform may bring about more childcare and increased access to childcare for women, but it will probably not help women achieve gender equality in the labour market or at home. What this reform reveals is that the real policy objectives are demographic and economic (that is, addressing the problems of low fertility and rapidly ageing population) rather than social (that of addressing the needs of families with small children). However, more importantly, the current childcare reform underlines a need seriously to rethink the real underlying issues, which relate to changes in women's employment patterns, shifts in gender relations, and how these are affecting the national birth rate in the first place. Data show that Japan's birth rate continues to decline despite the government's efforts to promote childbirth. What it suggests is that the Japanese government has yet to consider the underlying causes of the low fertility and engage in a freer public debate on the solutions to the low birth rate and rapidly ageing population.

Notes

1 I am grateful to Thomas Boje, Pat Boling, Pat Evans, Hiroyasu Hayashi, Arnlaug Leira, and Andre Sørensen for their support and comments on this chapter.
2 The procedure to qualify for public childcare in Japan is as follows. First, a parent must go to the local government office and make an application. The applicant then undertakes a needs assessment to prove that the child is truly 'lacking in care'. This usually involves providing the proof of employment, citizenship (that is a proof that the applicant is a registered citizen of the local area), and proof and an affidavit that there is nobody who can look after the child while the parents are working. Finally, the application is reviewed by the childcare review board set up by the local government which will give the final decision about whether the application is accepted or not.
3 Since the 1996 childcare reform legislation only began to be implemented in April 1998 and is still in the process of being implemented, I shall refer to the current or existing childcare system as the system that existed before the 1996 reform.
4 In Japan almost all of the certified childcare centres are in the form of day-care centres. Currently, among 22,000 or so certified childcare centres across the country, only thirty-eight are what is called evening childcare centres (*yakan hoikujo*) that provide childcare during the evening hours. The government regulations include those related to the building, for example, it cannot be built in wood, it has to have a certain number of fire escapes and exits, etc. and a minimum space allocation per child, and the ratio of childcare workers to children based on the ages of the children.

5   Since all the certified childcare centres run on the basis of providing full-time childcare (and for that reason until the reform only the children of full-time working mothers were considered 'lacking in care'), they are required to provide hot meals as a part of the childcare service. This has meant that childcare centres must hire at least one full-time cook/nutritionist. With the reform of 1996, however, certified childcare centres are allowed to contract out meals from catering companies as a way to cut costs.

6   The registered uncertified childcare centres are those which are registered with the Ministry of Health and Welfare as providing childcare services. Although these childcare centres do not have to meet all the requirements set for certified childcare, they are 'advised' to follow the minimum requirement conditions set out in the government guideline. These childcare centres may be inspected by the government officers from time to time. Some of these childcare centres may also receive some public grants to support their activities. However, most of their income comes from other sources.

7   Although kindergartens are an important form of childcare in Japan, I shall restrict my discussion here to childcare centres. The reason is that kindergartens come under the jurisdiction of the Ministry of Education and, as a result, the regulations governing them are based on a completely different set of legislation. Also, the 1996 childcare reform only applies to childcare centres.

8   On the other hand, under the current system, certified childcare centres are not allowed to hire part-time childcare workers, and since childcare workers (*hoikushi*) in Japan are government certified and licensed professionals, it means that there is some measure of quality childcare in these places. The uncertified childcare centres are not bound by this regulation.

9   There is, however, a large regional difference in the level of access to childcare. Because local governments act as the gate-keepers, deciding who can put their children into certified childcare, they can decide how they wish to interpret the legal definition of the child 'lacking in care'. For example, in recent years some progressive local governments have begun to relax their rules concerning childcare eligibility and have begun to allow children of part-time working mothers to qualify for certified childcare. In special cases, such as the city of Chiba, the local government has introduced a new policy which ensures certified childcare space for all children who need it regardless of their parents' employment status.

10 It should be pointed out here that, while the state (local government) has been functioning as the gate-keeper for certified childcare, the mismatch in the actual childcare places and the number of children registered is not evenly spread across the country. In reality, in the large cities there are huge waiting lists while in some rural areas certified childcare centres are not able to get enough children because of the decline in the proportion of young families. For example, in 1998, the enrolment rate for childcare centres across the country was about 88 per cent, but there were about 40,000 children on the waiting list across the country. A breakdown of the waiting lists shows that it is highest among under one-year-olds. Approximately 11 per cent of children under the age of one were not able to get into a certified childcare place in Japan. The figure varies from as low as zero in rural areas such as Niigata, Kanazawa, Miyazaki and Fukuyama cities, to over 50 per cent in Okinawa, Tokyo's Adachi ward, Musashino and Kohira cities, and Sakai city in Osaka (Hoikujoho 1998, 1999).

11 This was a piece of legislation drafted into Japan's postwar constitution by the US-led occupying government (GHQ). The purpose of this legislation was legally to force the Japanese state to provide social welfare for its people.

12 This was to match with another plan, called the Gold Plan, launched in 1989 which involved a large expansion in the public sector services for elderly people, and a large infusion of public money for private businesses to develop services for the elderly.

13 However, this does not mean that their children will necessarily be placed in their choice of childcare centres. The placement decision will still be made by local government. It simply means that parents will now be formally asked about the childcare centres in which they wish to register their children and the local government will respect their choice as much as possible.
14 The exchange rate for the yen in 1999 was on average ¥110 = US$1, or ¥120 to euro 1, although in reality the yen fluctuated between ¥105 and ¥125 to US$1 during that year. The average male income for 1998 was about ¥5.5 million, and the average household income was about ¥7.5 million.
15 The average non-subsidized cost of childcare for a child under the age of 1 is approximately ¥140,000 per month.
16 This year was notorious as the year of the fire-breathing horse (*hinoe uma*). It is believed that girls born in that year will shorten their husbands' lives. Such years occur only rarely; in the twentieth century there was only one, in 1966.

References

Anme, T. (1996) *Shoshika Jidai no Kosodateshien to Ikuji Kankyo Hyoka* (*An Evaluation Study of Childrearing Support and Childrearing Environment in the Age of Declining Birth Rate*), Tokyo: Kawashima Shoten.
Boling, P. (1998) 'Family Policy in Japan', *Journal of Social Policy*, 27, 2: 173–90.
Gordon, A. (1997) 'Managing the Japanese Household: the New Life Movement in Postwar Japan', *Social Politics*, 4, 2: 245–83.
Hoikujoho (1999) 'Joho Fairu' (Information File), *Hoikujoho*, vol. 265, March.
Hoikujoho (1998) '1998-nen 4-gatsu 1-nichi Genzai no Taikijisu Akiraka ni' (The Children on Childcare Waiting List as of 1 April 1998), *Hoikujoho*, vol. 261: 20–22 November.
Hoikukai (1994) 'Kodomo Mirai Zaidan ni Tsuite' (About Kodomo Mirai Zaidan). *Hoikukai*, vol. 243, November: 6–7.
(1996) *Kokumin Seikatsusenkodo Chosa* (*National Survey of Life Satisfaction*), Tokyo: EPA.
Japan – Economic Planning Agency (1997) *Kokumin Seikatsu Chosa* (*National Household Survey*), Tokyo: EPA.
Japan – Ministry of Health and Welfare (1981) *Baby Hotel Jittai Chosa* (*Survey of the Conditions of Baby Hotels*), Tokyo: Ministry of Health and Welfare.
Japan – Ministry of Health and Welfare (1994) *Riyo Shiyasui Hoikusho wo Mezashite* (*Towards an Accessible Childcare*), Tokyo: Ministry of Health and Welfare.
Japan – Ministry of Health and Welfare (1994b) *21 Seiki Fukushi Bijon* (*The 21st Century Welfare Vision*), Tokyo: Ministry of Health and Welfare.
Japan – Ministry of Health and Welfare (1995) *Jido wo Torimaku Setai no Jokyo: kokumin seikatsu kisochosa tokushu hokoku* (*The Conditions of Families with Children: a special report from the National Household Survey*), Tokyo: Ministry of Health and Welfare.
Japan – Ministry of Health and Welfare (1996) *Kokumin Seikatsu Jittai Chosa* (*National Household Income Survey*), Tokyo: Ministry of Health and Welfare.
Japan – Ministry of Health and Welfare (1996b) *Shakai Hosho Kozo Kaikaku no Hoko* (*The Direction for Social Security Restructuring*), Tokyo: Ministry of Health and Welfare.
Japan – Ministry of Health and Welfare (1997) *Kosei Hakusho: Kenko to Seikatsu no Shitsu no Kojo wo Mezashite* (*White Paper on Health and Welfare: Towards an Improvement of Health and Standard of Life*), Tokyo: Ministry of Health and Welfare.

Japan – Ministry of Health and Welfare (1998) *Kosei Hakusho: shoshi shakai wo kangaeru* (*White Paper on Health and Welfare: Issues of Low Birth Society*), Tokyo: Ministry of Health and Welfare.

Japan – Rodosho (1997) *Hataraku Josei no Jitsujo* (*The Reality of Working Women*), Tokyo: 21-seiki Shokugyo Zaidan.

Japan – Somucho (1992) *Shakai Seikatsu Kihon Chosa* (*Basic Survey of Social Life*), Tokyo: Somucho.

Japan – Somucho (1995) *1995 Genzai Suikei Jinko* (*1995 Current Population Data*), Tokyo: Somucho.

Jolivet, M. (1996) *Japan, The Childless Society?: The Crisis of Motherhood*, London: Routledge.

Kashiwame, R. (1997) *Jido Fukushi Kaikaku to Jicchitaisei* (*Child Welfare Reform and Its System of Implementation*), Tokyo: Minerva.

Kato, Y., Tanimukai, M., Shibano, M., Hamaya, A., Takaishi, J., Tomota, H. and Hirata, Y. (1997) 'Gyakutai Boshi Denwasodan no Assessment Kisochosa wo Moto ni Shite – Kosodateshien Sabisu no Teigen' (Towards Establishment of Childrearing Support Services: Based on a Preliminary Survey of the Abuse Prevention Telephone Hotline), presented at the 45th Annual Japan National Social Welfare Association Conference, Ryukoku University, Kyoto, Japan, 25–26 October.

Kusatake, A., Kainou, T., Wakano, N. and Yoshida, A. (eds) *Kazoku Detabokku* (*Family Data Book*), Tokyo: Yuhikaku.

Murayama, Y. (1998) 'Hoikusho' (Childcare Centres), in Nihon Fujin Dantai Rengokai (ed.) *Fujin Hakusho* (*White Paper on Women*), Tokyo: Horubu Publisher.

Murayama, Y. (1997) 'Jidofukushiho "Kaisei" no shoten: hoikusho sochi seido wo megutte' (Child Welfare Law 'Reform' and its Focus: the Childcare Centre sochi seido), in Nihon Kodomo wo Mamoru Kai (ed.) *Kodomo Hakusho* (*White Paper on Children*), Tokyo: Soudo Bunka.

Nihon Jido Mondai Chosakai (1992) *Minkan Kosodateshien Sabisu Riyosha Chosa* (*A Survey of Private Sector Childrearing Support Services Users*), Tokyo: NJMC.

Ohinata, M. (1995) 'Saikin no Kodomo wo Aisenai Hahaoya no Kenkyukara Mietekuru Mono' (Research on the New Mothers who Cannot Love their Children: From a Psychological Perspective) *Kazoku Kenkyu Nenpo*, no. 20: 20–31

Peng, I. (1997a) 'Impacts of Welfare Restructuring in Japan, 1980–1995: Dilemmas of Welfare Transition', in Peter Saunders and Tony Eardley (eds) vol. 2 (Proceedings of the National Social Policy Conference, Sydney, 16–18 July).

Peng, I. (1997b) 'Impact of Welfare Reform in Japan since 1980: with Focus on the Issue of the Ageing Society', *Japanese Journal of Social Services*, no. 1: 99–119.

Shakai Hoshoseido Shingikai (1995) *Shakai Hosho Taisei no Saikochiku – Kankoku* (*The Restructuring of the Social Security System: Recommendations*), report of the Minister of Health and Welfare, 4 July.

Shimoebisu, M. (1994) 'Kazokuseisaku no Rekishitekitenkai: Ikuji ni Taisuru Seisakutaiou no Hensen' (Historical Development of the Family Policy: Changes in Policies Concerning Childcare), in Shakai Hosho Kenkyujo (ed.) *Gendai Kazoku to Shakaihosho* (*Today's Family and Social Security*), Tokyo: University of Tokyo Press.

Tamura (1997a) 'Hoikushoseido Kaikakuan no Mondaiten' (Issues Related to the Childcare Reform Policy Legislation), *Hoiku Joho*, vol. 243, 5–11 May.

Tamura (1997b) 'Koseisho Nyushotetsuzukihoshin wo do Yomunoka' (How to Understand the Ministry of Health and Welfare's Policies on Childcare Application Procedures), *Hoiku Joho*, vol. 250, December: 6–17.

Zenkoku Hoikudantai Rengokai and Hoikukenkyusho (eds) (1997) *Hoiku Hakusho 1997 (White Paper on Childcare 1997)*, Tokyo: Sodo Bunka.

9 Lone mothers

How do they work and care in different welfare state regimes?

Jørgen Elm Larsen

Introduction

During the past decade lone mothers have increasingly been the subject of social scientists' research. Broadly speaking, research on lone mothers has been divided into two streams. One category of research concentrates in a relatively limited way on lone mothers: their numbers, makeup and development, living conditions and in association with these factors, the extent of poverty and policies implemented. The other category utilizes lone mothers as a 'border case' to characterize the relationships between the state, the market and the family in a number of different types of welfare states. The treatment and wellbeing of lone mothers is used as a litmus test of how women in general fare in a given welfare state. However, there is not a sharp divide between these two categories of research and in this chapter the aim is to integrate them with the purpose of clarifying in what way the case of lone mothers can be used to categorize welfare states as 'women-friendly'.

This chapter discusses some of the predominant models of welfare state typologies and their ability to account for lone mothers' poverty risks. The conclusion is that different policy regimes may have similar effects on lone mothers' poverty rates and similar regimes may have different effects on lone mothers' poverty rates.

New structures and changing everyday life: changes in gender relations and family life

In the last twenty to thirty years there has been a fundamental change in the structure of the family in the western world. Families has become less stable, and the size of families has shrunk. There has been an increase in divorce rates. Furthermore, there has been an increase in the number of single people with or without children. The number of marriages, and especially the number of remarriages after divorce, is falling, and marriage no longer provides life-long security. At the same time there has been an increase in the number of women participating in the workforce everywhere. This has changed the lives of women and also markedly altered the conditions of family life and the way of living in general. However, the participation of women in the workforce has not diminished their relative responsibilities and care duties around the home to take account of the paid work they have taken on. This, then, has given rise to a number of conflicts, for example between work and family life, between the sexes and for women themselves (Beck 1992; Beck and Beck-Gernsheim 1995).

Three tendencies with particular significance for relations between the sexes and for family structures can been pointed out:

- younger women are often better educated than older women and, due to the manner of their upbringing and labour market participation, they expect equality;
- two-income families have become a common strategy to maintain economic security not only for women but for the family as a whole;
- young mothers have been motivated to enter the labour force and stay there because of, for example, increasing instability in family patterns and hence within the expectation of having a male breadwinner. To have a job is a safeguard for oneself and one's children against the instability of marriage (Europaparlamentet 1994; Saraceno 1996).

Thus, the way marriage is looked upon by individuals has changed considerably since the Second World War. Women's increasing economic independence brings with it not only the fact that the value of marriage has fallen with regard to its previous criteria, but also that there has been a change in the criteria within which marriage is measured. For example, the value of marriage as a source of economic security has decreased, whereas its value as a source of personal and intimate relationships has become more important (Giddens 1992).

However, the conditions for entering into marriage or leaving an unsatisfactory marriage are still of crucial importance for the possibilities of establishing and maintaining functioning, autonomous households for lone mothers.[1] These conditions vary greatly in different welfare states, and these differences have important consequences for lone mothers and their children.

Lone mothers and theories of welfare state regimes

Feminist welfare state research has shown that the origin and development of welfare states has not only been a question of regulating market forces and class relationships, but that regulation of relationships between the sexes has been an integral part of this process. Feminist welfare state research has – through criticism of the prevailing interpretations of the dynamics and the actors in the welfare state development process – attempted to reconstruct the existing paradigms so that they can encompass gender relations or develop alternative models, for example, the breadwinner model.

Lone mothers are often used as a strategic 'border case' in feminist research on welfare states because the lone mother category is extremely apt to describe the conditions for a social citizenship, which reflects gender: that is, the right and opportunity to establish and maintain an autonomous household without leading to marginalization, poverty and stigmatization. Thus, welfare states that support this right to establish and maintain a functioning, autonomous household in different and complementary ways are generally seen as 'women-friendly' welfare states.

Orloff (1993) argues that the decommodification concept developed by Esping-Andersen (1990) has to be subordinate to an overall concept of independence, which includes an individual's freedom from being forced into a number of suppressive conditions in different arenas. This assumes that the state mediates in a number of relationships from the economy to the family and race relations in the local community. Orloff expands and revises Esping-Andersen's dimensions of analysis by adding two new dimensions: access to paid work and the possibility and capacity to create and maintain an autonomous household. The demand for capacity to establish and maintain an autonomous household is especially related to poverty risks due to the absence of a husband (divorced or deceased). Lone mothers' financial vulnerability is – past and present – proof of this.

Lewis (1997a) is, however, of the opinion that it is not sufficient to make changes to Esping-Andersen's and others' analyses of welfare state regimes by drawing women into the representation of and connection between work, welfare and decommodification. For example, it would probably not be the case that access to paid work in itself would lead to financial autonomy for women. Some feminist studies of the welfare state have therefore launched alternative gender-specific models that use another set of criteria to construct welfare regimes. Lewis tries, as a starting point, to find some rough indicators for the relationship between paid work, unpaid work and welfare. This approach looks at how far away from the traditional male breadwinner model different countries have moved. She points to three types of welfare states: strong male breadwinner models (e.g. Germany, the UK and the Netherlands), moderate male breadwinner models (e.g. Belgium and France), and weak male breadwinner models (e.g. Denmark and Sweden) (Lewis and Ostner 1994).

Sainsbury (1994) is critical of Lewis's and Ostner's typologies on the grounds that they are based on one common dimension: the strength of the male breadwinner model in the shape of the traditional division of labour between the sexes, and its implication for social rights.[2] Sainsbury identifies ten dimensions as the basis for defining variations in breadwinner and care regimes: for example, family ideology, the basis for rights, unity (individual/family) for benefits and contributions, whether employment and wage policies give priority to men or are directed at both sexes, whether care is primarily private or whether the state is heavily involved, and whether the care work is paid or has a paid element.[3] Including all these parameters in the analysis gives a more comprehensive and complex insight into women's position in different welfare states. Looking at things in this way, there is a sharp division between Sweden on the one hand and the UK, the US and the Netherlands on the other, but also significant divisions between the latter three countries. In the Netherlands the family is the unit for social benefits, while the individual is the unit in the US and the UK. Sainsbury, therefore, concludes that the male breadwinner model cannot be the only reference point for looking at the welfare state's gender regimes and shows the advantages gained by using comparisons that are based on a number of different dimensions.

The notion of defamilialization

In a later work Sainsbury (1996) attempts a distinction between the breadwinner model and the individual model. The two models characterize how social benefits and services either underpin the family or support the individual's chance of achieving or right to have autonomy. It has been argued that 'defamilialization' is a more useful concept compared with the decommodi-fication concept, in that defamilialization 'is about the terms and conditions under which people engage in families, and the extent to which they can uphold an acceptable standard of living independently of (patriarchal) "family" participation'. (McLaughlin and Glendinning 1994: 65). As family responsibilities in modern society typically rest on a smaller extended family and on more fragile family ties, then the extent of defamilialization can be a deciding factor for families' and individuals' welfare, as well as the strength of family obligations in themselves. The concept of defamilialization concerns the right not to give care as well as the right to do so. Defamilialization does not mean that a total breakdown in family relationships is occuring:

> The issue is not whether people are completely 'defamilialized' but rather the extent to which packages of legal and social provisions have altered the balance of power between men and women, between dependents and non-dependents, and hence the terms and conditions under which people engage in familial or caring arrangements.
>
> (McLaughlin and Glendinning 1994: 66)

It also concerns forming the framework for the family and its members, so they can take care of each other and manage the voluntary responsibilities they take on without the development of power imbalances, unbalanced dependency relationships, and the impossibility of leaving the relationship.

Lewis (1997b) agrees that there are problems connected with feminist politics that argue for the right to receive social benefits as a 'care-giving person' (see, for example, Knijn 1994), because status as a care-giving person also makes women dependent on men's income, or lone mothers totally dependent on public benefits, and may create obstacles for entering or re-entering the labour market in the future. However, it is necessary to include care regimes in any welfare state analysis that has relations between the sexes as a pivotal point (Anttonen and Sipilä 1996). This is particularly clear in relation to lone mothers, who have to be financially self-sufficient and manage childcare as well. To avoid the situation where lone mothers are forced to 'choose' between paid work or care – as they are in many countries – it is necessary that they, on the one hand, have the possibility to negotiate an 'income package' made up of income contributions from the children's fathers, from paid work and from social benefits, and that they, on the other hand, are supported by policies that facilitate their employment; especially through publicly subsidized childcare facilities.

Poverty regimes and policy regimes in relation to lone mothers

The concepts of policy regime and poverty regime are here used to explain how and why routes to the capacity to establish and maintain an autonomous household can be paved in different ways for lone mothers. I understand poverty regimes as an outcome of the logic of policy regimes. Different policy regime logics may, however, have the same effect on the level of poverty but different outcomes in terms of the capacity to establish and maintain an autonomous household. Policy regimes must, therefore, be related both to their ability to combat poverty and to their ability to create pathways to autonomous households. This is basically a question of how the resources and services to avoid poverty are generated: that is the specific combination and level of resources from the market, the state and the family. However, autonomy and wellbeing are also affected, for example, by the legal framework around the family institution and by public discourses in relation to lone mothers.

Poverty regimes

The question of what constitutes the risks to lone mothers of having low incomes and living in poverty can only be answered by considering the relationship and the interaction between the labour market, family structure and the state. Lone mothers obtain their incomes from three different sources: private sources, paid work and social security payments. However, the relative proportions of these three sources vary significantly from country to country as well as from individual to individual within the group of lone mothers (Wong *et al.* 1993).[4] It is the overall configuration of income sources and the social infrastructure that, in combination, can affect these sources (for example, childcare facilities), and determine the character and extent of the poverty risk that confronts lone mothers.

Table 9.1 puts together the approximate overall effects of labour market participation and policy regimes on poverty risks to lone mothers. The extent of poverty among lone mothers varies significantly among the wealthy developed nations, but in all countries there is a tendency for lone mothers to be poorer than two-parent families irrespective of whether the proportion of lone mothers in employment is greater than that of married mothers in two-parent families (Lewis 1997a).

The ranking for the 15 countries in Table 9.1 has the Scandinavian countries at one end and the US at the other.[5] In the US approximately half of all lone mothers and their children live below the poverty line. In those countries where

Table 9.1 Lone mothers: poverty, labour market participation and public provisions

Ranking	Poverty	Labour market participation	Public provisions
1	Sweden (a)	Sweden	Sweden
2	Norway (a)	Denmark	Norway
3	Denmark (a)	France	France
4	Netherlands (b)	Portugal	Luxembourg
5	Belgium (b)	Norway	Denmark
6	Luxembourg (c)	Luxembourg	Belgium
7	Greece (c)	US	UK
8	France (c)	Italy	Germany
9	Spain (d)	Germany	the Netherlands
10	Italy (d)	Greece	Italy
11	Ireland (d)	Belgium	USA
12	Germany (d)	Spain	Portugal
13	UK (d)	UK	Ireland
14	Portugal (d)	the Netherlands	Greece
15	US (e)	Ireland	Spain

Notes: Ranking according to poverty rates (from low to high), labour market participation (from high to low) and degree of public provisions (from high to low). Trends from the 1980s to the beginning of the 1990s.

Since the poverty rates differ in the studies referred to, the ranking of countries in Table 9.1 should be seen only as relative as indicated by country-group ranking from (a) to (e):

(a)   Low: under 10 per cent
(b)   Low+: 10–15 per cent
(c)   Medium–: approximately 15–20 per cent
(d)   Medium+: approximately 20–30 per cent
(e)   High: approximately 50 per cent.

There are a significant number of studies about lone mothers and poverty. However, few of these are comparative. It is difficult to make comparisons between different studies of poverty, because they often build on different definitions of poverty, different methods of poverty measurement, and different data. Consequently the results also vary – and in some cases quite significantly so.

Sources: Bak 1997; Lewis 1997a; Bradshaw *et al*. 1996; Millar 1996; Baker 1995; Martin 1995; McLanahan *et al*. 1995; EU 1994; Hobson 1994; Ramprakash 1994; Sørensen 1994; Borchorst 1993; Bradshaw *et al*. 1993; OECD 1993; Oppenheim 1993; Wong *et al*. 1993; Millar 1992; Roll 1992; and Smeeding *et al*. 1990.

the incidence of lone mothers' poverty is lowest there exists either a high degree of labour market participation combined with generous supplementary public benefits, as in Sweden and Denmark, or a high level of public benefits, as in the Netherlands and Belgium.

Policy regimes

There is no overall gender model which can explain the complex mix of contributions to lone mothers' incomes and services from the welfare state, the market and the family. Overall it is, however, possible to identify four types of policy regimes for lone mothers:

- those that aim to support lone mothers exclusively as mothers;
- those that aim to have lone mothers choose between paid work and mothering;
- those that aim to support lone mothers both as paid workers and as mothers;
- those where the family institution is the nexus of lone mothers' livelihoods.[6]

The construction of the four types of policy regimes attempts to characterize the kind of roles and relationships lone mothers are either encouraged or forced to engage in by state policies or lack of state policies. However, it is only when these 'role models' are related to poverty rates that it is possible to make important distinctions both between and within the four policy regimes. By combining policy regimes and poverty regimes it becomes possible to measure the degree to which lone mothers can achieve independence from a male breadwinner and at the same time avoid poverty.

Policy regime 1: lone mothers exclusively as care-givers

This regime can be subdivided into two qualitatively different types:

- countries with high levels of poverty among lone mothers – the UK and Ireland;
- countries with relatively low levels of poverty among lone mothers – Belgium and the Netherlands.

The UK and Ireland demonstrate similar characteristics with respect to labour market participation, in that it is low in both countries for lone mothers and even lower for married and cohabiting mothers.

This type of policy regime is selective and directed towards poor families. Social security benefits are given to all poor families on the assumption that mothers – irrespective of whether they live in one- or two-breadwinner families – will stay at home with their children. By generally meeting the needs of poor families, lone mothers are also assisted because they often belong to the group of poorer families. The norm in the UK is that lone mothers stay at home. Almost half of lone mothers' income originates from public benefit payments. British policies can be characterized as 'poverty entrapping policies', as they eliminate low-paid part-time work as an economic possibility. The policy creates a dichotomy between homemakers and full-time low-paid mothers. Lone mothers are either unsupported workers or mothers (Duncan and Edwards 1997).

Belgium and the Netherlands are not identical, but are sufficiently similar to be considered together, and differ from the other categories of countries. The incidence of poverty is relatively low. The welfare state system is specifically directed towards lone mothers with modest incomes. It is founded on the assumption that most women would prefer to be at home with their children, if it were financially possible, and that lone mothers have special problems that require special assistance. In the Netherlands the state plays a dominant role in lone mothers' maintenance, as labour market participation is low, and lower for lone mothers than for both married and cohabiting mothers.[7] In Belgium the state also plays a central role in lone mothers' maintenance, but their labour market participation is greater than in the Netherlands.

Policy regime 2: lone mothers as care-givers or workers –
Norway, France and Luxembourg

Norwegian social policy specifies that lone mothers must be able to choose between staying at home or taking a job. To support this policy an 'income package' has been established which includes a universal tax-free children allowance to lone mothers, education allowances to lone mothers, and rent assistance (Kamerman 1995). However, there is a shortage of day-care institutions in Norway and the number of hours children spend in school per day is low until the children reach 10 years of age. This is a big problem for lone mothers irrespective of their level of education. The relatively generous benefits for lone mothers need to be seen in the light of generous benefits to all mothers. The special 'transition benefit' for lone mothers can create problems when they are confronted with the labour market after the transition benefit ceases (Leira 1993). However, Norwegian women's employment rate increased during the 1980s and 1990s especially following the creation of good part-time jobs in the public sector. This made it easier for women with small children to manage both working and family life even though the coverage rate of public childcare for children below 2 years of age did not exceed 20 per cent in 1993 (Ellingsæter and Rønsen 1996).

In France and Luxembourg poverty rates are relatively low among lone mothers. Both countries have a relatively high level of labour market participation and well-developed social benefits and services. Policy regimes giving universal support for younger children aim to give financial support and job protection by way of maternity/paternity leave for parents with small children. This policy is based on the assumption that most mothers of younger children prefer to remain at home if they can, and that these children benefit from having parents who are at home because they want to be. This covers both married and unmarried mothers. French family policy is explicitly formulated in such a way that it benefits all families with two or more children, but it puts special emphasis on families with young children (under 3 years of age). In France, universal child benefits are given and there are means-tested additional supplements to low-income families (Kamerman 1995). The French policy supports lone mothers as mothers or as workers.

Policy regime 3: lone mothers as care-givers and workers

This regime can be subdivided into two qualitatively different types:

- countries with high levels of poverty – Portugal and the US;
- countries with low levels of poverty – Sweden and Denmark.

Portugal and the US display similarities. Lone parents have a high level of labour market participation in both these countries,[8] and public benefits in both countries are poor. Lone mothers in these countries are unsupported workers. That lone mothers in Portugal experience less poverty than in the US must be attributed to greater support from their families. While the proportion of lone mothers is high in the US, it is low in Portugal.

The US has a high rate of labour market participation for lone mothers (but in contrast with Denmark and Sweden a lower rate for lone mothers compared with married mothers), but at the same time has the highest incidence of poverty among the 15 nations included in this study. This is partially due to poor public benefits, little support from the father to the children, and low level of overall help from the family, as well as very low wages for those without education and work experience.

Denmark and Sweden are characterized by a low incidence of poverty and high labour market participation. In contrast with the US, and especially in Sweden minimum wages are high and these are further supplemented by income assistance, rental assistance, and day-care assistance; thus limiting the incidence of poverty and underpining lone mothers' labour market participation and basis for providing for their children.

This policy regime, which combines labour market and family policies, has established a number of benefits that support working families with children. The aim is to make it possible for both parents to enter and remain in the labour market. The basic assumptions of the policy regime are that only when paid work makes up a substantial part of the total income will the family have an adequate standard of living, and also that men and women should have an equal opportunity to participate both in paid work and in the home. Lone mothers are treated on the same terms as married/cohabiting mothers, in that they need to be self-sufficient through participation in the labour market. Sweden and Denmark have placed particular emphasis on full employment, and labour market and social policies have played a major role in reaching that objective, thus supporting lone mothers as workers (Duncan and Edwards 1997).

Policy regime 4: the family institution as the nexus of solo mothers'
livelihood – Germany, Greece, Italy and Spain

In Germany, Greece, Italy and Spain the family institution is very important for the livelihood of lone mothers. The family is a major contributor to lone mothers' income and, for those who participate in the labour market, the family provides childcare. Due to the family system in these four countries the poverty level of lone mothers is reduced considerably.

Italy and Germany are similar to each other in a number of ways. They are somewhere in the middle with respect to labour market participation, in the middle with respect to poverty, and in the middle with respect to the generosity of state benefits. That lone mothers in Italy apparently manage better than their German counterparts, then, is because the family usually plays a more central role in taking care of its members. However, the proportion of lone mothers is greater in Germany, and Italy has a low incidence of lone mothers.

Greece and Spain also have points of similarity. Public benefits to lone mothers are limited. Greek and Spanish lone mothers have low levels of labour market participation and relatively high risks of being in poverty. That Greeek and Spanish lone mothers actually do better than the German and Italian, then, is primarily due to greater support from their families. The proportion of lone mothers in these countries is, however, low.

Conclusion on poverty regimes and policy regimes

Most countries demonstrate characteristics from a number of models and within each model countries vary greatly in lone mothers' poverty rates, partly as a result of differences in the level of benefits paid to lone mothers. Table 9.2 shows the main findings from the study of poverty regimes and policy regimes in relation to lone mothers.

From Table 9.2 it can be concluded that the possibility of establishing and maintaining an autonomous household, also when children grow up and move away from home, is most developed in countries where there is either a chance

Table 9.2 Summary of the findings from the study of poverty regimes and policy regimes in relation to lone mothers

Policy regime	Poverty regime		
	Poverty low	*Poverty medium*	*Poverty high*
Mothers	Belgium The Netherlands		UK Ireland
Mothers or workers	Norway	France Luxembourg	
Workers and mothers	Denmark Sweden		US Portugal
Family institution		Germany Greece Italy Spain	

of choosing between work and care or where work and care can be combined. In countries where lone mothers are almost exclusively dependent on state, market or family support, the possibility of establishing and maintaining a well-functioning autonomous household is fragile or limited.

The position of lone mothers raise a fundamental question about the relationship between care and social citizenship rights. However, the summary in Table 9.2 shows how policy regimes can structure women's choice in relation to paid and unpaid work, and indicates the extent to which the various welfare states demonstrate an integrated or a dichotomous approach in relation to labour market participation and public benefits – especially in the southern European countries where the family is a central part of the total care configuration for lone mothers.

A lone-mother-friendly citizenship: politics of equality or difference?

Citizenship as defined by T.H. Marshall (1964) consists of civil, political and social citizenship rights. Citizenship rights are to create a more inclusive society (Lister 1990). Even though citizenship rights are based on equality principles they may. in reality, for example be practised within a gender-defined labour market, where the traditional old-fashioned worker was a full-time male worker, who was without care and housework duties.

The paradox in the feminist interest in the citizenship concept is that the actual idea of a 'female-friendly citizenship' is self-contradictory because the citizenship concept was from its inception 'female unfriendly', and because the category 'females' in itself represents a false generalization in line with the traditional construction of citizenship in a universal male model (Lister 1997). The continued prevalence of the idea concerns whether the universal citizen – in theory without social class, gender, ethnicity and sexuality, but in reality male, white and heterosexual – is a barrier for a gender-sensitive welfare state analysis. Jones (1990) argues that:

> In a democratic polity, citizens are meant to enjoy equal individual rights. Still, biological, social, and discursively defined differences make the granting of the same rights to different persons more likely to sustain a hierachy of rights than a uniformity of status.
>
> (Jones 1990: 796)

The solution which is proposed by some feminists is to define the citizenship concept in such a way that it can contain a full social citizenship for all members of society. This also requires a recognition that citizens as members of the community have care duties, and furthermore it requires a re-evaluation and redistribution of those care duties. The processes that need to be initiated in attaining such changes are very deep-seated, because they challenge the gendered division of work and care on which most family and welfare state systems are built. Which citizenship ideals can assist the removal of gender status as the basis for inequality, and which citizenship models can best promote women's active participation in all affairs of life? The deciding question here is whether citizenship can weigh up equality/equal status between society's different status groups – e.g. men and women – or whether citizenship should integrate individuals on the basis of difference and diversity. Lone mothers' dilemma between care and work illustrates in an exemplary way the problems there are in the balance between differences and equality.

Lone mothers caught up between care and paid work

A key characteristic of a 'lone mother-friendly' citizenship is the capacity both to establish and maintain an autonomous household and to reconcile family life and work life. This means that an inclusive citizenship for lone mothers has to combine politics of equality and of difference (universalism and particularism).

Lone mothers' relatively greater financial vulnerability and more stressed lifestyle (especially for lone mothers in full-time work) compared with two-breadwinner families can be alleviated but not eliminated when women's wages approach those of men and/or when low wages are supplemented with public benefits and services, and when there exist the possibilities for taking days off for family care. Even though the lone mother's income cannot be expected to be the same as in a two-breadwinner family, public policies can still partly reduce the differences, and poverty can be reduced to a minimum, or be totally eliminated. From a financial standpoint, lone mothers are better off in those countries where child benefits are generous – and this is especially the case where child benefits and services are universal. Lone mothers' financial welfare is best served where they have the opportunity to 'package' their income – i.e. income from both work and public benefits; where the benefits are universal for mothers and children and not categorized for lone mothers; and where the 'social benefit/wage' is high, especially with respect to publicly-financed childcare facilities. However, in many countries lone mothers do not 'package' their incomes in a balanced manner, because they are almost exclusively dependent on either state, family or market incomes.

In the Netherlands, for example, the possibility for lone mothers to establish and maintain an autonomous household is almost entirely dependent on support from the state. It is possible to have equality in wellbeing (measured in relation to the gender-determined poverty gap), even though a large proportion of women live alone, or are lone mothers. There exist large gender differences in wage levels in the Netherlands, partly because relatively few women participate in the labour market, and partly because of the large wage gap between men and women. Thus, equality is achieved mainly through the taxation system and redistribution via social benefit payments. A reasonably high basic level of income is obtainable by all, and generally this defines the lowest level of income in the marketplace (Sørensen 1995).

The possibility for lone mothers to establish and maintain an autonomous household in Germany is more limited than in the Netherlands. In Germany there is no guaranteed basic level of income. Thus, the gap between the incomes of men and women is much greater, even though taxation and transfer incomes to a large extent reduce these imbalances that otherwise would be the result of the uneven labour market relationships. As a reasonably high minimum income level for everyone is not available, the family and the male breadwinner remain very important factors for women's financial wellbeing.

In the US lone mothers' dependency on labour market participation makes it difficult or impossible, especially for unskilled lone mothers with wages below the poverty line, to establish and maintain an autonomous household. A key component in establishing and maintaining a well-functioning autonomous household for wage-earning lone mothers is the degree of recognition of their care work – such as childcare, care benefits, childcare benefits, and parental leave entitlements. The extensive poverty among lone mothers in the US can partly be explained by the lack of recognition of care work as a legitimate area of public responsibility. Thus, day-care possibilities, employment possibilities, and the way the welfare state generally socializes the costs of care, make up the one side of possibilities that lone mothers have. The other side comprises the ways in which the benefit types and levels are defined and laid in place (Hobson 1994).

The Scandinavian 'case'

The Scandinavian welfare states have in a number of ways come quite a long way in relation to gender equality: women's participation in the labour force is high, part-time work is subject to strong regulation and social protection compared with many other countries, and the differences between men's and women's wages are relatively limited compared with other countries'. Public childcare and parental leave arrangements, as well as conditions tied to flexible work-time, are significantly better than in other countries.

In Sweden the relatively small gender gap in the poverty level is achieved by a combination of relatively small differences in income levels and, thus, a limited redistribution between men and women in the family and a large redistribution via taxation. Sweden has mapped out a strategy for equal opportunities by changing from rights to make demands, based on differences, to politics based on equal treatment. This was an equal treatment strategy which was based on labour market participation, and which was underpinned by full employment policies. The mapping out of this strategy also opened the possibility for a greater recognition of women's care work within the family (Lewis and Åström 1992). This also marks a difference from Denmark, because care activities are supported much more in Swedish than in Danish policies. In Sweden, for example, women have a right to a long maternity leave and women with small children have a right to part-time jobs. This is not the case in Denmark. The Scandinavian, and especially the Swedish, welfare state in many ways combines principles of equality and difference. However, especially in the Danish case, it can be stated that there is too much emphasis on equality (the breadwinner model) and too little emphasis on difference (the care model), thus making it difficult for working lone mothers to reconcile working life and family life – and especially having time left for other things than working and caring (Larsen and Sørensen 1993). These two criteria are, especially for lone mothers, difficult to unite even with mediating policies such as maternity leave, parental leave and care leave, even though these policies are important elements in a social order which makes possible both equality and difference.

However, politics that place too great an emphasis on differences can, on the other hand, weaken women's long-term citizenship position. The balancing act thus consists of creating conditions so that both care and paid work can develop within the citizenship position. But as 'time' (paid-work time, housework time, care time, democratic and participation time and free time) is a central factor, the time dimension must also be an important part of the citizenship issue (Lister 1997). A more equitable gender-based division of labour would thus promote both similarities and differences: it would improve women's possibilities in the public sphere to put them on more equal terms with men and, at the same time, emphasize the importance of care duties as a part of citizenship. Feminist praxis must therefore be based in a 'politics of solidarity in difference' (Lister 1997), a 'transversal politics' (Yuval-Davis 1994) or a 'reflective solidarity' (Dean 1995).

Changes in the policy logic

The policy logic of welfare states is not cast in bronze. In those countries where the male breadwinner model has dominated, there has been a move towards treating lone mothers more as workers rather than as mothers. However, there remains great ambivalence in, for example, Germany and the UK with respect to defining the role that women with small children are to fulfil. In connection with a move to reduce the UK welfare state's social responsibility towards poor families, there has been a renewed move towards men's role as the breadwinner. This, however, is based more on the role of men as biological fathers and as breadwinners for their children than as a breadwinners for the family (see Millar in this volume). Most European countries do not rank lone mothers very high on their political agenda and they have not been the subject of comprehensive political discourse and measures. Only in the UK are lone mothers seen as a serious social problem and have been characterized and caricatured as 'welfare mothers'. However, it is most likely that a continued growth of lone mothers in, for example, Italy or Germany will increase focus on this group. This is also in connection with the fact that the European countries generally are experiencing more types of pressure which may force them to redefine and reorganize family policies: changes in gender roles, changes in family structure, integration of women into the labour market, inadequate social security systems and pressure on public budgets. As the situation is now, it is not possible to point out one, single, tendency regarding lone mothers in the US and the western European countries. It is just as easy to point out differences as similarities between the countries.

However, there is one tendency in policy regime development that does indicate that most countries are now moving away from purely income transfer methods to policies that encourage women to combine wage income with social benefits and services. If women are expected to work, then there has to be in place an adequate social infrastrucure which makes this possible. Those tendencies that have existed in a number of countries, to force people – including lone mothers – from social benefits into work ('work-fare'), have actualized the dilemma between care and work. Knijn (1994) has argued for the right to care time as a part of citizenship. Any forcing of people into work, of those who have care-giving duties, would thus constitute an example of the prioritizing of paid work over care in relation to inclusion and exclusion from citizenship rights. However, Lister (1997) sees a problem in Knijn's argument, as she fears the occurrence of exclusion from full citizenship unless the rights to engage in care are not limited. Lister is of the opinion that the balance between care and paid work must be established through the consideration of a person's lifetime development. This could, for example, happen by women with older children having the possibility for and right to enter the workforce, assuming that their employment is supported by adequate institutional arrangements.

If independence and self-sufficiency are the keys to citizenship, and if employment is the key to independence and self-sufficiency, then inequalities on the labour market, both in the form of access to, the conditions for, and the outcome of labour market participation, are crucial for lone mothers' wellbeing and their capacity to establish and maintain an autonomous household.

Social and health policies, for example in relation to care for dependent persons, are a factor in labour market participation both in relation to the opportunity to participate and for the type of participation for those individuals that are involved in care work. If wages, especially for unskilled people, are very low, if there are no, or very limited, additional social benefits to supplement the wage income, and if there is a poor infrastructure of publicly financed day-care facilities, the attempt to move or force lone mothers to work may actually worsen instead of improving their situation. The new Labour government's 'New Deal for Women' in the UK, for example, exposes exactly the gap between, on the one hand, intensions of promoting lone mothers' labour market participation and, on the other hand, low wages and lack of publicly funded day-care facilities which can make labour market participation a very poor deal for lone mothers (Levitas 1998; Lister 1999). Even in the most 'lone mother-friendly' welfare state, Sweden, lone mothers' living conditions have deteriorated from the 1980s to the 1990s. Due to rising levels of unemployment and cuts in welfare state spending in areas especially affecting benefits and services given to lone mothers, the poverty rate for lone mothers has increased considerably during the period from 1987 to 1994 (Socialstyrelsen 1997). Although the legal framework for establishing an autonomous household for lone mothers has generally improved in most countries, the possibility to maintain an autonomous household for lone mothers has been made more difficult in many countries during the 1990s, not least due to changes in both labour market conditions and in welfare state spending.

Conclusion

Feminist welfare state research has contributed to a better understanding of how welfare states are co-producers of commodification and decommodification, how stratification patterns not only must be seen in relation to social classes but also in relation to gender, age and ethnicity, and that the relationships between the family, the state and the market is not only a breadwinner relationship, but also offers a structure to gender relations and gender-based work divisions – especially when it concerns the relationship between paid work, unpaid housework and care tasks. However, an important question, which must be asked, is how meaningful is the use of such globalized concepts about welfare state regimes and citizenship rights – feminist or not – to characterize national welfare state configurations and institutions that do not necessarily demonstrate consistency for the various policy logics and citizenship rights, and thus can only diverge from one policy field to another and from one area of citizenship rights to another.

In connection with these issues, lone mothers become an interesting 'border case' because this raises some of the most central issues that are connected with the recognition of unpaid care work (or lack thereof), the manner in which paid and unpaid work is combined, and the states' responsibility with respect to the individual and the family. If lone mothers are taken as a starting point for a classification of regime types, then the placement of the individual countries looks somewhat different. Should we, then, have to abandon general theories of regime types? This study as well as other studies (for example, Nurmi 1997) show that welfare state regimes can only be generated on a very general level. As soon as more limited phenomena are analysed, such as lone mothers, then one can often conclude that countries need to be regrouped or differentiated in relation to the more general regime classifications. Taking as the starting point how lone mothers' risk of poverty is affected by family, state and the market, as well as the relationship between these spheres, I have shown that some of the most popular regime typologies cannot fully explain lone mothers' poverty risks in different nations' welfare states. Those policy regimes that are normally regarded as being homogeneous, for example France and Germany in Esping-Andersen's (1990) typology or, for example, the UK and the Netherlands in Lewis and Ostner's (1994) typology, produce very different effects in relation to lone mothers' poverty risk, and policy regimes that are normally regarded as being heterogeneous, produce quite homogeneous poverty risks for lone mothers, for example Denmark and the Netherlands in Lewis and Ostner's typology.

Therefore, one important conclusion to be drawn from this study is that a distinction has to be made between types of policy regimes and their outcomes. The same policy regime may produce very different outcomes, and different policy regimes may produce similar outcomes. The outcomes perspective on welfare state regimes or policy regimes is important for the understanding of how policy regimes work in practical terms.

It has, however, been claimed that even though comparative studies of gender and poverty, including feminization of poverty across countries, are important in that they allow prediction about basic gender inequalities, these studies often have a limited perspective on gender and the welfare state – especially if they only focus on how public policies either reduce or promote women's poverty risk. For example, Orloff (1996) is of the opinion that such a narrow focus on the relationship between gender and the welfare state is problematic, if one is concerned with the state's influence of gendered social institutions, e.g. gender-based work divisions and the gender power structure. This criticism is in principle correct, but it is at the same time double-edged, in that to the same extent it also strikes at the non-feminist and feminist attempts that have been made to classify different nations' welfare states into more general regime types. A more narrow focus on lone mothers and poverty risk is really a litmus test on whether it is more relevant to work with more limited topics and the possible policy regimes (or configurations between state, the market, and the family), that are attached to these. At the same time it is obvious that a general understanding of the prevailing gender and gender-based power relations in the welfare state and in citizenship rights are necessary to allow identification of the relationships between the different societal spheres and policy fields. However, one of the welfare state's fundamental characteristics must be whether it has been able to eliminate or reduce poverty to a minimum. Seen from a gender perspective, the deciding criterion for the welfare state's quality is whether lone mothers have low or high poverty rates, such that women have the possibility for choosing an alternative to marriage – or the possibility for existing without a male breadwinner.

Finally, it can be concluded that from the perspective taken on the evaluation there will be particular dimensions in the construction of the welfare state and the construction of society that will be more in focus than others, and with this certain limitations for their ability to be generalized and for theory formation. Therefore it is not possible to establish one and only one yardstick in relation to evaluating welfare states and their ranking in relation to various 'quality criteria', for example, decommodification, defamilialization or the breadwinner ideology. Evaluations of welfare states on the basis of different modes of stratification do not point to homogeneous rankings of countries, and the case of lone mothers emphasizes this conclusion. The case of lone mothers shows a demand for much more in-depth case studies. Thus, comparative welfare state research should cultivate more intensive case studies of demarcated phenomena and perhaps localities with the view to obtain more finely differentiated insights.

Notes

1 An autonomous household is here defined as a household where it is possible to have a high degree of independence, first of all from a male breadwinner but also an independence which is not based on another (new) form of 'hegemonic' dependency on either the state, the market or the family system. A high degree of autonomy is based on having choices and being able to combine income sources and services from the state, the market and the family without this leading to new forms of suppressive dependencies. The premise refers to the level of material resources and services available for lone mothers to establish and maintain an autonomous household and

does not refer to, for example, subjective feelings of wellbeing.

2 Hobson (1994) also refers to the typology problems, and she points out that the inclusion of the UK, the Netherlands and Germany as part of the group of strong male breadwinner states ignores differences in poverty among lone mothers that are residual in the male breadwinner model's ideology.

3 However, Sainsbury argues, like Lewis, that the potential for examining the interaction between the gender dimensions and those dimensions that are regarded as being important in mainstream research is most valid when gender is separated from, rather than being included in, mainstream theories and analyses.

4 An important, perhaps the most important, difference between lone mothers is in relation to their income-earning capacity. This is partially determined by level of education, training, proficiency, and work experience. The polarization effect is on the increase between lone mothers and married as well as cohabiting mothers, and also within the group of lone mothers: between those who can combine a wage income and other incomes with public benefits, and those who receive means-tested benefits, and who receive little or no private assistance (Scheiwe 1994).

5 It is important to point out that the poles represent uniformity with respect to the extent of lone mothers. The proportion of lone-mother families was almost identical in Sweden, Denmark, Norway and the US, and these countries are very clearly at the top among all the rich, developed countries.

6 These models do, in most cases, also apply to women in general and not only to lone mothers.

7 In the meanwhile, the Netherlands has changed its policies with respect to lone mothers. It now puts more emphasis on ability to be self-sufficient and has, therefore, started to implement 'workfare' policies for lone mothers (see Kremer 1994; Bussemaker *et al.* 1997).

8 The employment pattern of Portugese women is quite different from that of women in most other developed countries, as they are often self-employed and/or engaged in family businesses.

References

Anttonen, A. and Sipilä, J. (1996) 'European Social Care Services: Is It Possible to Identify Models?', *Journal of European Social Policy*, 6, 2: 87–100.

Bak, M. (1997) *Enemorfamilien*, Copenhagen: Forlaget Sociologi.

Baker, M. (1995) *Canadian Family Policies. Cross-National Comparisons*, Toronto: University of Toronto Press.

Beck, U. (1992) *Risk Society. Towards a New Modernity*, London: Sage.

Beck, U. and Beck-Gernsheim, E. (1995) *The Normal Chaos of Love*, Cambridge: Polity Press.

Borchorst, A. (1993) 'Working Lives and Family Lives in Western Europe', in S. Carlsen and J. E. Larsen (eds) *The Equality Dilemma. Reconciling working life and family life, viewed in an equality perspective*, Copenhagen: Munksgaard International Publishers.

Bradshaw, J., Ditch, J., Holmes, H. and Whiteford, P. (1993) *Support for Children. A Comparison of Arrangements in Fifteen Countries*, London: HMSO.

Bradshaw, J., Kennedy, S., Kilkey, M., Hutton, S., Corden, A., Eardley, T., Holmes, H. and Neale, J. (1996) *The Employment of Lone Parents: A Comparative Analysis in 20 Countries*, York: Commission of the European Communities/University of York.

Bussemaker, J., van Drenth, A., Knijn, T. and Plantenga, J. (1997) 'Lone Mothers in the Netherlands', in J. Lewis (ed.) *Lone Mothers in European Welfare Regimes. Shifting Policy Logics*, London: Jessica Kingsley Publishers.

Dean, J. (1995) 'Reflective Solidarity', *Constellations*, vol. 2, 1: 114–40.

Duncan, S. and Edwards, R. (1997) *Single Mothers in an International Context: Mothers or Workers?*, London: UCL Press.

Ellingsæter, A.L. and Rønsen, M. (1996) 'The Dual Strategy: Motherhood and the Work Contract in Scandinavia', *European Journal of Population*, 12: 239–60.

Esping-Andersen, G. (1990) *The Three Worlds of Welfare Capitalism*. Cambridge: Polity Press.

EU (1994) *Poverty Statistics in the Late 1980s: Research based on micro-data*, Luxembourg: Eurostat.

Europaparlamentet (1994) *Betænkning fra Udvalget om Kvinders Rettigheder. Om fattigdom blandt kvinder i Europa*, Luxembourg: Europaparlamentet.

Giddens, A. (1992) *The Transformation of Intimacy. Sexuality, Love and Eroticism in Modern Societies*, Cambridge: Polity Press.

Hobson, B. (1994) 'Lone Mothers, Social Policy Regimes, and the Logics of Gender', in D. Sainsbury (ed.) *Gendering Welfare States*, London: Sage.

Jones, K.B. (1990) 'Citizenship in a Women-friendly Polity', *Signs*, 15, 4: 781–812.

Kamerman, S.B. (1995) 'Gender Role and Family Structure Changes in the Advanced Industrialized West: Implications for Social Policy', in K. McFate, R. Lawson and W. J. Wilson (eds) *Poverty, Inequality, and the Future of Social Policy*, New York: Russell Sage Foundation.

Knijn, T. (1994) 'Fish without Bikes. Revision of the Dutch Welfare State and its Consequences for the (In)dependence of Single Mothers', *Social Politics*, vol. 1, no.1: 83–105.

Kremer, M. (1994) *Interpretations of Citizenship. Gender, Care and the Obligation to Work in the British, Danish and Dutch Welfare State*, Utrecht: University of Utrecht.

Larsen, J.E. and Sørensen, A.M. (1993) 'Lone Parents', in S. Carlsen and J.E. Larsen (eds) *The Equality Dilemma. Reconciling Working Life and Family Life, Viewed in an Equality Perspective*, Copenhagen: Munksgaard International Publishers.

Leira, A. (1993) 'Mothers, Markets and the State: A Scandinavian "Model"?', *Journal of Social Policy*, 22, 3: 329–47.

Levitas, R. (1998) *The Inclusive Society? Social Exclusion and New Labour*, London: Macmillan.

Lewis, J. (1997a) 'Introduction', in J. Lewis (ed.) *Lone Mothers in European Welfare Regimes. Shifting Policy Logics*, London: Jessica Kingsley Publishers.

Lewis, J. (1997b) 'Gender and Welfare Regimes: Further Thoughts', *Social Politics*, no. 3, Summer 1997: 160–77.

Lewis, J. and Åström, G. (1992) 'Equality, Difference, and State Welfare: The Case of Labour Market and Family Policies in Sweden', *Feminist Studies*, 18, 1: 59–86.

Lewis, J. and Ostner, I. (1994) *Gender and the Evolution of European Social Policies*, Zes-Arbeitspapier, nr. 4, Bremen: Universität Bremen.

Lister, R. (1990) *The Exclusive Society. Citizenship and the Poor*, London: Child Poverty Action Group.

Lister, R. (1997) *Citizenship: Feminist Perspectives*, London: Macmillan.

Lister, Ruth (1999) 'The Responsible Citizen: Creating a New British Welfare Contract', unpublished paper.

Marshall, T.H. (1964) 'Citizenship and Social Class', in T.H. Marshall *Class, Citizenship and Social Development*, New York: Doubleday.

McLanahan, S.S., Casper, L.M. and Sørensen, A. (1995) 'Women's Roles and Women's Poverty', in K.O. Mason and A.-M. Jensen (eds) *Gender and Family Change in Industrialized Countries*, Oxford: Clarendon Press.

McLaughlin, E. and Glendinning, C. (1994) 'Paying for Care in Europe: Is There a Feminist Approach?', in L. Hantrais and S. Mangen (eds) *Family Policy and the Welfare of Women*. Cross-National Research Papers, Loughborough: University of Loughborough.

Martin, C. (1995) 'Father, Mother and the Welfare State', *Journal of European Social Policy*, 5, 1: 43–63.

Millar, J. (1992) *Poverty and the Lone Parent: the Challenge to Social Policy*, Aldershot: Avebury.

Millar, J. (1996) 'Mothers, Workers, Wives: Comparing Policy Approaches to Supporting Lone Mothers', in E. Bortolaia Silva (ed.) *Good Enough Mothering? Feminist Perspectives on Lone Motherhood*, London: Routledge.

Nurmi, K. (1997) *Gender Equality and Welfare State Models: Outcomes Perspective*, Turku: University of Turku, Department of Social Policy.

OECD (1993) *Breadwinners or Child Rearers: The Dilemma for Lone Mothers*, Paris: OECD.

Oppenheim, C. (1993) *Poverty. The Facts*, London: Child Poverty Action Group.

Orloff, A.S. (1993) 'Gender and the Social Rights of Citizenship: The Comparative Analysis of Gender Relations and Welfare States', *American Sociological Review*, 58, no. 3: 303–28.

Orloff, A.S. (1996) 'Gender in the Welfare State', *Annual Review of Sociology*, 22: 51–78.

Ramprakash, D. (1994) 'Poverty in the Countries of the European Union: A Synthesis of Eurostat's Statistical Research on Poverty', *Journal of European Social Policy*, 4, 2: 117–28.

Roll, J. (1992) *Lone Parent Families in the European Community. The 1992 Report to the European Commission*, London: Family Policy Studies Centre.

Sainsbury, D. (1996) *Gender, Equality and Welfare States*, Cambridge: Cambridge University Press.

Sainsbury, D. (ed.) (1994) *Gendering Welfare States*, London: Sage.

Saraceno, C. (1996) 'Family Change, Family Policies and the Restructuring of Welfare'. Paper prepared for the OECD Conference: 'Beyond 2000: The New Social Policy Agenda', Paris: OECD.

Scheiwe, K. (1994) 'Labour Market, Welfare State and Family Institutions: The Links to Mother's Poverty Risks. A Comparison between Belgium, Germany and the UK', *Journal of European Social Policy*, 4, 3: 201–24.

Smeeding, T.M., O'Higgins, M. and Rainwater, L. (1990) *Poverty, Inequality and Income Distribution in Comparative Perspective. The Luxembourg Income Study (LIS)*, London: Harvester Wheatsheaf.

Socialstyrelsen (1997) *Social Rapport 1997*, SoS-rapport 1997: 14, Stockholm: Socialstyrelsen.

Sørensen, A. (1994) 'Women's Economic Risk and the Economic Position of Single Mothers', *European Sociological Review*, vol. 10, no. 2: 173–88.

Sørensen, A. (1995) 'Gender and Welfare in Europe', paper prepared for presentation at the 8th Scandinavian Social Policy Seminar at Hässelby Slott, Vällingby, Sweden, 10 February 1995.

Wong, Y.-L.I., Garfinkel, I. and McLanahan, S. (1993) 'Single-Mother Families in Eight Countries: Economic Status and Social Policy', *Social Service Review*, June 1995: 177–97.

Yuval-Davis, N. (1994) 'Women, Ethnicity and Empowerment', *Feminism and Psychology*, vol. 4, no. 1: 179–97.

10 Changing obligations and expectations

Lone parenthood and social policy

Jane Millar

Many countries have experienced very significant changes in the patterns of family formation and family structure in recent years. Couples are more likely to live together outside marriage, to marry later, to have fewer children, to separate and divorce, to remarry or live with a new partner, and individuals are more likely to live alone. Families have become more diverse and less stable. The 1996 report of the *EU Observatory on National Family Policies* (Ditch *et al.*, 1998: 9) summed up these trends as follows:

> Patterns of family formation and dissolution are changing throughout Europe, and although the changes have been much greater in some countries than in others, they appear to be moving in a common direction. In general, the changes point to a more diverse and complex set of behaviour in terms of forming families, and a greater degree of instability in such formations.

New family patterns create new and complex ties of love, care, obligation, duty and support across and between different families and households, and thus pose a number of problems or dilemmas for governments. In the UK these family trends have been particularly marked – the UK has one of the highest divorce rates in Europe, for example, and one of the highest rates of extra-marital births – and debate over the causes and consequences of changing family patterns has become an increasingly prominent political and policy issue, one that creates strong feelings and polarized attitudes. Some argue that the government should seek to resist family change and restore the 'traditional' family, with marriage promoted by tougher divorce laws, and by more financial support for marriage and less for cohabitation. Others have argued that policy cannot turn back the clock in this way but can only respond to, or maybe even positively support, new family forms (see Millar 1997; and Smart 1998 for further discussion of these debates).

This ambivalence about the policy response to family change is further complicated by the fact that, at a time of welfare state restructuring, the role of the family as welfare provider has assumed a new political importance. Families may have changed significantly but they are also being asked to play an increasingly important role in the provision of welfare. More emphasis on family obligations and responsibilities, by design or by default, is an inevitable outcome of reducing state welfare provisions (Millar and Warman 1996). Thus countries that have been seeking to cut back on welfare spending have increasingly looked to the family to provide alternative forms of support. Countries that already rely heavily upon family support for welfare look anxiously upon these family trends which might undermine the support that families – or to be more accurate, women – are willing, and able, to give (Papadopoulos 1997). Moreover changes in the nature of families raise questions about where these family obligations should fall, and whether they should be based on legal ties (such as marriage), or biological ties (such as parenthood), or social ties (such as cohabitation). High rates of divorce and unmarried parenthood make it very likely that governments will have to address these questions directly and so make much more visible and explicit the normative foundations of policy – and hence, perhaps, open these up to disagreement and debate. This chapter explores the relationship between family change, family obligations and government policy, drawing on recent policies towards lone parents in the UK as the main example but also seeking to set this in a wider cross-national context. The first section discusses the nature of the UK policy debates raised by family change, while the second and third focus on two policy areas – parental support for children in lone-parent families and lone mothers and employment – as illustrative of these issues in practice.

Family change, family obligations and the state

The rise in lone parenthood has been the most visible sign of changing family patterns in the UK. In the early 1970s there were about half a million lone-parent households in the UK, most of them headed by divorced or separated women. By the mid-1990s this had risen to about 2.7 million, or 24 per cent of all families with children, and included an increasing proportion separated not from marriage but from cohabitation (Haskey 1998). The rise in lone parenthood has thus been at the heart of anxieties about the impact of family change (Duncan and Edwards 1997; Ford and Millar 1998; Kiernan *et al.* 1998).

There have been three main areas of concern. The first relates to the extent to which government policy, especially liberal divorce laws and the financial and housing support offered to lone-parent families, has created or sustained these trends. The writings of US authors such as Murray (1984), who argued that family instability is a 'rational' response to the disincentives to marriage in the tax and transfer systems, found a ready audience in some UK policy circles. This view of the state as usurping the family has been a thread running through policy discussions and popular discourse for a number of years, especially during the 'new right' era of the 1980s (Abbott and Wallace 1992; Lister 1996). Second there has been concern over the impact of family change on children. Lone parenthood – whether it be as a result of divorce or as a result of a birth outside marriage – is often depicted as something that is chosen by adults but inflicted on children and children are thus perceived as the innocent victims of the selfish choices of adults. Third, there is anxiety about the changing relationships between women and men and in particular about the extent to which the rise in lone motherhood can be interpreted as reflecting a rejection of men by women. State benefits and support for lone parents are seen as giving women the choice to live, and bring up their children, without men. Instead they are 'married to the state' (*The Sunday Times* 1993) or having 'babies on benefit' (*Panorama* 1993). It is suggested that men who are rejected by women in this way, and who may also be rejected by the labour market, have no clear role to play at home or at work and thus no ties to bind them to society (Dennis and Erdos 1992; Morgan 1995).

These anxieties mean that policy responses to family change in the UK have tended to be rather confused and uncertain. In general the relationship between family change and social policy is by no means clear. As Kamerman and Kahn (1997: 27) point out, 'family change has posed problems for policy-makers and families but has not assured a response. Some family policies are responsive to family change, some apparently to other factors.' We should probably be wary of seeking too clear a causal line from family trends to policy measures. Although behaviour and policy may be adrift from each other, policy-makers are necessarily willing or able to close the gap: doing nothing is a common, and probably the safest, policy response to situations of competing demands and interest groups. Nevertheless, in recent years, there have been some significant changes in the assumptions about the family, and gender roles within the family, underlying and framing UK social policy.

First, as marriage has become more insecure and unstable, there has been an increasing focus on the duties and obligations of parenthood. Marriage has declined in legal significance and parenthood has become increasingly defined as the relationship that confers life-long and unconditional obligations (Hale 1998). Maclean and Eekelaar (1997) examine three indicators of the legal status of marriage (the degree of regulation of entry into and exit from marriage, the extent of differences in the legal status of marriage and cohabitation, and the existence of 'no-fault' divorce) and conclude that marriage has become a more private relationship in the UK with less state involvement and fewer rights and duties specifically attached to marital status. In particular, marriage is not construed as a life-long relationship but as a contract that either partner can terminate. Second, there has been a growing recognition of the dual role of women as workers and mothers, and the need for government support for this, particularly for lone mothers. Married women have been entering the UK labour market in steadily increasing numbers for many years but, in the absence of state support, have largely 'solved' the problem of reconciling work and family life by taking part-time rather than full-time jobs. Lone mothers do not have this option and can only take paid employment if they can make arrangements for the care of their children. Many also require cash support to supplement their wages, which may be insufficient to support a family. Thus, there have been a number of policy measures introduced that are intended to encourage and support employment among lone mothers, especially since the late 1980s (Ford and Millar 1998).

Shifting the policy focus from marriage to parenthood seems to be a rational and coherent response to the declining importance of marriage in patterns of family formation. Supporting lone mothers to be wage-earners makes sense if it is no longer possible to rely upon a male 'breadwinner'. But such policies are not without their own tensions and problems and some of these dilemmas are well illustrated by two recent pieces of legislation: one dating from the 1980s, during the period of Conservative government and focusing on family support issues; and the other forming part of the post-1997 Labour government's welfare reforms and focusing on employment issues.

Child support for children in lone-parent families

The first example concerns the maintenance of children after parental divorce, or when parents are unmarried, and the obligations of non-resident parents to contribute to the costs of supporting their children. This emerged in the late 1980s as a key part of the Conservative policy agenda. The impetus was partly moral (to ensure that divorced and separated fathers could not simply 'desert' their children) and partly financial (if fathers paid more then the government could pay less). Thus the 1991 Child Support Act aimed to ensure that all separated fathers paid child maintenance at higher levels than had hitherto been expected. The amounts to be paid would be set according to a standard formula, this would be administered through a specially created agency, and all fathers – whatever their circumstances or the circumstances of their separation – would be required to pay something towards the cost of supporting their children.

There was, in general, much apparent agreement with the principle that fathers should support their children financially from all those involved: politicians and policy-makers, the public at large, the separated fathers and the lone mothers. However, once this legislation started coming into effect there was an immediate and quite overwhelmingly hostile response, and child support was second only to the 'poll tax' in the negative reaction it created (Millar 1996a). Many separated fathers viewed the measures as unfair, either because the amounts of money were considered to be too high or because they felt that, in their particular case, there were special circumstances that should be taken into account. Many lone mothers wanted to see fathers paying but often felt that, in their particular case, any money received was probably not worth the problems caused. Views about the principles that should underpin child support were not translated into support for this policy in practice.

By now, several years later, the hostility seems to have died down somewhat, not least because of the concessions made to the separated fathers, who proved to be an effective pressure group, much more so than lone mothers. Thus, for example, the average child maintenance award fell from about £41 to about £28 a week between 1995 and 1997, partly as a consequence of final assessments generally being lower than initial assessments but also because changes to the rules have reduced the contribution of the absent parents (CSA

1997). There is virtually no performance indicator that shows the scheme to have been a success. At an aggregate level the proportions of lone parents in receipt of child maintenance has scarcely changed. Bradshaw and Millar (1991) found about 29 per cent of their sample of lone parents in the late 1980s were receiving child maintenance. This was before the child support scheme was introduced. Marsh, Ford and Finlayson (1997) found the same proportion in receipt in 1994, after the scheme had been in operation for about three years. This has not improved and many separated fathers are still waiting to be assessed, or have been assessed and found to have incomes that largely exempt them from payment (DSS 1997). Over 70 per cent of lone mothers on income support seek to avoid a child support assessment and in 1993/4 only £15 million was paid through the CSA to children compared with over £200 million through previous arrangements in 1992/3 (DSS 1998a). The Labour government has promised to simplify the formula and speed up the system (DSS 1998a, 1999), but whether this will solve the problem of lack of consent remains to be seen.

The UK child support legislation focuses on parenthood as the primary relationship and seeks to enforce the obligations of parenthood, regardless of marriage. The experience of implementation highlights some of the problems and difficulties that can arise from a shift of focus. Three in particular stand out. First, the legislation treats all fathers, never-married and ex-married, in the same way. But some critics of the scheme have argued that biological fatherhood alone should not always create an unconditional financial obligation to children. There is some evidence that unmarried fathers do not feel the same degree of obligation to their children as married fathers (Maclean and Eekelaar 1997). This does not necessarily mean that they should not have the same legal obligations but it may be very difficult to enforce obligations that are not accepted as legitimate (Finch 1989). Focusing on biological, rather than social, ties to create financial obligations may prove difficult to enforce in practice. Second, the CSA defines the rights and duties of fathers purely in financial terms and ignores obligations to care and the issue of ongoing contact between the separated parent and the child. Again some critics argue that if fathers are to play a greater role in childrearing after parental separation then perhaps the state should be defining and enforcing parent–child contact in the same way as it is seeking to enforce parent–child financial transfers (Burgess 1998). Third, because there is no state guarantee of the child support payments, the income of the women is directly dependent on whether and what the men pay. In this respect the women remain financially dependent upon the men, just as within marriage (Millar 1994). Although in theory gender-neutral (in that the provisions apply in the same way to absent mothers as they do to absent fathers), in practice the question of dependency is not necessarily avoided by focusing on parenthood rather than marriage. Much depends on the way in which the parental obligation is put into practice. For example, the use of 'advanced maintenance payments' in a number of countries (including Sweden, Denmark, Austria,

France, Germany) puts the children's need for an adequate income first and makes the child support obligation a debt to the state rather than a transfer between individuals (Millar 1996b). This means that the payment is guaranteed by the state, and so is received whether or not the separated parent pays. By contrast, in the UK, if the separated parent does not pay then the lone parent receives no money.

The issue of the obligations of separated parents to their children is an area where law and policy have been changing in a number of countries. Millar and Warman (1996) suggest that many countries are moving towards defining these obligations as irrespective of, rather than contingent upon, the marital status of the parents. Nevertheless there is much variation in practice. For example, in no European Union countries are unmarried fathers automatically given the rights and duties of parenthood in the same way as married fathers. An unmarried father who establishes paternity can usually acquire some of these rights and duties but there is quite considerable variation across countries, as Table 10.1 shows. In some countries the assumption is that both parents should share parental rights and duties, as married couples do. In other countries such sharing may be permissible but is not automatic. And in others the unmarried father can gain some, not all, the rights and duties of parenthood but only at the discretion

Table 10.1 Parental rights: non-married and divorced couples, various EU countries, late 1980s/early 1990s

Non-married couples		*Divorced couples*	
Presumption that both parents should share rights and responsibilities	Denmark Finland France* Norway Portugal Sweden UK	Presumption that both parents should share rights and responsibilities	Finland France Spain Italy Greece Sweden
Sharing permissible	Austria France* Luxembourg Netherlands Spain	Joint parental responsibility permissible and encouraged	Norway Denmark Netherlands UK
Unmarried fathers some rights at discretion of courts	Germany Greece Ireland Italy	One parent only to have parental responsibility	Austria Belgium Germany Luxembourg

Note: * Depends on length of cohabitation.

Source: Millar and Warman (1996).

of the courts. There is similar variation in the possible legal arrangements after divorce. In some countries only one parent can be the legal guardian of the child after divorce while in others either both parents automatically retain parental responsibility after divorce or joint parental responsibility after divorce is becoming more common and encouraged.

Issues of the financial support of children after parental divorce have attracted increasing attention in some countries in recent years (Barnes *et al.* 1998; Corden 1999). This is particularly so outside Europe (the US, Australia, Canada, New Zealand have all introduced some version of 'child support' schemes) but also in some European countries (Sweden, Norway and the Netherlands have all reviewed their systems of child maintenance payments). In other countries, however, child maintenance after divorce has not so far become a visible policy issue. This is not necessarily because existing systems work well. The available evidence is limited, but what there is suggests that most systems are not very effective in ensuring payment. That this has become an issue in some countries but not (yet) in others probably relates more to different demographic and economic contexts, to different values accorded to family privacy, and to different paradigms of family policy. However, if it is correct that there is an increasing convergence around the importance of parenthood in determining obligations, then the child maintenance issue is likely to come onto the policy agenda in many more countries in the future.

In relation to all these issues, the rights of men, women and children are increasingly likely to come into direct conflict. The UN Convention on the Rights of the Child (1989) includes 'the right from birth to a name . . . the right to know and be cared for by his or her parents' (Article 7); and 'the right of a child who is separated from one or both parents to maintain personal relations and direct contact with both parents on a regular basis, except if it is contrary to the child's best interests' (Article 9). The right to an identity – to a name and to know one's parents – may come into conflict with different views about the appropriate rights of unmarried parents, especially unmarried fathers. Children have the right to contact with both parents but joint parental responsibility may mean a loss of rights and autonomy for the caring parent (usually the mother) as it gives the other parent (usually the father) the right to intervene in decisions without the obligation to join in the day-to-day care. Parents may have a general obligation to support their children, but individual parents may have to enforce that obligation against each other, and thus maintain their own dependent relationship.

Arguably, a policy focus on parenthood rather than marriage reflects the way in which marriage is becoming culturally less important, with people increasingly likely to perceive their personal and sexual relationships as contingent and temporary, private arrangements to be entered into voluntarily and exited at will (Giddens 1992; Beck and Beck-Gernsheim 1995). Parenthood now holds the quality of permanence once accorded to marriage. However, there are clearly many new and morally complex issues to be faced if governments are to take a more active role in defining and enforcing the rights and duties of parenthood.

Motherhood and paid work: the 'New Deal for Lone Parents'

Central to the social policy agenda of the UK Labour government is the idea of the 'active welfare state'. In such a welfare state the main role of policy is to enable people to support themselves. As Tony Blair put it in his first speech as prime minster: 'work is the best form of welfare – the best way of funding people's needs, and the best way of giving them a stake in society'. In the Green Paper, *A New Contract for Welfare*, the very first of eight key principles set out to guide reform is that 'the new welfare state should help and encourage people of working age to work where they are capable of doing so.' (DSS 1998b). This applies to lone parents as much as it does to other groups. Indeed it is lone parents, young people, the long-term unemployed and people with disabilities who are the main target groups for 'welfare-to-work' policies. The 'New Deal for Lone Parents', implemented nationally from the autumn of 1998, seeks to encourage and help lone parents with school-age children to find employment.

The goal of increasing employment among lone parents is very much part of a more general policy emphasis on 'work, work, work' but the New Deal for Lone Parents also builds upon previous policy initiatives intended to encourage higher rates of employment among this group. Although ambivalent about lone mothers and employment, by the early 1990s the Conservatives had embarked upon a policy of seeking to encourage employment through increasing the financial incentives to paid work. The extension of Family Credit to part-time workers in 1992 was a key policy change. Family Credit (introduced in 1988) is a wage supplement payable to low-wage workers with children. Initially confined to those working for at least twenty-four hours a week, in 1992 it was extended to those working sixteen or more hours per week. Rather than having what was more or less an all-or-nothing choice between benefits and full-time employment, lone parents could now more readily combine income from benefits and from part-time working. Part of child maintenance payments and of childcare costs were ignored when assessing entitlement to family credit, which added to the financial incentives to employment. The number of lone parents receiving Family Credit rose rapidly, especially after 1992, and by November 1996 there were about 316,000 lone mothers and 13,000 lone fathers receiving Family Credit, at levels ranging from an average of £49 a week for one-child families to £95 for four-plus child families (DSS 1997).

The underlying assumption of this approach is that employment levels can be increased simply by ensuring that those in work are better off financially than those out of work. However, the research evidence, of which there is a considerable amount, suggests that things are much more complex than this (Bradshaw and Millar 1991; Ermisch 1991; Marsh and McKay 1993; McKay and Marsh 1994; Ford *et al.* 1995; Ford 1996; Shaw *et al.* 1996; Bradshaw *et al.* 1996; Duncan and Edwards 1997). These various studies reach some common conclusions about the determinants of employment among lone mothers – the importance of the age of youngest child is clear, as are 'human capital' assets in the form of education and work experience. State provisions play a role, but no one factor (replacement ratios, childcare provision, etc.) dominates for all lone parents. The message is that lone parents are very diverse – in their personal characteristics, their 'stage' of lone parenthood, their attitudes, the nature of their households, their social and neighbourhood networks, the labour markets they live in, their knowledge and understanding of their benefit entitlements, and their personal cost-benefit assessments of the risks and rewards of employment.

The New Deal for Lone Parents seeks to try to recognize and respond to this diversity. It is part of an increasing commitment towards 'active' labour market policies for all benefit claimants (Gardiner 1997; Eardley and Thompson 1997; McCormick and Oppenheim 1998). These policies are based on the idea that each claimant is an individual with specific needs and assets. The best way to improve employment opportunities is therefore through 'tailor-made' packages that suit the specific needs of that individual at that particular time. Claimants are very likely to find it difficult to construct such packages themselves and so the role of advisers includes providing information and support, encouraging claimants to become more active in their search for work, and monitoring their claims. The New Deal advisers will thus act as channels for advice, information and other services. The target group are lone parents with children of school age (i.e. aged 5 and above) and lone parents newly claiming income support, as well as existing claimants, are invited to attend a New Deal interview, where they are offered the opportunity to take part in the scheme. The 'raw' statistics show that, up to February 2000, about 133,000 lone parents had attended an initial New Deal interview. Of those who have left the scheme, 39 per cent had gone into employment and 43 per cent returned to Income Support. Almost half of those in employment are continuing to receive Personal Adviser support. The evaluation of the prototype scheme, which was running in eight areas of the country in the year before the national scheme was introduced, found that there was a small reduction in the numbers of lone parents claiming Income Support (of about 3.3 per cent compared with control areas). The additional employment effect – i.e. those who would not have found work without the programme – was estimated at 20 per cent (Hales *et al.* 2000).

The New Deal is being implemented alongside other policies also intended to support employment. These include measures to 'make work pay', in the form of a national minimum wage and a tax credit for low-wage families, and a 'national childcare strategy'. The latter includes the introduction of a childcare tax credit worth up to £70–105 a week; additional expenditure of £300 million to extend after-school care for up to half a million children; the promise of a nursery place for every 4-year-old; £100 million investment in training for child-care workers (DfEE 1998; Minster for Women 1998).

However, the extent to which these policies will enable a substantial number of lone parents to enter employment remains to be seen. The New Deal is already in operation although neither the minimum wage, the tax credits, nor the childcare strategy are yet in place. The New Deal for Lone Parents does not offer any incentive to employers to create jobs and to take on lone parents, unlike the New Deal for unemployed people, which does include employment subsidies. There must also be questions as to whether the New Deal for Lone

Parents can overcome some of the more intangible factors that might act as barriers to employment. Many non-employed lone mothers lack confidence in their employment abilities. Others may be suspicious of government intentions and thus be unwilling to participate in government schemes. Lone parents have been subject to much adverse comment from politicians, media and some policy 'think-tanks' and highly negative images of these families have been very strong in the UK (Duncan and Edwards 1997). The disruption and difficulties caused by the Child Support Agency will deter some lone parents from any further contact with government bodies, beyond what is essential. The Labour government has so far done little to dispel these negative views and the fact that they implemented cuts to lone parent benefits as one of their first acts of social security policy was widely seen as an attack upon these families.[1] The replacement of family credit by a tax credit will improve the financial returns from work but it may prove difficult in practice to deliver these new forms of in-work wage supplementation (Meadows 1997; Millar 1998).

Nor can it be said that a policy consensus has been reached. At present the New Deal for Lone Parents is voluntary and targeted at parents with children of school age. But the question of compulsion is often raised and a pilot scheme to require all benefit claimants, lone parents included, to attend an initial interview with a New Deal advisor will be put into operation in 1999 (DfEE 1999). However, more drastic steps such as compulsion to seek work and compulsory 'workfare' (i.e a requirement to work in return for benefits) do not look likely options for lone parents at least for the immediate future. Other critics, however, suggest that even New Deal policies may go too far in encouraging employment and in doing so fail to recognize the contribution and value of the unpaid work of parenting. If paid employment is defined as the central way in which individuals can make a contribution to the common good then other contributions, such as providing care for others who need that care, are likely to be devalued. Equity issues – comparing support for lone mothers with support for married mothers, and support for lone parents with support for other unemployed groups – may also become controversial, especially perhaps if the New Deal policies are successful.

Shifting practice may thus take some time. Nevertheless these measures represent a very significant policy shift for the UK. During the Conservative era women's employment was seen very much as a private issue. If women with children wanted to go out to work it was their responsibility to make the necessary arrangements for childcare and so on and neither the government nor employers were seen as having much of a role to play (Lister 1996). This view has now been firmly rejected by the Labour government and the acceptance that government has a central role to play in ensuring that high quality childcare is available and affordable is a major new development. Such care has traditionally been seen as the responsibility of the family, and not the state, and so this is a significant redrawing of state/family boundaries in the UK. Similarly the New Deal for Lone Parents is based on a view that motherhood and paid employment are not incompatible, except perhaps for the mothers of very young children. For lone mothers, the long-standing mothers-or-workers dilemma (Lewis 1989) is becoming resolved in favour of the mother-and-worker model. The policy props needed to support this in practice are not fully in place, but the outline is clear. Crucially, it is part-time rather than full-time employment that is expected or, more accurately, the definition of 'full-time' work has been sharply reduced. Anyone working over sixteen hours a week is considered to be in full-time work and so is eligible to receive financial support to make up their wages to a level that they can live on. Having the vast majority of lone mothers in employment of around sixteen to twenty hours a week, receiving wage supplements and private transfers from their ex-partners, and with access to child-care places and subsidies – this is now the goal of UK policy.

Indeed, it is now generally the case that, in most western countries, lone mothers are being expected, or compelled, to seek paid employment rather than being able to rely on long-term state support. Some lone mothers are excluded from this obligation, generally by reference to the age of the youngest child in the family, as summarized in Table 10.2. Again there is some variation across countries, but many countries require lone mothers to seek work when their children reach nursery or school age. Others have no fixed age but generally expect employment. For example, in the US benefits are now time-limited and, in many states, all lone mothers are expected to seek work, regardless of the age of their children. Some countries do not expect lone mothers to seek employment until their children reach secondary, or even school-leaving age, but even in these countries there is an increased emphasis on encouraging employment. For example, in New Zealand the age limit as been reduced from 16 to 14 and lone parents with children aged between 7 and 13 are required to attend an annual interview to discuss their employment plans (Baker 1998). In Australia and Ireland (as in the UK) the sixteen year limit still holds but policy is shifting in both these countries. In Australia the JET (Jobs, Education and Training) programme which was aimed at increasing employment has been running since the mid-1990s and child-care support has been increased substantially (McHugh and Millar 1997). In Ireland there is increasing policy interest in the employment issue, albeit with a recognition that encouraging higher rates of employment among lone mothers may be difficult to achieve in the context of a low employment rate for mothers generally (McCashin 1997; McLaughlin and Rodgers 1997).

The UK is thus far from alone in the way in which policy is defining lone mothers as both workers and mothers. As Bussemaker *et al.* (1997) note in relation to similar policy shifts in the Netherlands, this approach:

> forms a clear break with the idea that lone mothers of young children should, and could, focus their undivided attention on caring for their children regardless of how they became lone mothers. The new legislation stresses the lone mother's responsibility for self maintenance and entitlement to benefits is increasingly linked to availability for work.
>
> (Bussemaker *et al.* 1997: 110–11)

Table 10.2 Lone parents: requirements to work, various countries, early 1990s

Work test generally regardless of age of children (with some discretion)	Denmark Italy Spain Sweden US
No work test if children are under 3 years of age	Austria Finland France Germany
No work test if children are under 5, 6 or 8 years of age (i.e school starting age)	Canada (most provinces) Luxembourg Netherlands Norway
No work test if children are under 14/16	Australia Ireland New Zealand UK

Source: Baker 1998; Bradshaw *et al*. 1996; Bussemaker *et al*. 1997.

And, in some countries, it is not just for lone mothers that there have been changes in policy expectations. In Australia, married women can no longer receive benefits solely as dependants of their husbands. Since 1995 both members of a couple are required to establish individual eligibility for benefit, either as someone seeking work or as someone at home caring for a child (aged under 16). From 1998 this latter benefit – the Parental Allowance – can be paid to either married or lone mothers (or fathers) and the separate sole parent pension has been abolished. Thus lone and married mothers are now treated in the same way (Millar 1998). In the Netherlands, both members of couples are expected to seek work unless there is a child aged under 5, in which case one of the parents would be exempt from this requirement (Bussemaker *et al*. 1997).[2]

The approach in Sweden and Denmark, where lone mothers are seen not so much as a separate category of family where different rules should apply, but more as a particular type of one-earner family (Stoltz 1997; Hobson and Takahashi 1997) may be becoming more commonplace in other countries.

Conclusion

Family change has been very rapid in the UK and the policy response somewhat ambivalent and confused, with much controversy surrounding policy choices in this area. The attempt to introduce a more stringent system of child support for children of separated parents was a failure and is currently under review. Policies to support and sustain employment among lone mothers are less controversial, although by no means universally supported, and may prove difficult to implement in practice. Both sets of policies have their roots, and their problems, in the existing UK provisions and values. But they are also specific examples of some more general trends in policy found elsewhere. In many countries there is an increasing emphasis on parenthood as an unconditional and life-long relationship that creates rights and duties on the basis of biological ties. At the same time there is an increasing emphasis on employment obligations for all adults, whether parents or not, whether married or not. There are still many significant differences across countries, of course, and in particular the 'family' is placed rather differently in law and policy in the countries of southern Europe (Guillén 1996; Millar and Warman 1996; Papadopoulos 1997; Martin 1997). However, in many countries these are active issues of debate and often concern. Behaviour, attitudes, law and policy are all fluid, and changes in one feed back into changes in the others, with no single causal direction apparent. Sometimes it seems that law and policy are 'ahead' of behaviour and attitudes but sometimes law and policy lag 'behind' behavioural and attitudinal change. The situation at any one time is a mixture of both the old and the new, and so there are often contradictions and inconsistencies between different areas of law and policy.

In many countries where policy changes have been taking place, these are often justified as part of a modernization of the welfare state, necessary to take account of the changing nature of the family, the changing status and position of women, and to create a welfare state that is well adapted to the more insecure and divided labour market. However, these reforms may raise new problems and areas of potential dispute. An increasing focus on the obligations and duties of parents, in the context of more unstable family structures, makes visible and explicit a complex set of issues about the relative roles of mothers and fathers in providing for and caring for children; and about whether, and how, the state should replace or enforce these. The increasing focus on the employment obligations of adults makes visible issues about caring work and how this can be combined with paid work. It is not clear what will happen to obligations to care (or 'rights to give and receive care', as Knijn and Kremer 1997, put it) if all working-age adults are expected and required to engage in paid labour. Paid employment is the most significant route out of poverty and, for this reason alone, employment-related policy strategies are very important for lone mothers and indeed women generally. But care work is increasingly becoming one of the most significant routes into poverty. Who bears the costs of children and who bears the costs of care are likely to be among the most central policy questions of the next century.

Notes

1 The measures abolish the existing 'one-parent benefit' (a small increase to child benefit for lone parents) and the 'lone parent premium' (an additional sum paid to lone parents in receipt of income support). These cuts were first proposed by the then Conservative government but implemented by the Labour government amid much controversy. A number of Labour MPs voted against these cuts but the government argued not only that were they bound by their promise not to increase public expenditure above planned levels for 2 years but also that New Deal policies were a far more effective and appropriate way of helping these families.

2 In the UK the government has recently proposed that the partners of unemployed claimants should also be subject to work tests and have access to training schemes, etc. This proposal, so far, refers only to those without children.

References

Abbott, P. and Wallace, C. (1992) *The Family and the New Right*, London: Pluto Perspectives.

Baker, M. (1998) *Poverty, Social Assistance and the Employability of Low-Income Mothers: Cross-National Comparisons*, Canada: Division of Human Resources Development.

Barnes, H., Day, P. and Cronin, N. (1998) *Trial and Error: A Review of UK Child Support Policy*, London: Family Policy Studies Centre.

Beck, U. and Beck-Gernsheim, E. (1995) *The normal chaos of love*, Cambridge: Polity Press.

BBC Television (1993) 'Babies on benefit', *Panorama* report, October.

Bradshaw, J. and Millar, J. (1991) *Lone Parent Families in the UK*, London: HMSO.

Bradshaw, J., Kennedy, S., Kilkey, M., Hutton, S., Corden, A., Eardley, T., Holmes, H. and Neale, J. (1996) *The Employment of Lone Parents: a Comparison of Policy in 20 Countries*, London: Family Policy Studies Centre.

Burgess, A. (1998) *A Complete Parent: Towards a New Vision Of Child Support*, London: Institute for Public Policy Research.

Bussemaker, J., van Drenth, A., Knijn, T. and Plantenga, J. (1997) 'Lone Mothers in the Netherlands', in J. Lewis (ed.) *Lone Mothers in European Welfare Regimes*, London: Jessica Kingsley.

Bussemaker, J. (1998) 'Rationales of Care in Contemporary Welfare States: The Case of Childcare in the Netherlands', *Social Politics*, 5, 1: 70–96.

Child Support Agency (1997) *Quarterly statistics, November 1997*, London: CSA.

Corden, A. (1999) *Making Child Maintenance Regimes Work*, London: Family Policy Studies Centre.

Council of Europe (1995) *Report on a European Strategy for Children*, Luxembourg: Council of Europe Doc 7436.

Dennis, N. and Erdos, G. (1992) *Families Without Fatherhood*, London: Institute of Economic Affairs.

Ditch, J., Barnes, H., Bradshaw, J., and Kilkey, M. (1998) *A Synthesis of National Family Policies 1996*, Brussels: Commission of the European Communities.

Department of Education and Employment (1998a) *Childcare: a Framework and Consultation Document*, London: The Stationery Office.

Department of Education and Employment (1999) *The Gateway to Work*, London: The Stationery Office.

Department of Social Security (1997) *Social Security Statistics*, London: The Stationery Office.

Department of Social Security (1998a) *Children First: a New Approach to Child Support*, London: The Stationery Office.

Department of Social Security (1998b) *New Ambitions For our Country: A New Contract for Welfare*, London: The Stationery Office.

Department of Social Security (1999) *A New Contract for Welfare: Children's Rights and Parent's Responsibilities*, London: The Stationery Office.

Duncan, S. and Edwards, R. (1997) *Single mothers in international context; mothers or workers?*, London: UCL Press.

Eardley, T. and Thompson, M. (1997) *Does Case Management Help Unemployed Job Seekers? A Review of The International Evidence*, Sydney Australia: Social Policy Research Centre.

Ermisch, J. (1991) *Lone Parents: An Economic Analysis*, Cambridge: CUP.

Finch, J. (1989) *Family Obligations and Social Change*, Cambridge: Polity Press.

Ford, R. and Millar, J. (1998) (eds) *Private Lives and Public Responses: Lone Parenthood and Future Policy in the UK*, London: Policy Studies Institute.

Ford, R. (1996) *Childcare in the Balance: How Lone Parents Make Decisions About Work*, London: Policy Studies Institute.

Ford, R., Marsh, A. and McKay, S. (1995) *Changes in Lone Parenthood*, London: HMSO.

Forssén, K. (1998) *Children, Families and the Welfare State*, Helsinki: STAKES.

Gardiner, K. (1997) *Bridges from Benefit to Work, a Rreview*, York: Joseph Rowntree Foundation.

Giddens, A. (1992) *The Transformation of Intimacy: Sexuality, Love and Eroticism*, Cambridge: Polity Press.

Guillén, A. (1996) 'Citizenship and Social Policy in Democratic Spain: The Reformulation of the Francoist Welfare State', *Southern European Society and Politics*, 1, 2: 253–71.

Hale, B. (1998) *Private Llives and Public Duties: What is Family Law For?*, The 8th ESRC Annual Lecture.

Hales, J., Lessop, C., Roth, W., Gloyer, M., Shaw, A., Millar J., Barnes, M., Elias, P., Hasluck, C., McKnight, A. and Green, A. (2000) *Evaluation of the New Deal for Lone Parents: Synthesis Report*, London: DSS Research Report No. 11.

Haskey, J. (1998) 'One-Parent Families and their Dependent Children in Britain' in R. Ford and J. Millar (eds) *Private Lives and Public Responses: Lone Parenthood And Future Policy in the UK*, London: Policy Studies Institute.

Hobson, B. and Takahashi, M. (1997) 'The Parent–Worker Model: Lone Mothers in Sweden', in J. Lewis (ed.) *Lone Mothers in European Welfare Regimes*, London: Jessica Kingsley.

Kamerman, S.B. and Kahn, A.J. (1994) 'Family Policy and the Under-3s: Money, Services and Time in a Policy Package', *International Social Security Review*, no. 47: 3–4, 31–43.

Kamerman, S.B. and Kahn, A.J. (1997) *Family Change and Families Policies in Great Britain, Canada, New Zealand and the United States*, Oxford: Clarendon Press.

Kiernan, K., Land, H. and Lewis, J. (1998) *Lone Mothers in Twentieth Century Britain: From Footnote to Front Page*, Oxford: Oxford University Press.

Knijn, T. and Kremer, M. (1997) 'Gender and the Caring Dimension of Welfare States: Towards Inclusive Citizenship', *Social Politics*, 4, 3: 328–61.

Lewis, J. (1989) 'Lone Parent Families: Politics and Economics', *Journal of Social Policy*, 18, 4: 595–600.

Lister, R. (1996) 'Back to the Family: Family Policies and Politics under Major', in H. Jones and J. Millar (eds) *The Politics of the Family*, Aldershot: Avebury.

Maclean, M. and Eekelaar, J. (1997) *The Parental Obligation: A Study of Motherhood Across Households*, London: Hart Publishing.

Martin, C. (1997) 'Social Welfare and the Family in Southern Europe: Are There Any Specificities?' in B. Palier (ed.) *Comparing Welfare Systems in Southern Europe, volume 3*, Paris: Mire.

Marsh, A. and McKay, S. (1993) *Families, Work and Benefits*, London: Policy Studies Institute.

Marsh, A., Ford, R. and Finlayson, L. (1997) *Lone Parents, Work and Benefits*, London: The Stationery Office

McCashin, A. (1997) *Employment Aspects of Young Lone Motherhood in Ireland*, Dublin: Irish Youth Work Press.

McCormick, J. and Oppenheim, C. (1998) *Welfare in Working Order*, London: Institute for Public Policy Research.

McHugh, M. and Millar, J. (1997) 'Single Mothers in Australia: Supporting Mothers to Seek Work', in S. Duncan and R. Edwards (eds) *Single Mothers in International Context; Mothers or Workers?*, London: UCL Press.

McKay, S. and Marsh, A. (1994) *Lone Parents and Work*, London: HMSO.

McLaughlin, E. and Rodgers, P. (1997) 'Single Mothers in the Republic of Ireland: Mothers Not Workers', in S. Duncan and R. Edwards (eds) *Single Mothers in International Context; Mothers or Workers?*, London: UCL Press.

Meadows, P. (1997) *The Integration of Taxes and Benefits for Working Families with Children: Issues Raised to Date*, York: Joseph Rowntree Foundation.

Millar, J. (1994) 'State, Family and Personal Responsibility: the Changing Balance for Lone Mothers in the UK, *Feminist Review*, 48: 24–39.

Millar, J. (1996a) 'Poor Mothers and Absent Fathers' in H. Jones and J. Millar (eds) *The Politics of the Family*, Aldershot: Avebury.

Millar, J. (1996b) 'Mothers, Workers, Wives: Comparing Policy Approaches to Supporting Lone Mothers' in E. Silva (ed.) *Good enough mothering?*, London: Routledge.

Millar, J. (1997) 'Social Policy and Family Policy', in P. Alcock *et al.* (eds) *The Social Policy Companion*, London: Social Policy Association.

Millar, J. (1998) *Integrated Family Benefits in Australia*, York: Joseph Rowntree Foundation.

Millar, J. and Warman, A. (1996) *Family Obligations in Europe*, London: Family Policy Studies Centre.

Minister for Women (1998) *Focus on Childcare*, London: Minister for Women.

Morgan, P. (1995) *Farewell to the Family?*, London: Institute of Economic Affairs.

Murray, C. (1984) *Losing Ground*, New York: Basic Books.

Papadopoulos, T. (1997) 'Family, State and Social Policy for Children in Greece', in J. Brannen and M. O'Brien (eds) *Children in Families: Research and Policy*, London: Falmer Press.

Philips, M. (1997) *The Death of the Dad*, London: The Social Market Foundation.

Shaw, A., Kellard, K. and Walker, R. (1997) *Moving Off Income Support: Barrier, Bridges and Behaviour*, DSS Research Report no. 53, London: HMSO.

Smart, C. (1998) 'Wishful Thinking and Harmful Tinkering. Sociological Reflections on Family Policy', *Journal of Social Policy*, 26, 3: 1–21.

Stoltz, P. (1997) 'Single Mothers and the Dilemmas of Universal Social Policies', *Journal of Social Policy*, 26, 4: 425–44.

Sunday Times (1993) 'Wedded to Welfare', 11 July.

United Nations (1989) *UN Convention on the Rights of the Child*, Geneva: UN.

Index